Protest and Survive

Vietnam, Love It and Leave. Artist: Tony Auth. *Source: Broken Arrow* 2, no. 1 (12 July 1970): 8.

Protest and Survive

Underground GI Newspapers during the Vietnam War

JAMES LEWES

Westport, Connecticut
London

Library of Congress Cataloging-in-Publication Data

Lewes, James, 1959–
    Protest and survive : underground GI newspapers during the Vietnam War / James Lewes.
        p. cm.
    Includes bibliographical references and index.
    ISBN 0–275–97861–3 (alk. paper)
    1. Vietnamese Conflict, 1961–1975—Journalism, Military—United States. 2. Vietnamese Conflict, 1961–1975—Protest movements—United States. I. Title.

    DS559.46 .L48 2003
    959.704'31—dc21   2002028311

British Library Cataloguing in Publication Data is available.

Library of Congress Catalog Card Number: 2002028311

ISBN: 0–275–97861–3

First published in 2003

Praeger Publishers, 88 Post Road West, Westport, CT 06881
An imprint of Greenwood Publishing Group, Inc.
www.praeger.com

Printed in the United States of America

The paper used in this book complies with the Permanent Paper Standard issued by the National Information Standards Organization (Z39.48–1984).

10 9 8 7 6 5 4 3 2 1

Copyright Acknowledgments

The author and publisher gratefully acknowledge permission to reprint the following:

Excerpts from *Working-class War: American Combat Soldiers in Vietnam* by Christian G. Appy. Copyright © 1993 by the University of North Carolina Press. Used by permission of the publisher.

Excerpts from *The Paper Revolutionaries* by Laurence Leamer. © 1972. Reproduced with permission of the Century Foundation.

Excerpts from *Uncovering the Sixties*, edited by Abe Peck, copyright © 1985 by Abe Peck. Used by permission of Pantheon Books, a division of Random House, Inc.

Excerpt from Gloria Emerson's, *Winners and Losers*. Random House, 1977. Reprinted by permission.

Chapter 6 appeared as "Envisioning Resistance: . . . " by James Lewes, in *Media History,* 7:2 pp. 137–151 © 2001. Taylor and Francis http://www.tandf.co.uk.

Every reasonable effort has been made to trace the owners of copyright materials in this book, but in some instances this has proven impossible. The author(s) [editor(s)] and publisher will be glad to receive information leading to more complete acknowledgments in subsequent printings of the book and in the meantime extend their apologies for any omissions.

To Helen and Max,
without whom none of this would have been possible.

We were not sticklers for accuracy . . . but our factual errors were not the product of any conspiracy to mislead the young, but of our own lack of organization, shorthandedness, and impatience with grueling research efforts. Facts are less important than *truth* and the two are far from equivalent. . . . Let's suppose . . . we are watching Walter Cronkite . . . who . . . calmly asserts that the Allied Command (!) reports 112 American soldiers were killed in the past week in Vietnam, 236 South Vietnamese died in the same period, and Enemy (*not* Vietnamese?) deaths were "put at" 3,463. Now, I doubt the *accuracy* of that report, but I know it doesn't come *close* to the *truth;* in fact it is an obscene, inexcusable lie.

Raymond Mungo,
Famous Long Ago: My Life and Hard Times with Liberation News Service

Contents

Illustrations

CHARTS

Introduction

ACTIVE DUTY DISSENTERS

On 8 March 1965, 1,500 advance troops from the Ninth Marine Expeditionary Brigade flew into the American air base in DaNang. The Brigade was brought up to full strength the next day, when the remaining 2,000 men waded ashore in full battle gear.[1] Instead, of the expected Viet Cong and North Vietnamese troops, "they were met by city officials from DaNang, curious Vietnamese, Special Forces Advisors . . . and groups of American airmen who had erected signs of welcome."[2] Like tourists,[3] these persons watched as the marines assaulted "the beach in full battle array."[4]

While the United States had supported the South Vietnamese military with men and material since 1954,[5] these were the first combat troops stationed "in country."[6] Their arrival meant that "the floodgates were [now] open. Johnson had managed to surmount the final obstacles [standing] in the way of [an] American takeover of the war."[7] Within a year there were more than one quarter of a million U.S. troops stationed in Southeast Asia.

Over the last thirty years, American military historians—including Colonels Robert Heinl, Shelby Stanton, and Harry Summers—have gone to great lengths to prove this was the "finest military force the United States had ever sent abroad."[8] What they ignore, however, is the fact that these men, from the lowliest private to the highest-ranking officer, arrived in South Vietnam unprepared to fight a war of attrition against an elusive guerilla army. First, the U.S. military had trained them to fight a ground war in Central Europe against the Soviets, not a war of attrition against peasants in South Vietnam. Second, in spite of being warned against "going in there thinking [they were] . . . John Wayne,"[9] many of these troops arrived expecting the war to be like the movies.

Third, encumbered by history[10] and racist stereotypes inherited from World War II,[11] many officers and senior noncommissioned officers arrived in Vietnam expecting to "win this brushfire war, and win it . . . very quickly. I guess we [had] believed . . . our own publicity. There was nothing we could not do because we were Americans, and for the same reason, whatever we did was right."[12]

As attested to by Philip Caputo, Bill Ehrhart, and other Vietnam veterans, these illusions evaporated amidst the jungles and rice paddies of South Vietnam, where GIs learned that

Their mission was not to win terrain or seize positions, but simply to kill: to kill Communists and to kill as many of them as possible.[13]

Having seen comrades and close friends, who "wiped out by seventeen years of war movies" had come to "Vietnam . . . [to] get wiped out for good,"[14] many GIs "acquired a contempt for human life and a predilection for taking it."[15]

Likewise, those officers who had believed they "could win this brushfire war, and win it quickly" soon discovered that the men they "had scorned as peasants . . . were, in fact, a lethal, determined enemy. By autumn, what had begun as an adventurous expedition had turned into an exhausting, indecisive war of attrition in which we fought for no cause other than our survival."[16]

In his review of Vietnam veteran memoirs and oral histories, Lloyd Lewis argues that these GIs came to see the war as "shapeless, disjointed, fragmented—a reality wholly other than any they had known or were prepared to meet. It seemed to many as though they had been ripped out of one world in which the familiar order of cause-effect, means-end, premises-conclusions operated and had been transported to another planet for their thirteen-month tour of duty. . . . As one soldier commented, 'It was no orderly campaign, as in Europe, but a war waged in a wilderness without rules or laws.'"[17]

Every GI appears to have responded to this formless war differently. Most tried to survive their tour of duty by "block[ing] the war from their minds."[18] Others embraced the war and slipped into a state of barbarism. For example, a veteran reported to Mark Lane that he "had a friend that had a pet skull. He chopped the head off and he used to keep it in his tent."[19] A minority went berserk and "lost all concern for the safety of others, as much as for [themselves]."[20] And some began to question why they should have to fight in a war that "was unwinnable . . . for a bunch of corrupt politicians in Saigon."[21]

Christian Appy argues that rank-and-file troops in Vietnam were radicalized in the aftermath of the 1968 Tet offensive, as an increasing number of them questioned whether the war in Vietnam was worth the life of a single GI. This, he claims, can clearly be seen in the fact that "by 1969 combat avoidance increasingly developed into direct 'combat refusals,' the military's euphemism for mutiny."[22]

This shift in attitude had to have been known to the Pentagon brass because in April 1969 the Pentagon had commissioned a committee of army historians to interview GIs in the field and assess their attitude toward the war. The committee reported that GIs believed "the war is about the biggest blunder the United States has ever made."[23] They felt the government should "get all the boats and planes that we have, put every American GI on it, and get us out of here as fast as we can."[24]

While there is no evidence the committee's report had any effect on either the Pentagon or the administration, their finding that GIs felt "if there is a chance we might get [killed] we shouldn't take the chance,"[25] was not concocted out of thin air. In fact, GIs began measuring "the success of an operation . . . not by how many enemy were killed but by how few Americans, not by how much fighting but by how little."[26]

The fact that GIs had begun to deliberately avoid contact with "the enemy" cannot be explained away as merely a survival tactic. Instead, it suggests these men had come to doubt the legitimacy of their officers' command and control. As Michael Herr observed—during the siege of Khe Sanh—these men felt there was nothing their officers could do to them that was any worse than being stationed in Vietnam:

> "Fuck the lieutenant," Mayhew said. "You remember from before, he ain't wrapped too tight."
> "Well he wrapped tight enough to tear you a new asshole."
> "Now what's he gonna do to me? Send me to Vietnam?"[27]

Once legitimate command disintegrated, there was nothing to stop GIs in Vietnam turning on their officers and "fragging"[28] them for real and supposed slights. In fact, according to one Vietnam veteran, after 1969, traditional relations of power in Vietnam all but disappeared. "If you mess with my partner as an NCO or something like that, in the unwritten code there, I had the right to blow your brains out. And the guys would do it. Those lieutenants and the CO didn't mess with nobody in the field."[29]

Unfortunately, the Pentagon claimed that these behaviors proved "deliberate efforts [were] being made to introduce the divisiveness found in our society into the army."[30] For GI activists, such claims were absurd. The editor of *The Ally*, for example, wrote that it was not civilians but "the war [that] created the anti-war GI. Men do not need the kind of stupid discipline the military hands out if they believe in what they are doing. When men are asked to fight an unjust war and are then harassed and abused while doing it, they begin to ask questions."[31]

In 1971, the Pentagon commissioned the Research Analysis Corporation to identify the causes of dissent amongst Vietnam-era servicemen. Employing findings from a survey of 844 soldiers at five bases in the United States, the Research Analysis Corporation reported "that *more than half of all soldiers* . . . became involved in some form of resistance activity [emphasis mine]."[32] When questioned about their involvement, 58 percent cited their opposition to the Vietnam War and 38 percent blamed "the way the army treats the individual."[33]

In the three decades since the war, the fact that a plurality of GIs not only opposed U.S. intervention in Southeast Asia but got "involved in some form of resistance activity" has been ignored by historian and commentator alike. So long as debates about the Vietnam War are dominated by those who claim that GIs "had been denied permission to win,"[34] no one will be able to hear those GIs who believed that the war was not worth winning:

We were angry about what the Army was doing—the stupidity of haircuts, the long hours of KP, the constant harassment, the utter lack of usual rights and the total disrespect for us as human beings. We also knew the war was crap—that it wasn't being fought to save the Vietnamese or to protect America. We saw clearly that it was the rulers of our country—the big businessmen—using us to maintain their control of another country. But that wasn't all, we also knew that all wasn't right in America. We were aware that 35 million of our people lived in poverty, and that 22 million of our Black brothers and sisters were kept on the bottom—used and abused as the white power structure saw fit—and put down brutally if they objected. Some of us had worked before we came in so we knew that long hours and overtime was the only way to have some extra spending money. We wanted a decent life when we got out—something we knew wasn't waiting for us. A Job that meant something, not just selling 40–50 hours a week to the highest bidder. We wanted a decent living, not one taxed away to nothing because of a war that was making someone else rich. But the thing of it was, we were in the Army. What could we do? Wait two or three years? We were tired of wasting time, tired of waiting for things to get better and knowing they never would. So we decided to try and stop some of the stuff that was coming down, see what we could do to change things.
That was the . . . motivating force behind our paper.[35]

This book focuses on this and other GI-produced underground newspapers.

WHY THE GI PRESS

I have chosen to concentrate on the GI underground press because it provided a unique space where GIs—without fear of retribution—could question the logic, and criticize the praxis, of those who ruled their lives.

For the editor of *The Logistic*, his and other GI papers were the GI's last best hope. Among other things, these papers provided GIs with:

... [W]hat is lacking in the intellectual void of military service—what might be termed as an intellectual counterpart to military logistics.

Our "mental" logistics will be characterized by facts and ideas. Instead of moving troops, we will move minds. Instead of supplying troops, we will supply the facts-about the army, about the country, about the world. Instead of quartering troops, we vow to make our paper a forum for your ideas and viewpoints. Then and only then will this post have a paper which brings the true issues into light. We aren't interested in telling you what to think, but we do wish to inform you about what others are thinking so that you can make your own decisions and form your own opinions.[36]

This book draws on, and is grounded by, a sample of 720 articles written between 1968 and 1970 for publication in more than 130 different newspapers.[37] These offer a unique window on to the activities and concerns of the GI movement and its struggle for GI rights.

The papers announced demonstrations months in advance and later reported on them as major victories. They viewed any judicial or disciplinary action on the part of military authorities toward GIs as attempted repression. Most important, they visualized hard and fast boundaries between who could and could not be part of the GI movement:

A Note for Lifers: We want you to understand that when we talk about lifers, we're referring to the stereotypical lifer or known pig. If you are in fact not one of these people but a real live human being, and you would like to stand up and be counted, we'll be happy to do the counting.[38]

Finally, the fact that GI newsworkers often chose to use generic military commands as titles for their papers meant they deliberately subverted traditional military discourse. Titles such as *About Face!* and *All Ready on the Left* not only identified "the general nature of the newspaper to prospective readers." They also capitalized "on possible anti-military dissidence already experienced by alienated or otherwise dissatisfied members of the armed forces."[39]

These activities did not take place in a sociocultural vacuum but in an embedded environment whose inhabitants had been drafted or had enlisted to avoid the draft.[40] These servicemen[41] came from cities and small towns across the United States whose populations were often polarized between those who wholeheartedly supported the war and those who became progressively critical of the need for Americans to be involved in Vietnam.

Given the fact that the draft did not distinguish between recruits who did or did not support the war, it was only a matter of time before the military had to cope with an antiwar movement of its own making. Unfortunately, the Pentagon viewed movement activists as little more than common criminals and lumped them in with rapists, murderers, and forgers. Consequently, it is impossible to accurately assess just how many GIs took part in antiwar activities.

In an effort to gauge the depth of such dissent, GI activists at Fort Lewis McChord petitioned their base commander to allow the distribution of an opinion poll:

We are now seeking that permission, and we publicly challenge the army to let us . . . take a poll on Fort Lewis to determine how enlisted men regard the war in Vietnam. *LET US SEE, ONCE AND FOR ALL, WHO IS INTERESTED IN FINDING OUT THE TRUTH AND WHO IS AFRAID OF THE TRUTH!* We dare the army to test its repeated claims that only a few soldiers oppose the war. We dare the army to let the men who have to fight this war express their opinions about it to the public. We dare the army to try and find out the truth [emphasis in the original].[42]

It is my contention that I can reconstruct how these enlisted men expressed their opinions to the public through a close examination of the editorials and statements of purpose published in the GI press.

In spite of the fact that Vietnam veteran's memoirs are chock full of unrest and dissent, scholars have ignored this antimilitarist subculture and its media.[43] The costs of this inside, and outside, the academy, have been far ranging and debilitating. I shall briefly touch on three.

First, it delimited historians and academics to an inadequate and fallacious intellectual sphere, whose contours have been assiduously constructed by politicians, historians, high-ranking military personnel, and media critics. As has been effectively illustrated by Jeffrey Kimball, Christian Appy, and James William Gibson,[44] these persons continue to hold that the United States military was "stabbed in the back" by fifth columnists and their liberal allies.

Second, it has resulted in the effective disenfranchisement of a whole class of activists—most of who opposed the war at great personal risk.

Third, it has reduced the activities of the antiwar movement to a handful of spectacular moments and, thus, obscures the institutional substructure of such a protest movement.

Without explaining every facet of the GI movement, it is my position in this book that the GI movement can neither be reconstructed nor understood without the environs within which this movement emerged. This project pays special attention to those military and civilian support groups and institutions founded to abet GI activists. The most important of these were the antiwar coffeehouses, founded mostly by veterans and a few civilian sympathizers, and the GI press.

The influence and effect of both were emphasized in an untitled proposal,[45] distributed at the 1970 National Convention of the U.S. Antiwar Movement.[46] The authors first assessed the breadth and range of GI movement activities and the influence and effect of its relationship with the larger civilian movement:

The radicalization of servicemen in the last few years has produced a phenomenon unprecedented in U.S. history, an anti-war movement within the military. Nearly every major base in America now has an activist group of soldiers bravely attempting to publish journals, organize rallies and establish peace centers and coffeehouses. . . . These activities are of critical importance to the national effort which we are presently waging in order to end the war.[47]

They then suggest that the civilian antiwar movement had been unable to profit from, or abet, these GIs, because all too few of them "are aware of the specific activities in which they can participate."[48] To remedy this separation they present a number of recommendations, which they "hope . . . will give direction to renewed efforts on behalf of the [GI] Movement"[49]:

[1] We urge civilian organizations to help the GI Press Service raise the funds necessary to publish a petition against the war currently being circulated among active duty servicemen. . . . [2] We urge that every serious anti-war group establish contact with GIs at bases in all parts of the country, that every organization (student, labor, women's group etc.) make a serious effort to communicate with servicemen at nearby military bases. . . . Organizations should obtain lists of the more than 60 GI newspapers and organizations now in U.S. bases. By contacting these papers or organizations, local groups can meet with, and assist GIs who oppose the war. . . . Through activities such as these civilian groups can attempt to reach more servicemen and expand the antiwar movement. We urge peace activists in every section of the country to establish contacts with the large number of GIs who oppose the war and who will express their feelings if given the opportunity.[50]

SOME REMARKS ABOUT TERMINOLOGY

For GI newsworkers, it was crucial to differentiate "GIs"[51], "grunts"[52] and enlisted men—who they claimed to represent—from those "lifers"[53] and "the brass"[54] who in effect ruled their lives. For example, the editors of *A'bout Face*, a Black-Panther influenced paper, claimed the paper was "Published by GI's for GI's."[55] Likewise, the editors of *Attitude Check* claimed that their paper spoke "for all . . . 'active duty personnel' . . . [including] permanently based male and female Marines, Schools battalion personnel as well as those Marines in transient undergoing preparatory training for duty in the Republic of Vietnam."[56] Finally, the editor of *Duck Power* claimed that his paper was "published in the interests of the enlisted man."[57]

The term "the movement" needs to be read as standing in for the civilian antiwar movement. Likewise, "GI movement" refers to those GIs who publicly opposed the war and called for a radical transformation of the military from an authoritarian/hierarchical organization to a democratized one. For the editor of the GI paper *As You Were*, this movement was "similar to the older Black and Brown struggles in that it was born out of oppression and fear this Movement manifests itself in many ways and on many levels."[58]

"Underground press" is a covering term that describes a number of different publications produced under different conditions and intended for different audiences whose only common other was their shared opposition to the Vietnam War. For the purposes of this book, these publications fall into two general types: one produced by civilians and the other produced by GIs with the assistance of concerned civilians and Vietnam veterans.

Consequently, I use the terms "civilian press" and "civilian paper" to refer to those underground papers that were produced by civilians. Likewise, I use "GI press" and "GI paper" to refer to GI-produced underground papers. The civilian press arose between 1964 and 1968 within an expanding counterculture and a movement that was increasingly politicized, occupying oppositional stances to all forms of authority. The GI press arose between 1967 and 1970 within an expanding GI peace movement, whose stance opposed militarist authority and the Vietnam War. The phrase "underground newsworker" is used for those who worked for nonmilitary underground newspapers. Likewise, "mainstream newsworker" is used to refer to persons who worked for any nonunderground paper, be it *The New York Times*, *Iowa City Press Citizen*, or *Stars and Stripes*. "GI newsworker" refers to those GIs involved in the production and distribution of the GI press.

Lastly, I use the labels "critical communication scholars" and "critical communication scholarship" to refer to the work of contemporary Western Marxists whose work addresses the ideological influence and effect of mainstream media. This includes the work of former New Left activists such as Stuart Hall and Todd Gitlin and former students at Birmingham University's Center for Contemporary Cultural Studies, such as Dick Hebdige and Phil Cohen.

A PRELIMINARY DEFINITION

In this book, I use the label "underground press" generically to stand in for and describe a variety of newspapers published by—and serving the interests of—a multitude of different groups and associations. While the great majority of these papers were published between 1967 and 1971, the earliest such publication, *The Los Angeles Free Press*, appeared on 1 May 1964.

Most publications were members of the Underground Press Syndicate (UPS), subscribers of Liberation News Service (LNS), or both. Through association with a variety of foreign and domestic press services,[59] UPS and LNS gave these papers access to a wealth of national and international news not covered by Associated Press, United Press International, or Reuters. While some of the smaller underground papers came to rely on UPS/LNS materials for the bulk of their content, the majority used such news and information to supplement local events and activities.

The degree to which these papers were countercultural community newspapers cannot be overstressed. For instance, most underground newspaper publishers, editors, and reporters lived in—and saw themselves as part of—the same countercultural communities that they reported on. As was illustrated by *The New York Rat*'s coverage of the Columbia University occupation in April 1968, underground press newsworkers were active participants in the events they covered.

With few exceptions, these papers were actively interested in the myriad of political struggles of the period. Their reporting favored the claims of demonstrators and activists over those of the authorities. While the editorial staffs were more often than not leftist or ultraleftist, their opposition to these authorities stemmed from their experiences as participants in the actions they described. For example, LNS took advantage of the October 1967 March on the Pentagon to meet with a gymnasium full of underground press editors and publishers who had come to Washington, D.C., to participate in the march.[60] Likewise, the Chicago underground newspaper *The Seed* served as the national coordinating office for the Festival of Life.

When the papers discussed cultural events, they treated the latest "happening" record release or rock concert with the same seriousness that Harold Rosenberg brought to his art criticism, viewing them as inherently political moments. The producers and performers of such events were interviewed with the same reverence as politicians on Sunday morning talk shows, and the pronouncements of Mick Jagger or Bob Dylan, among others, were seen as political theory.

But defining the media this way does not imply that they were carbon copies of each other. Instead they reflected the diversity of the counterculture and—depending on the intended audience—emphasized certain issues over others.

In closing, I need to draw a distinction between notions of antimilitary and antimilitarist. The former connotes a stance opposing all forms of military activity, as well as those involved, however directly or tangentially, with the military. Antimilitarist, on the other hand, connotes an opposition to the synthesis of military action with the goals and needs of corporate imperialism.

Claiming GI movement activists were antimilitarist does not mean they were opposed to the use of military power for political ends. These GI antiwar activists, had they been born earlier, would have fought in the Second World War. Given their class background coupled with their ideological position, many would probably have served with the Lincoln Brigade. The stance they took in the 1960s was because they found the situation in Vietnam intolerable and rejected the proviso that it was vital to America's survival.

NOTES

1. For a description of the Ninth Marine Expeditionary Brigade's deployment to Vietnam, see Philip Caputo, *A Rumor of War* (New York: Ballantine Books, 1978).

2. Douglas Welsh, *The History of the Vietnam War* (New York: Galahad Books, 1981), 69.

3. Elizabeth Diller and Ricardo Scofidio argue that while "tourism and war appear to be polar extremes of cultural activity—the paradigm of international accord at one end and discord at the other. The two practices . . . often intersect: tourism of war, war on tourism, tourism as war, war targeting tourism, tourism under war, war as tourism are but a few of their interesting couplings." (Elizabeth Diller and Ricardo Scofidio, eds., "Introduction," in *Back to the Front: Tourisms of War* [New York: Princeton Architectural Press, 1994], 18. Also published in French in *Visite aux armées: Tourismes de guerre* [New York: F.R.A.C. Basse-Normandie]).

4. Welsh, *The History of the Vietnam War*, 69.

5. According to Langguth, the Ninth Marine Expeditionary Brigade brought the number of U.S. troops in South Vietnam to 27,000 (Jack Langguth, "Force 'Strictly Defensive' Arrival Is Protested by Hanoi and Peking; U.S. Marine Units Arrive in DaNang," *The New York Times* [3 March 1965]: 1, 3).

6. "In Country: Vietnam." (Downloaded from Vietnam Veteran's Terminology and Slang web page at [http://www.vietvet.org/glossary.htm].)

7. Welsh, *The History of the Vietnam War*, 70.

8. Ronald H. Spector, *After Tet* (New York: Vintage Books, 1993), 26.

9. Caputo, *A Rumor of War*, 44.

10. Caputo writes that "for Americans who did not come of age in the early sixties, it may be hard to grasp what those years were like—the pride and overpowering self-assurance that prevailed. . . . We went overseas full of illusions, for which the intoxicating atmosphere of those years was as much to blame as our youth" (Caputo, *A Rumor of War*, xiii–xiv).

11. See John Dower, *War without Mercy: Race & Power in the Pacific War* (New York: Pantheon Books, 1986).

12. Caputo, *A Rumor of War*, xiii–xiv.

13. Ibid., xix.

14. Michael Herr, *Dispatches* (New York: Avon Books, 1978), 209.

15. Caputo, *A Rumor of War*, xix.

16. Ibid., xiv.

17. Lloyd Lewis, *The Tainted War: Culture and Identity in Vietnam War Narratives* (Westport, Conn.: The Greenwood Press, 1986), 72.

18. Christian Appy, *Working-Class War: American Combat Soldiers and Vietnam* (Chapel Hill, N.C.: The University of North Carolina Press, 1993), 207.

19. See Mark Lane, *Conversations with Americans* (New York: Simon and Schuster, 1970) and the testimony given before the Winter Soldier Hearings in February 1971.

20. Johnathan Shay, *Achilles in Vietnam: Combat Trauma and the Undoing of Character* (New York: Athaneum, 1994), 90.

21. Caputo, *A Rumor of War*, 317.

22. Appy, *Working-Class War*, 242.

23. Ibid., 233.

24. Ibid., 233.

25. Ibid., 233.

26. Ibid., 232.

27. Herr, *Dispatches*, 116.

28. The murdering of a fellow serviceman or a superior with a fragmentation grenade.

29. Mark Baker, ed., *NAM* (New York: Berkley Books, 1983), 171.

30. "Growth of GI Power," in *The Ally* 1, no. 17 (June 1969): 3.

31. Ibid., 3.

32. David Cortright, "GI Resistance," in *Give Peace a Chance: Exploring the Vietnam Antiwar Movement*, eds. Melvin Small and William Hoover (Syracuse, N.Y.: Syracuse University Press, 1992), 117.

33. Ibid., 119.

34. Ronald Reagan cited by Jeffrey Kimball, "The Stab-in-the-back Legend and the Vietnam War," in *Armed Forces and Society* 14, no. 3 (Spring 1988): 39.

35. "An FTA Birthday," in *Fun Travel Adventure* 9 (June 1969): 1.

36. "Editorial," in *The Logistic* 1 (ca. 1968): 1.

37. For a complete list of GI underground papers published in this period, see Appendix 2: GI Publications, 1967–1970. This includes place and date of publication.

38. "A Note for Lifers, " in *Broken Arrow* 1, no. 6 (2 October 1969): 6.

39. Harry W. Haines, "Soldiers against the War in Vietnam: The Story of *Aboveground*," in *Voices from the Underground: Volume 1, Insider Histories of the Vietnam Era Underground Press*, ed. Ken Wachsberger (Tempe, Ariz.: Mica Press, 1983), 188.

40. Appy notes that "The Selective Service System was the most important institutional mechanism in the creation of a working-class army. It directly inducted more than 2 million men into the military, and just as important, the threat or likelihood of the draft *directly induced millions more* to enlist. These "draft motivated" volunteers enlisted because they had already received their induction notices or believed they soon would, and thus they enlisted in order, they hoped, to have more choice as to the nature and location of their service. Even studies conducted by the military suggest that as many as half of the men who enlisted were motivated primarily by the pressure of the draft [emphasis mine]" (Appy, *Working-Class War*, 28).

41. By delimiting my remarks to servicemen, I do not mean to leave the impression that servicewomen supported the war.

42. "A Counterpoint Challenge," in *Counterpoint* 2, no. 14 (7 August 1969): 8.

43. The exceptions to this are David Cortright, *Soldiers in Revolt* (New York: Anchor Press, 1975) and Appy, *Working-Class War.*

44. See Kimball, "The Stab-in-the-back Legend," Appy, *Working-Class War,* and James William Gibson, *Warrior Dreams* (New York: Hill and Wang, 1994), 1–121.

45. Found among the David Cortright Papers (D.C.P.), housed at the Swarthmore College Peace Collection.

46. This was organized by the National Peace Action Coalition.

47. Untitled report, signed by thirteen GIs. Unfortunately, except for David Cortright, the signatures are indecipherable.

48. Ibid., 1.

49. Ibid., 1.

50. Ibid., 1–3.

51. GI: government issue. (Downloaded from Vietnam Veteran's Terminology and Slang web page at [http://www.vietvet.org/glossary.htm].)

52. Grunt: a popular nickname for an infantryman in Vietnam; supposedly derived from the sound one made from lifting up his rucksack. (Downloaded from Vietnam Veteran's Terminology and Slang web page at [http://www.vietvet.org/glossary.htm].)

53. Lifers are those servicemen who had decided to make a career out of the military but could never rise above the rank of sergeant.

54. The brass are the officer corps.

55. "Untitled Note," in *A'bout Face* 1, no. 1 (4 July 1970): 1; "Disclaimer," in *A'bout Face* 1, no. 1 (4 July 1970): 1.

56. "Check Us Out," in *Attitude Check* 1, no. 1 (November 1969): 3.

57. "Untitled Note," in *Duck Power* 1, no. 3 (24 September 1969): 1.

58. "As You Were—A Mirror of Non-Violent Revolution in America," in *As You Were* 13 (April 1970): 1.

59. In 1970, Liberation News Service (LNS) included the following news services and informational clearing houses as being affiliated with LNS: the Africa Research Group, the Arab Information Service, the College Press Service, the GI Press Service, the North American Congress on Latin America, Prensa Latina.

60. See Raymond Mungo, *Famous Long Ago: My Life and Hard Times with the Liberation News Service* (Boston: Beacon Press, 1970), 17–20.

Chapter 1

Theoretical Frameworks

INTRODUCTION

To break the "massive dependence" of postwar British social sciences "on American theories and models,"[1] Stuart Hall and his colleagues focused on youth subcultures. These, they argued, "take shape around the distinctive activities and 'focal concerns' of groups. They . . . have reasonably tight boundaries, distinctive shapes . . . focal concerns and territorial spaces. When age and generation also distinguish these tightly defined groups, we call them 'youth sub-cultures'."[2]

While they were not the first British social scientists to focus on the activities and concerns of youth culture,[3] they were the first to examine them on their own terms and in their own right. The importance of this shift in focus cannot be overemphasized, as it provided them with the necessary tools to challenge these American theories and models.[4]

Within a decade, by the end of the 1970s, the Birmingham School had swept these "American models and theories" out of the English academy. While Stuart Hall is reluctant to claim the credit for this "creative disintegration . . . of sociology,"[5] he does accept that he and his colleagues "were prescient in sensing, quite early, that the whole armour-plated craft of structural-functionalism was less seaworthy than it had appeared."[6]

During the 1980s, British cultural studies began to percolate through the American academy. While in Britain, it had been fairly easy to dispatch the Americans; in the United States it was another matter. Here, Hall and his colleagues were not only academic insurgents doing battle against an entrenched orthodoxy, but they were also doing it in the "environment that [had] produced functionalism as a major theoretical position and [whose] practitioners . . . dominated the field . . . of communication. . . . It was a perspective imbued with optimism . . . based on the belief in the perpetuity of the social system and the capacity to overcome instabilities or disorders."[7]

For example, Charles Wright argued, in the *Sociology of Mass Communication*, that American mass media had successfully bridged the distance between the need to make a profit and the unspoken requirement they "provide the public with information and discussion on important social issues and to avoid activities harmful to the public welfare."[8] This information and these discussions were central to and necessary for the construction and reproduction of the American democratic polity in two ways. On the one hand the media are able to alert the public to possible threats. Such information enables the "population [to] mobilize and avert destruction."[9] Because this knowledge and information was made available to the whole population, the media were able to foster and support "feelings of egalitarianism within the society."[10]

While it is reassuring to know that mass media foster "feelings of egalitarianism," there are a number of problems that force one to question the validity of such claims. First, given that it is impossible, because of cultural, economic, temporal, and spatial constraints, for the mass media to alert all the public to all these "imminent threats and dangers," Wright and his colleagues not only leave it up to gatekeepers and senior mainstream newsworkers to prorate these threats, but also to foster "feelings of egalitarianism" by heaping "prestige upon individuals who make the effort to keep themselves informed about events."[11] This ignores the very real influence of those class interests, which lead persons to take the time to be informed in the first place. Third, by arguing that as a social institution, mass media are separate to and different from the economic structure, family, and government. Wright not only quarantines, neutralizes, and de-ideologizes the media, he, in fact, deliberately masks the influence and effect of class and power.

Critical communication scholars found such claims to be problematic. Influenced by "long-forgotten or unknown 'Western Marxist' texts,"[12] these scholars returned "to the agenda the key question of the determinate character of culture and ideologies—their material, social and historical conditions of existence."[13] From this perspective, the mass media were not only the ideological state apparatus par excellence. As such, they cannot be considered in isolation of the economic structure, family, and government.

Likewise, gatekeepers do not merely share the interests of the elite; they are central to their production and reproduction. Consequently, these persons do not merely legitimate a way of walking, thinking, interpreting, consuming, and speaking. They in fact delimit one's range of possible alternative choices to those they promote.

Despite appearing natural, these practices and behaviors are fraught with hegemony and framed through ideology. The effects of this are twofold: they ensure the continuation of an already existing set of relations of subordination and domination. Simultaneously, they mythologize these practices and behaviors and therefore make them appear to be natural.

THEORETICAL ROOTS AND CONCERNS

While it is not my purpose in this chapter to trace the theoretical roots of critical communication scholarship, I briefly explore the influence of Louis Althusser, Roland Barthes, George Herbert Mead, and V. N. Volosinov upon their position. In looking at these theorists, I concentrate on their critique of ideology, as it lies at the heart of the break made by critical communication scholarship with the claims and expectations of Functionalist theory:

These texts marked a decisive . . . break in Cultural Studies: the break into a complex Marxism. They restored the debate about culture a set of theorizations around the classical problem of ideologies. They returned to the agenda the key question of the determinate character of culture and ideologies—their material, social and historical conditions of existence. They therefore opened up a necessary reworking of the classical Marxist questions of 'base' and 'superstructures'—the decisive issue for a non-idealist or materialist theory of culture. This reworking of Cultural Studies on the ground of the 'base/superstructures' metaphor was a highly significant moment, which had a formative impact on the Centre's work.[14]

The importance of Althusser and Barthes for the development of cultural studies and later critical communication scholarship was to be found in their analysis of the construction and reproduction of ideology.[15] In exploring this, Althusser and Barthes revisit Marx's proposition that the structure and interests of the corporate institutions of a state rest upon, are shaped by, and reflect the ruling economic interests of the epoch:[16]

The ideas of the ruling class are in every epoch the ruling ideas, i.e. the class which is the ruling material force of society, is at the same time its ruling intellectual force. The class which has the means of material production at its disposal, has control, at the same time, over the means of mental production, so that . . . the ideas of those who lack the means of mental production are subject to it. . . . Insofar . . . as they rule as a class and determine the extent and compass of an epoch, it is self-evident they do this in its whole range, hence among other things rule also as thinkers, as producers of ideas, and regulate the production and distribution of the ideas of their age: thus their ideas are the ruling ideas of the epoch.[17]

For Althusser, the production, reproduction, and distribution of these ideas were facilitated through those institutions, including the culture industry, which "function massively and predominantly *by ideology*."[18]

Given the fact Marx died in the 1870s, his exposure to the culture industry would have been rudimentary at best. He could not have imagined the influence and effect of the culture industry's colonization of our "work, rest and play."[19]

Barthes, on the other hand, argued this colonization had, in effect, voided Marx's temporal differentiation between time spent at work and time spent living.[20] We now interpret both as a sequence of moments, pre-scripted for us "through the press, the news [to] become the very norm as dreamed; though not actually lived . . . at the cost of an immobilization and an impoverishment of consciousness."[21]

As opposed to Functionalist media theorists, whose work has "served to provide knowledge about the use of messages and media for purposes of maintaining control [and] preserving the status quo,"[22] Althusser and Barthes offer a critique, grounded by the proposition that the institutions cultural production cannot be examined—let alone understood—in isola-tion of the relations of production and power in society.

While I agree that mainstream media refract, reflect, and reproduce the ruling ideas in society, I quibble with Barthes' suggestion that we have been duped into accepting "a world . . . without contradictions because it is without depth, a world wide open and wallowing in the evident."[23] To do otherwise means I accept his premise that we are institutionally entrapped in webs of meaning not of our own making, which have "turned reality inside out, emptied it of history and . . . removed from things their human meaning, so as to make them signify a human insignificance."[24]

Although Barthes is never attacked as an elitist, there is little difference between these remarks and Adorno's observation that the culture indus-try had reduced the "most intimate reactions of human beings so that per-sonality scarcely signifies anything more than shining white teeth and freedom from body odor and emotions."[25] There is evidence that this posi-tion has merit, but it does not and cannot account for the kinds of resis-tance tracked by Stuart Hall, Dick Hebdige, Greil Marcus, and John Savage, among others.

This was not the case, however, with George Herbert Mead, whose sug-gestion that we are embedded in environments of meaning that we navi-gate by learning the various "rules of the game" is most relevant to this discussion. As Mead himself points out, it is only when we have learned these rules that we can take on the attitudes of those around us and par-ticipate in communal activities and events.[26]

Despite the fact that Mead rejected historical materialism as antithetical to democracy,[27] his discussion of the "generalized other" can be read as a critique of the construction and reproduction of ideology. Furthermore, his proposition that we need to learn the rules of the game before we are able to internalize the generalized other suggests that these rules conform to—and are shaped by—the ruling ideas of society.

In his discussion of "The Self,"[28] Mead differentiates between the gener-alized other of one's social group and that of organized society. While he suggests that the internalization of the former is a prerequisite for individual's integration into the body social, he notes that one only need internalize the generalized other of one's social group to develop a complete self.

Interestingly, Mead—like Gramsci, Volosinov, Hall, and Hebdige—argues that the rules of the game are not set in stone but are open to negotiation.[29] Consequently, these ruling ideas can only "be maintained so long as the dominant classes 'succeed in framing all competing definitions within their range' . . . so that subordinate groups are, if not controlled; then at least contained within an ideological space which does not seem at all 'ideological'."[30]

Despite the best efforts of the elite, these definitions are open and interpreted by "differently oriented social interests within one and the same sign community, i.e. by the class struggle. Class does not coincide with the sign community. . . . As a result, differently oriented accents intersect in every ideological sign. Sign becomes the arena of class struggle."[31]

This is because the sign, like its material equivalent, the commodity, is the product of human intervention and manipulation. Like the commodity—which is the product of institutionally organized human labor—the sign is the product of communicative interaction between two or more persons who are "organized socially."[32]

Given that "consciousness takes shape and being in the material of signs created by an organized group in the process of its social intercourse,"[33] it should come as no surprise that the generalized other of the social group may not only be incompatible with that of organized society, it may in fact be contrapuntal. It is at this point that the generalized other of the organized society is not only challenged, it can in fact be transformed.

While I have barely scratched the surface of these various positions, the influence and effect of their claims and propositions on critical communication scholarship cannot be overstressed. For example, Althusser's argument that ideological claims and aspirations are constructed, transmitted, internalized, and reinforced through "structures like the family, cultural and political institutions"[34] was adapted and applied, by Phil Cohen (1972),[35] Paul Corrigan (1986),[36] and Dick Hebdige (1979),[37] to the cultural and political ecology of subcultures. In fact, as was noted by Cohen, subcultures cannot be understood in isolation of "the relationship between culture and community in the perspective of a class struggle."[38]

Volosinov's argument that the ruling ideas in society were conditioned "above all by the social organization of the participants involved and also by the immediate conditions of their interaction"[39] was interpreted by Hall and his colleagues to mean these ideas were not set in stone. Instead, they open to reinterpretation by members of subordinate subcultures, their peers, and their parents.[40]

Last, and by no means least, critical communication scholars have been keenly interested in the differently oriented representations and visualizations of these "differently oriented accents" by different media to a variety of different social groups, classes, and communities. As is best illustrated by the response of the British public to the Sex Pistols in 1976 and 1977,[41] these differently oriented representations do generate a range of differently oriented responses and reactions.[42] Some will be actively interested and sympathetic to the subculture, some will be actively interested and opposed, and some will be oblivious to the subculture and ignore it.

MAINSTREAMING MEDIA

While most persons get their information from the mass media, *some do not!* Unfortunately, traditional communication theory, with its emphasis on interindividual and mass communication, has overlooked at best—and ignored at worst—the visualization of "differently oriented accents" outside of the mass media. Consequently, the communicative interactions of those persons who do not turn to these media as their primary source of information are more often than not ignored.

I am not suggesting that communication scholarship has completely ignored these accents. It has not. A number of scholars, including Todd Gitlin and Dick Hebdige, have explored them. Unfortunately, these same scholars subsequently dismissed alternative media as ineffectual when compared to mainstream media.

This shift may be the consequence of there being few, if any, institutional rewards to be gained from a concentration on alternative media. It is not clear, however, what—if any—are the intellectual rewards of ignoring these media. One only need compare and contrast Todd Gitlin's terse dismissal of the underground press in *The Whole World Is Watching*, with his rich and vibrant epitaph for the underground press—*The Underground Press and Its Cave-in*—to get a sense of the cost.[43]

Equally problematic is the attempt on the part of these same scholars to not only equate mainstream with alternative media but also do so while avoiding any discussion of these alternative media. These scholars seem to be riding the laurels of their—and their colleagues'—earlier writings. For example, while Dick Hebdige's discussion of *The Face*[44] provides a cogent and insightful analysis of a mass-market music magazine, it reads very differently when framed against his earlier writings.

For the remainder of this chapter, I elaborate on the intellectual costs and consequences—for communication studies—of focusing on mainstream media to the exclusion of other media sources and forms. In so doing, I am not concerned with communication studies per se, but with the subset of communication scholarship influenced by Gramsci and the Birmingham School.

Hebdige's Face and His Retreat from Style

While it could be argued that Hebdige's "Bottom Line on Planet One: Squaring up to *The Face*" stands apart from his better known earlier writings,[45] it needs be considered in the light of these. When viewed from this light, his attempt to equate *The Face* with earlier punk rock fanzines cannot stand the test of scrutiny. Unlike these fanzines, *The Face* was not "produced on a small scale as cheaply as possible, stapled together and distributed through a small number of sympathetic retail outlets."[46]

For example, in *Subculture: The Meaning of Style*, he argued that punk fanzines provided "an alternative critical space within the sub-culture itself to counteract the hostile or at least ideologically inflected coverage . . . in the [mainstream] media."[47] *The Face*, which he described as a "gentrified cut-up,"[48] offers no such space. It, in fact, offers a passive/voyeuristic audience of consumers a window onto "a world where [their] actual presence is unnecessary."[49]

Unfortunately, in his discussion of *The Face*, Hebdige let surface stand in for substance. To return to his example of the punk fanzine, Hebdige argued that this critical space, so long as it remained under the control of the core subculture, resulted in these subcultural activists being able to "consciously invert values . . . deliberately challenge assumptions [and] falsify expectations."[50]

Unfortunately, such control can only be maintained so long as the subculture and its patterns of cultural production and consumption remained below the media horizon. Once noticed and caught under the glare of the mass media, the subculture inevitably loses control of its own constructions. These are then "manufactured from above instead of being spontaneously created from within."[51] These new publications tend to be edited and published by corporate appointees with little or no subcultural experience. Likewise, they are aimed at an audience of outsiders who have been alerted to the subculture by the mass media.[52]

In *The Meaning of Mod*, Hebdige observed that "when a Mod Magazine could declare authoritatively that there was a 'New Mod Walk' then one had to acknowledge, reluctantly, that this particular white negro[53] had, somewhere along the line, keeled over and died."[54] Given that *The Face* was obsessively concerned with 1980s versions of these same walks, it was no more than a revamped and updated mod magazine! Unfortunately, Hebdige seems to miss this correlation. What is missing from "The Bottom Line on Planet One: Squaring up to *The Face*" is any concern with the subcultural roots of cultural phenomena.

Unlike his former colleagues, Angela McRobbie and Iain Chambers— who have thrown the baby of cultural studies into the postmodern waters[55]—Hebdige wants to keep at least one foot grounded in the modernist camp.[56] On the one hand he tentatively commits himself to McRobbie's position that postmodernism offers "a wider, and more dynamic, understanding of contemporary representation than other accounts to date."[57] On the other hand, he, like Stuart Hall, wants to hang on to and revive the project of Western Marxism.[58]

Unfortunately, he selects *The Face* as the stage on which to resolve these intellectually incompatible positions. He does not help himself by comparing and contrasting it with *The Tatler*, which has always been concerned with the comings and goings of debutantes and their various suitors and lovers. Consequently, his claim that *The Face* is "infinitely better, more popular, significant, influential and socially plugged in than *The Tatler*"[59] is meaningless.

During the 1970s, best illustrated by his description of a "mod magazine," Hebdige would have dismissed claims that publications like *The Face* were cutting edge and/or radical.[60] Instead, he would have argued it represented the commodified edge of subcultural colonization. Stripped of style and innovation through commodification, recuperation, and repression, it was inevitable that *The Face*, or a publication much like it, would step in and sell the subculture back to these former subcultural activists.

Despite the fact this is driven by commercial as opposed to political concerns, its effects were felt throughout the subculture. Most importantly—because of advertising revenues from cigarette, alcohol, fashion, and record companies—*The Face* was able to skim off the cream of punk fanzine newsworkers by paying them salaries. This stripped the ground from under these fanzines, leaving them to compete with no money, substandard writers, and second-rate critics.[61]

While no one has tracked the effect this had on the punk subculture and its publications in the late 1970s and early 1980s, Abe Peck and Lawrence Leamer have documented the effect that such "over the counter culture" publications had on the underground press of the 1960s. It was nothing less than devastating.[62]

Not Ready for Prime-Time Radicalism

The problems outlined above are not unique to the work of Hebdige; they also plague Gitlin's discussion of the influence and effect of mainstream media on the career of the 1960s New Left. For example, Gitlin argued in *The Whole World Is Watching* that "in a floodlit society, it becomes extremely difficult, perhaps unimaginable, for an opposition movement to define itself and its world view, to build up an infrastructure of self-generated cultural institutions, outside the dominant culture."[63]

By trying to have it both ways, Gitlin's position is problematic and intellectually delimiting. On the one hand, he acknowledged that the underground press was indispensable for the construction, articulation, and communication of counterhegemonic demands and stances. On the other hand, he argued that its influence and effect was effectively subsumed and eclipsed by a mainstream media interested in and committed to reinforcing the status quo.

By drowning out the underground press, Gitlin argued, the mainstream media contained and constrained its influence. By refusing to acknowledge or discuss the content or validity of these counterhegemonic demands and stances, the mainstream media were free to transform the producers and consumers of such attitudes into folk devils worthy of moral panics. Once these producers and consumers have been contained and vilified, their ideas and attitudes were open to commodification.

This concentration on the mainstream media has effected scholars and their work in a number of ways. In spite of pretensions to being objective and value free, scholars effectively set themselves up as arbiters of what is and what is not communication. If scholars delimit communication in this way, how can they begin to unpack, or hope to interpret, the construction of those environments of meaning discussed above?

Most problematic, this results in academics becoming complicit in the reinforcement and reproduction of "an ideological space that does not seem at all 'ideological': which appears instead to be permanent and 'natural', to lie outside history, to be beyond particular interests."[64]

Herbert Menzel's Neglected Realm

Unlike Hebdige and Gitlin, Herbert Menzel argued that academics *had to attend* to that socially vital communication that is "intermediate between . . . mass and interpersonal communication."[65] Such a focus would enable scholars to highlight issues and concerns missing from, or downplayed by, mainstream scholarship. These include the diversity of media within a given country or geographic region; how these media enable specific groups to tailor their message for particular audiences; and what—if any—feedback the producers had received from their intended audience.

Lastly, and most importantly for this book, such a study could focus on the role of these media in the evolution and career of social unrest. As Menzel noted, during periods of social unrest, quasi mass media:

. . . [H]ave specific functions to perform. Presumably, there must be some kind of dissatisfaction which *must be shared.* The people involved *must be able to express* themselves. They *must be able to organize.* They *must receive some kind of recognition.* For all these things to happen, there *must be communication channels* which . . . link together the kinds of people who can play the roles requisite at each phase of the movement, and yet can do so without detection, or at least interference [emphasis mine].[66]

While Menzel attempts to differentiate and unpack these intermediate communications from mainstream media, there are problems with his approach that delimit its utility for this study. Among these are his treatment of all intermediate communications as one and the same. Consequently, he cannot differentiate underground and/or radical newspapers and newsletters from those "speakers who take part in election campaigns . . . salesmen approaching a succession of potential buyers . . . storefront information centers, literary agents . . . and numerous others."[67] What differentiates these from mass and interpersonal communication has nothing to do with content, intention, or ideology; it is purely a matter of size, distribution, and influence.

He also remains committed to a mainstream model of communication with a sender, a message, and a receiver. While it is true that he does allow for some feedback from the receiver, he suggests this will have little effect on the sender who can be sure this feedback "will correspond to a preconceived plan."[68]

Finally, he implies there is no difference between the "interaction in social unrest . . . [which] has the character of an excitable and mercurial groping for a social arrangement whose character is as yet shadowy and uncertain"[69] and the interaction between gatekeepers, their advisers, and hangers on.

Envisioning and Empowering Others

For Herbert Blumer, Stan Cohen, and Stuart Hall, on the other hand, such an equivocation is not only wrong headed, but also can never exist. Gatekeepers, who decide what is or is not fit to print, not only disapprove of those involved in this mercurial groping, but also do their level best to ensure the desired social arrangement can never come about by deliberately whipping up a "moral panic":

Societies appear to be subject, every now and then, to periods of moral panic. A condition, episode, person or group of persons emerges to become defined as a threat to societal values and interests; its nature is presented in a stylized and stereo-typical fashion by the mass media; the moral barricades are manned by editors, bishops, politicians and other right-thinking people; socially accredited experts pronounce their diagnoses and solutions; ways of coping are evolved or (more often) resorted to; the condition then disappears, submerges or deteriorates and becomes more visible. Sometimes, the object of the panic is quite novel and at other times it is something which has been in existence long enough, but suddenly appears in the limelight. Sometimes the panic is passed over and is forgotten, except in folklore and collective memory; at other times it has more serious and long-lasting repercussions and might produce such changes as those in legal and social policy or even the way society conceives itself.[70]

Interestingly, these media-directed crusades do not merely reproduce and reinforce the ruling ideas and institutions. They also attract previously uncommitted individuals who associate themselves with the claims and aspirations of those same activists the mainstream media paint as deviant and socially unacceptable.

This does not mean, however, that mass media legitimate the demands and aspirations of those persons. On the contrary, they "seek to neutralize all potential opposition by assimilating and redefining it, by pre-empting national consciousness with the spectacle's own image of opposition."[71] They do so with ease, because opposition movements, and the quasi mass media they produce, attempt to legitimate their demands and aspirations by framing them against the ruling ideas in society.

Given the limited audience for and distribution of these quasi mass media, their producers and consumers are powerless to effect the recuperation of their demands and aspirations by the culture industry. Once recuperated, they are then utilized to support and relegitimate those ruling ideas under attack.

As was noted by Blumer, the ideas expressed in quasi mass media are more often than not articulated to the body social through their presentation in the mass media, and, thus, become contained and constrained by the practices of such institutions:

The position of the general public is dependent on how the social movement and its manifestations are defined to the public and by the public. Generally, the public is uninformed about the given case of social unrest, is unfamiliar with the experiences of those at the center of the unrest and consequently is not able to put itself in the position of those voicing the protest. These limitations have a double effect on the general public. First, they shield the public from seeing the protested social arrangement as improper or illegitimate. Second, ignorance of the conditions provoking the unrest and unfamiliarity with the experiences of those caught in it make the general public easy prey to the way in which it is characterized to them. The depiction of the unrest and of the protesters through the various media of communication is very influential in shaping the public outlook. Since the media of communication are particularly open to use by authorities and to the representatives of special-interest groups unsympathetic to the social unrest, the definitions that are presented usually lead the general public to an unfavorable characterization of the unrest and its exponents.[72]

This claim that the mass media constrain the public's understanding of the meanings developed in social unrest is the central thesis of Richard Ericson, Patricia Baranek, and Janet Chan's *Visualizing Deviance*. For them the media "do not merely reflect others' efforts to designate deviance and effect control, but are actively involved themselves as social control agents. As such, media play a key role in constituting visions of order, stability, and change and in influencing the control practices that accord them these visions. In sum, they are central agents in the reproduction of order."[73]

An element of this process of reproduction through visualization is that both dominant and alternative meanings are presented objectively in the coverage of social unrest. This does not result, however, in alternative sets of meaning being presented as valid; instead, such meanings are framed in the context of the dominant set of meanings.

This allows "journalists to act as watchdogs, policing organizational life or deviations from their conceptions of the order of things. In turn this watchdog role allows journalists to bring into relief the normal or expected state of affairs, acknowledging order and contributing to community consensus."[74]

The grounding of alternative meanings against the dominant meanings occurs to reinforce the dominant meanings and delegitimate the alternative set of meanings. The result of this process—for Ericson et al.—is that the dominant meanings come to be reinforced and, thus, reproduced.[75]

A similar thesis is presented by Gitlin (1980), who argues that the media constrain alternative sets of meaning through the elevation of individual activists to leaders. The claims and aspirations of these leaders—and, in effect, the movement itself—are then invalidated by being grounded against the positions and predictions of persons in authority.

Despite the fact that these scholars acknowledge the existence of alternative sources of information, Blumer, Ericson, and Gitlin share a common problem. They do not consider these alternative sources as being worthy of analysis when compared to the role of mass communication. Although Blumer argues that to examine the articulation and development of social unrest, one has to acknowledge the role played by alternative media in the construction of alternative meanings, he adds that its effect upon the general public is negligible when compared to the effect of mass communication.

Likewise, Gitlin posits that the alternative media transmit alternative sets of meaning beyond the participants in social unrest. However, the latter number in the hundreds of thousands, while mainstream media consumers number in the tens of millions.

CONCLUSION

While the above models are treated by mainstream scholarship as fitting within the concerns of the academy, their framing of the counterculture sets them apart from the work of other scholars. This is clearly the case with Gitlin, whose concern with the ideological effect of the mass media led him to conclude that the New Left was hoodwinked into believing it had "to take the media into account in planning actions, choosing

leaders . . . and articulating positions."[76] Once hoodwinked, the movement was easy prey for the media to "package it and retail it as titilla-
tion . . . for the Americans' rage and bewilderment."[77]

Gitlin's position is not dissimilar to that of Dick Hebdige, who noted that
subcultural activists, because they deliberately flaunt public mores and values, are a magnet for the media. Once caught under its floodlit glare, the
subculture not only bifurcates into leaders and followers, it inevitably suc-
cumbs and is "cheated and exploited at every level. [Their] consumer rituals . . . [come] to involve the use of commodities directed specifically
at . . . [them] by a rapidly expanding pop industry. . . . Style [is] manufactured from above instead of being spontaneously created from within."[78]

Unfortunately, they offer no respite for rank and file activists, who—
because they do not fit the media's notions of what a movement radical or
subcultural activist should look or behave like—are anonymously
entrapped in a web of meanings not of their own making. As Gitlin himself noted in passing, such scholarship "cannot do justice to the whole of
the movement. . . . [T]here are very important dimensions of the movement's history and cultural identity which" it does "not discuss at all. Not
least there are the movement's *own* media, the hundreds of weekly photo-
offset 'underground' papers that sprang up in the later sixties and early
seventies."[79]

The failure of these scholars to consider these underground papers does
not mean they emerged and disappeared in a critical vacuum. On the contrary, there exists a rich and detailed literature that developed outside academic circles, which attempts to identify and explain the counterculture
and movement to a variety of audiences. This includes groups and individuals sympathetic to, and active in, the counterculture/movement.
Likewise, it includes groups and organizations that were ignorant of or
hostile toward the counterculture/movement and its goals. I examine
these claims and counterclaims in the next chapter.

NOTES

1. Stuart Hall, "Cultural Studies and the Centre: Some Problematics and Problems," in *Culture, Media, Language: Working Papers in Cultural Studies*, 1972–1979,
eds. Stuart Hall, Dorothy Hobson, Andrew Lowe, and Paul Willis (London:
Hutchinson, 1980), 20.

2. John Clarke, Stuart Hall, Tony Jefferson, and Brian Roberts, "Subcultures,
Cultures and Class: A Theoretical Overview," in *Resistance through Rituals: Youth
Subcultures in Post-War Britain*, eds. Stuart Hall and Tony Jefferson (London:
Hutchinson University Library, 1986), 14.

3. For an overview of the concerns and interests of these scholars, see Stan
Cohen, ed., *Images of Deviance* (Harmondsworth, U.K.: Penguin Books, 1971).

4. In the paper "Youth and Class: The Career of a Confusion," Graham Murdock and Robin McCron note "it was left to Talcott Parsons (1942) to coin the term

'youth culture.'" (In *Working Class Youth Culture*, eds. Geoff Mungham and Geoff Pearson [London: Routledge Direct Editions, 1976], 12). Unfortunately, these authors argue that Parson's influence on British and by implication European social sciences was to put it at the service of U.S. foreign policy. As they note "The Cold War was not only a political but also an ideological struggle. Essentially this centered on the contrast between the image of American society as a pluralist democracy and the image of Soviet society as a totalitarian state. . . . Parson's formulation fit well with . . . Cold War concerns." (Ibid., 12–13).

5. Hall, "Cultural Studies and the Centre," 26.

6. Ibid., 26.

7. Hanno Hardt, *Critical Communication Studies: Communication, History & Theory in America* (London: Routledge, 1992), 14.

8. Charles Wright, *Mass Communication: A Sociological Perspective* (New York: Random House, 1975), 26.

9. Ibid., 11.

10. Ibid., 11.

11. Ibid., 15.

12. Hall, "Cultural Studies and the Centre," 25.

13. Ibid., 25.

14. Ibid., 25.

15. For the purposes of this discussion I am using Roland Barthes' essay "Myth Today," in *Mythologies,* trans. Annette Lavers (New York: Noonday Press, 1988) and Louis Althusser's "Ideology and Ideological State Apparatuses (Notes towards an Investigation)," in *Lenin and Philosophy,* trans. Ben Brewster (New York: Monthly Review Press, 1971).

16. In *The Eighteenth Brumaire*, Marx observed that: "Upon the different forms of property, upon the social conditions of existence, rises an entire superstructure of distinct or peculiarly formed sentiments, illusions, modes of thought and views of life. The entire class creates and forms them out of its material foundations and out of the corresponding social relations" (Karl Marx, *The Eighteenth Brumaire of Louis Bonaparte* [New York: International Publishers, 1984], 47).

17. Karl Marx and Friedrich Engels, *The German Ideology* (New York: International Publishers, 1985), 64.

18. Louis Althusser, "Ideology and Ideological State Apparatuses (Notes towards an Investigation)," in *Lenin and Philosophy,* trans. Ben Brewster (New York: Monthly Review Press), 145.

19. This is borrowed from a British Mars Bar commercial, in which a stern voice advises the audience that "A mars a day helps you work, rest and play."

20. For Marx, time was spent at work "to secure the necessary means of subsistence to enable him to exist" (Karl Marx, *Wage Labour and Capital* [Peking: Foreign Language Press, 1978], 18). Concomitantly, he argued: "Life begins where this activity ceases, at table, in the tavern, in bed" (Ibid., 20).

21. Barthes, *Mythologies,* 141.

22. Hardt, *Critical Communication Studies,* 17.

23. Barthes, *Mythologies,* 143.

24. Ibid., 142–43.

25. Max Horkheimer and Theodor Adorno, eds., "The Culture Industry: Enlightenment as Mass Deception," in *Dialectic of Enlightenment* (New York: Continuum, 1989), 167.

26. George Herbert Mead argues a person cannot become fully social unless he or she cannot only take "the attitudes of other human individuals toward himself and toward one another within the human social process," (154) but also "in the same way . . . take their attitudes toward the various phases of aspects of the common social activity or set of social undertakings in which, as members of an organized society or social group, they are all engaged" (154–55). (George Herbert Mead, *Mind Self and Society* [Chicago: University of Chicago Press], 1967).

27. See Andrew Reck, ed., *Selected Writings: George Herbert Mead* (Chicago: University of Chicago Press, 1981), 291.

28. Mead, 1.

29. Ibid., 155–72.

30. Dick Hebdige, *Subculture: The Meaning of Style* (London: Methuen, 1979), 16.

31. V. N. Volosinov, *Marxism and the Philosophy of Language* (Cambridge, Mass.: Harvard University Press, 1973), 23.

32. Ibid., 12.

33. Ibid., 13.

34. Hebdige, *Subculture: The Meaning of Style*, 12.

35. See Phil Cohen, "Sub-Cultural Conflict & Working Class Community," in *Working Papers in Cultural Studies* 2 (1972): 5–52.

36. See Paul Corrigan, "Doing Nothing," in *Resistance through Rituals: Youth Subcultures in a Post-War Britain*, eds. Stuart Hall and Tony Jefferson (London, Hutchinson, 1976), 103–5.

37. Hebdige, *Subculture: The Meaning of Style*, chapter 1.

38. Cohen, Sub-Cultural Conflict," 6.

39. Volosinov, *Marxism and the Philosophy of Language*, 21.

40. For example, Hall and his colleagues note: "It is important to stress that, as sub-cultures, they continue to exist within, and coexist with, the more inclusive class from which they spring. Members of a sub-culture may *walk, talk, act, look* 'different' from their parents and . . . some of their peers: but they belong to the same families, go to the same schools, work at much the same jobs, live down the same 'mean streets' as their peers and parents." (Clarke et al., "Subcultures, Cultures and Class," 14).

41. See Fred Vermorel and Judy Vermorel, *Sex Pistols: The Inside Story* (London: Omnibus Press, 1987).

42. See Greil Marcus, *Lipstick Traces* (Cambridge, Mass.: Harvard University Press, 1989); Jon Savage, *England's Dreaming: Anarchy, Sex Pistols, Punk Rock, and Beyond* (New York: St. Martins Press, 1992); Vermorel and Vermorel, *Sex Pistols*.

43. Gitlin describes these papers as being "vibrantly alive" and "a marvelous adventure, full of infectious enthusiasm." They were "a political and cultural breakthrough," that "embodied the brave and winsome spirit of that moment" and "the best of the late-Sixties revolt." (Todd Gitlin, "The Underground Press and Its Cave-in," in *Unamerican Activities*, eds. Anne Janowitz and Nancy Peters [San Francisco: City Lights Books, 1981], 21).

44. See Dick Hebdige, "The Bottom Line on Planet One: Squaring Up to *The Face*," in *Hiding in the Light* (London: Comedia, 1988), 155–76.

45. Unlike his earlier work, Hebdige's focus in "The Bottom Line on Planet One" is with a publication as opposed to a subculture's [ab]use of commodities.

46. Hebdige, *Subculture: The Meaning of Style*, 110.

47. Ibid., 111.

48. Hebdige, "The Bottom Line on Planet One," 161.

49. Ibid., 161.

50. Dick Hebdige, "The Meaning of Mod," in *Resistance through Rituals: Youth Subcultures in Post-War Britain,* eds. Stuart Hall and Tony Jefferson (London: Hutchinson, 1976), 88.

51. Ibid., 94.

52. It was here that *The Face* marked a break with tradition in that it was edited, published, and packaged by former subcultural activists and aimed at both insider and outsider audience.

53. "White negro" is used by Dick Hebdige not out of racist malice but as a term borrowed from Norman Mailer's essay of the same name. (Hedbidge, "The Meaning of Mod," 94).

54. Ibid., 94.

55. See Iain Chambers, *Border Dialogues: Journeys in Postmodernism* (London: Comedia Books, 1990) and Angela McRobbie, *PostModernism and Popular Culture* (London: Routledge, 1994).

56. See Dick Hebdige, "Postmodernism and the Other Side," in *Stuart Hall: Critical Dialogues in Cultural Studies,* eds. David Morley and Kuan-Hsing Chen (London: Routledge, 1996), 174–200.

57. Angela McRobbie, "Postmodernism and Popular Culture," in *Terminal Zone* 1 (1986): 25–34.

58. For Hebdige, Stuart Hall's (and by implication his) vision of Marxism "bears little or no relation to the caricatured, teleological *religion* of Marxism which—legitimately in my view—is pilloried by the Post. A Marxism without guarantees is a Marxism which has suffered a sea change. It is a Marxism which has 'gone under' in a succession of tempests that include the smoke and fire of 1968 and the shrinkage of imaginative horizons in the monetarist 'new realism' of the 1980s and yet it is a Marxism that has survived, returning perhaps a little lighter on its feet . . . more prone . . . to listen, learn, adapt and to appreciate, for instance, that words like 'emergency' and 'struggle' don't just mean fight, conflict, war and death but birthing, the prospect of new life emerging: a struggling to the light." (Hebdige, "Postmodernism and the Other Side," 199).

59. Hebdige, "The Bottom Line on Planet One," 175.

60. Dick Hebdige, "Aspects of Style in the Deviant Sub-Cultures of the 1960s," these were reprinted as *CCCS Stenciled Occasional Papers* nos. 20, 21, 24, and 25 through the Centre for Contemporary Cultural Studies.

61. For example, in 1969—because she had been interviewed *Life, Look,* and *Time*—Janis Joplin did not see why she would "want an interview in a little old hippie publication?" and refused to grant the editor of the *New York Rat* an interview. (Lawrence Leamer, *The Paper Revolutionaries* [New York: Simon and Schuster, 1972], 66).

62. Abe Peck argues that by 1970, in part because of the interrelated pressures of commodification, recuperation, and repression many "underground papers" had become "themselves alienated, alienating institutions. 'We started fighting with our audience,' recalls Eliot Wald. . . . 'It became the movement and not the readers. There was a tremendous amount of pressure to be pure and right, and I always felt I wasn't quite adequate because I didn't want to take up the gun and

didn't analyze everything in terms of the Revolution.'" (Abe Peck, *Uncovering the Sixties* [New York: Pantheon Books, 1985], 262).

63. Todd Gitlin, *The Whole World Is Watching* (Berkeley: University of California Press, 1980), 3.

64. Hebdige, *Subculture: The Meaning of Style*, 16.

65. Herbert Menzel, "Quasi-Mass Communication: A Neglected Realm," in *Public Opinion Quarterly* 35, no. 4 (1971): 407.

66. Ibid., 408–9.

67. Ibid., 407.

68. Ibid., 407.

69. Herbert Blumer, "Social Unrest and Collective Protest," in *Studies in Symbolic Interaction* 1, no. 1 (1978): 19.

70. Stan Cohen, *Folk Devils and Moral Panics: The Creation of the Mods and Rockers* (New York: St. Martins Press, 1980), 9.

71. Norman Fruchter, "Games in the Arena: Movement Propaganda and the Culture of Spectacle," in *Liberation* (May 1971): 8.

72. Ibid., 25.

73. Richard Ericson, Patricia Baranek, and Janet Chan, *Visualizing Deviance: A Study of News Organization* (Toronto: University of Toronto Press, 1987), 3.

74. Ibid., 5.

75. This reproduction is pervasive, according to Ericson, who reports an interview he had with the editor of an alternative newspaper in Toronto. This editor complained that it was impossible to find writers with an alternative perspective on journalistic norms; as a result, submissions tended to resemble articles published in *The Times*. (See Ericson et al., *Visualizing Deviance*, chapter 4.)

76. Gitlin, *The Whole World Is Watching*, 15.

77. Todd Gitlin, "Sixteen Notes on Television and the Movement," in *TriQuarterly* 23/24 (winter/spring 1972): 361.

78. Hebdige, "The Meaning of Mod," 94.

79. Gitlin, *The Whole World Is Watching*, 16.

Chapter 2

The Literature of the Underground Press

INTRODUCTION

In the preceding chapter, I sketched the failure of Herbert Blumer, Todd Gitlin, and Dick Hebdige to adequately credit the contribution of underground media to movements for social change. This does not mean, however, that they have ignored this phenomenon; they have not. Likewise, they are not the only scholars to have paid attention to the underground press.

Among others, historians who focus on the pre-Revolutionary period in America cannot ignore the influence of those pamphlets and broadsides produced between 1760 and 1775. In fact, they are drawn to these materials by John Adams, who claimed that the revolution was won "in the minds of the people . . . [through] the pamphlets [and] newspapers in . . . the colonies."[1] Likewise, historians of the antislavery movement cannot ignore the influence and effects of the abolitionist newspapers.[2]

Given that the production and consumption of underground publications has continued from the founding of the Republic to the present, historians are not the only scholars to have examined these materials. During the late 1960s and early 1970s, for example, scholars (Robert Glessing and Lawrence Leamer), journalists (Jack Nelson and John Berks), and cultural critics (Ethel Romm and Gary Allen) envisioned the underground press for a number of different publics.[3] I focus on these writings in this chapter.

I begin with a comparison of Robert Glessing's *The Underground Press in America*, Lawrence Leamer's *The Paper Revolutionaries*, and Roger Lewis's *Outlaws of America*. In looking at their respective visualizations, I focus on their treatment of the underground press's evolution, paying special attention to their evaluation of *The Village Voice* and *Rolling Stone*.

I then turn my attention to the treatment of the underground press in mass communication textbooks, readers, and survey histories. I close my literature review with a comparison of the press's treatment by mainstream newsworkers and their underground counterparts. Having introduced these competing depictions, I shall focus on what it meant to be underground and whether or not the label was applicable to publications produced in the United States, where the citizen's right to publish is a constitutionally protected privilege.

For me, these papers shared certain characteristics that marked them as distinct from most other publications produced in America in the late 1960s. They were countercultural community newspapers whose staffs lived in—and saw themselves as part of—the same countercultural communities that the papers chronicled. Likewise, underground press newsworkers were active participants in the events they covered.

With few exceptions, these papers were actively interested in the myriad of political struggles of the period. Their reporting favored the claims of demonstrators and activists over those of the authorities. While the editorial staffs were more often than not leftist or ultraleftist, their opposition to these authorities stemmed from their experiences as participants in the actions they described. Lastly, and most importantly, there was not one underground press, there were many. Taken together, these newspapers reflected the diversity of the counterculture and, depending on the intended audience, emphasized certain issues over others.

LITERATURE REVIEW

Histories of the Underground Press

Of the five histories of the underground press published since 1970, only one, Abe Peck's *Uncovering the Sixties*, was printed after 1973. The other four—Robert Glessing's *The Underground Press in America*, Roger Lewis's *Outlaws of America*, Lawrence Leamer's *Paper Revolutionaries*, and Ethel Romm's *The Open Conspiracy*—appeared in print between 1970 and 1972. Given their sudden appearance, and equally sudden disappearance, one is left with a nagging suspicion that the attention paid to the underground press from 1970 to 1973 reflects its being viewed as a fad.

Despite this rush to publication, most of these visualizations offer little insight into either the history of the underground press, the goals and intentions of underground press newsworkers, or the relationship among these persons, their publications, and their public. To illustrate this, one only need consider the following from Francis Watson's *The Alternative Media:*

The development of countercultural papers was encouraged by the Underground Press Syndicate. This New York operation was founded in 1966 by a small group of underground editors and activists who frequented the office of the drug-culture

paper, *East Village Other.* Tom Forcade [sic], who later founded a slick-paper magazine for drug users, called *High Times,* was the Underground Press Syndicate's
first full-time coordinator.[4]

While the Underground Press Syndicate (UPS) obviously supported
the underground press, it was more interested in facilitating communication among existing papers than in encouraging new papers. Once a
paper had been founded, however, UPS did encourage it to join with
other underground papers by becoming a member. Only two of the six
founder members of the UPS lived in New York—the other four lived in
California (two) and Michigan (two)—so they could not have frequented
the offices of the *East Village Other.* Tom Forcade (whose last name is
actually spelled Forçade) was not at that meeting, and under his stew-
ardship UPS was based in Phoenix, where he lived on a bus, and not in
New York.

Lastly, Watson leaves the reader with the impression that the underground press was obsessed with drugs, but this is not the case. For example, the *East Village Other's* coverage of drugs and drug-related issues
declined from a high of 11.4 percent of its total content in 1966, to 5.6 percent in 1967, and 2.9 percent in 1968. The *Los Angeles Free Press's* coverage
of drugs in this same period went from 0.8 percent in 1967 to 1.6 percent in
1968. This fell to 0.3 percent in 1969.[5]

While this may strike the reader as nitpicking on my part, the problems
identified with Watson recur throughout the literature. The exception to
this is Lawrence Leamer's *The Paper Revolutionaries,* which remains the
best introduction to the underground press.

This is because Leamer did not attempt to mold the press to fit his preconceived notion of what the underground press was. Instead, he allowed
underground press newsworkers, editors, and publishers to define the
press for themselves. This is not the case with Roger Lewis, who had a ten-
dency to gush effusively while saying nothing. Unlike Leamer, who care-
fully differentiated among the papers in terms of content and ownership,
Lewis clumped them together with no concern for such subtleties.

Consequently, while Leamer was concerned with how the press reflected,
inflected, and influenced the ideological and cultural complexities that tore
the movement and its media apart, Lewis was not. For example, Lewis
offered the following explanation for the split in *The Berkeley Barb:*

Underground staffers are working . . . because it pleases them. These distinct
mental attitudes are evident in the publications that employ their talents. The kind
of split that occurred in the *Voice* and led to the foundation of *E.V.O.* occurred, on
another level, at the offices of the *Berkeley Barb.* Some of the people who worked for
the *Barb* in 1969 alleged that its owner . . . [Max Scheer] a freak of some principle
had been ripping off excessive profits for himself. They struck and eventually
founded their own paper, the *Berkeley Tribe.*[6]

Lawrence Leamer, on the other hand, described the same split thusly:

In June 1969 . . . Scheer was netting $5,000 a week. Even Scheer will admit that he was making "a hell of a lot of money"—very little of which was going to a staff still subsisting on movement wages. . . . [After] six weeks of negotiations . . . on July 11, 1969, the 12-page *Barb on Strike* appeared. It featured as its logo not Don Quixote but Scheer spurring his mount forward with a spear to the buttock, dollar bills trailing off behind the galloping editor.

"Capitalist pig Max Scheer has locked us, some 40 members of the *Berkeley Barb* staff, out of our office and fired us for trying to turn the *Barb* into a model of the people's revolution," wrote Steve Haines in the *Barb on Strike*. "We felt that it is sheer hypocrisy for the *Barb* to mouth the words of revolution while lining Max's pockets with the people's cash. We felt that *Barb* profits should go for bail funds, legal defense funds, [and] medical clinics. . . . For us, the staff, we wanted enough bread to pay our rent and groceries. . . . Max refused to give us anything substantial.[7]

The relative strengths and weaknesses of these scholars are brought into stark relief by their treatment of the *Village Voice* and *Rolling Stone*. While Leamer did credit the *Voice* for enabling "a new literary journalism . . . that has affected a generation of [underground] journalists and writers,"[8] he argued it never had "pretensions to being" an underground newspaper and "inhabits a no-man's land between the Establishment"[9] and the underground press. Despite the fact that Leamer's position mirrored the claims of underground press newsworkers,[10] it runs counter to the claims of Robert Glessing, Roger Lewis, Ethel Romm, and Francis Watson, who insisted that "the first underground publications in modern day America were the *Village Voice* and *The Realist*."[11]

Likewise, Leamer rejected the commonly held opinion that *Rolling Stone* was an underground newspaper. Noting that American culture has the unique ability to package even the most radical claims and aspirations, Leamer argued that *Rolling Stone* took the "visions, ideals and aspirations" of the counterculture "and packaged them in a commercially palatable form . . . a Bohemianism of style . . . [that] has a simply uncanny ability to smooth off the rough radical edges of any youth phenomenon to make it manageable and neutral."[12]

Robert Glessing, Ethel Romm, and Roger Lewis, on the other hand, each argued that *Rolling Stone* was not only an underground newspaper, but that it was also profitable. Robert Glessing, for one, considered the magazine to be an outstanding example "of what the underground press can do with in-depth reporting."[13] Francis Watson argued that *Rolling Stone* was not only an underground paper, but it also had, along with the *Village Voice*, "more to do with the promulgation of the cultural and political ideas of the underground . . . than . . . any . . . [other] underground"[14] newspaper.

Importantly, Leamer argued that the press's evolution and its biases were inseparable and that its modes of production were the consequence of the publisher's politics, not its economics. To support this, he identified two waves of papers, which he labeled first- and second-generation underground newspapers.

The first-generation of papers, including the *Berkeley Barb*, the *East Village Other*, and the *Los Angeles Free Press*, were all founded before 1967 and run hierarchically. They were owned, published, and edited by the same people. While this would eventually prove to be a problem, these original owners did not view this as a conflict. Instead they felt that they were publishing for a community to which they belonged.[15]

The second-generation of underground newspapers,[16] on the other hand, were all founded after 1967. They were collectively owned and ideally edited by a committee consisting of all the paper's staff in accordance with the principle of participatory.

Whereas the first generation had been founded to service and celebrate the burgeoning counterculture, the second generation developed out of what was perceived to be a growing revolutionary movement, and by 1968 many of these publications came to view their role as organs of propaganda. For example, in 1968 the Liberation News Service collective elected to align itself with Students for a Democratic Society because

It seemed that this might be accomplished by a movement given a degree of organizational coherence by SDS in which the formulation of a revolutionary strategy could develop. While LNS never regarded itself as an official organ of SDS, it recognized SDS hegemony over advanced sectors of the movement, utilized SDS contacts in its work and followed the internal polemics of the organization with keen interest.[17]

The shift from the first to second generation can be seen most clearly in the abandonment of the term "counterculture" and its replacement with the term "movement." Among other things, the change resulted in an escalation of rhetoric. These papers crackled with exaggerated claims for the effectiveness of the movement, which some believed was on the verge of seizing power through the violent overthrow of the state. As late as 1971, in fact, Roger Lewis claimed that

A very real underground [exists] . . . within the United States. . . . The energy and exuberance of the press makes one feel that America will rise to a *'new morning'*. It is an optimistic affirmation that recognizes that revolution exists as much as a state of mind as in tangible, physical form. In America mind and body are coming together.[18]

In drawing this distinction, Leamer introduces the internecine struggle between those who believed in the primacy of a cultural revolution and those who believed in the primacy of political struggle.[19] Leamer did not claim that this split was unique to either the United States or the 1960s. In fact, as he himself notes,

This debate . . . is as old as the nineteenth-century debate between Marxists and anarchists. The lesson of modern radical history is that the . . . [fists] are correct *in terms of strategy.* You don't successfully overthrow a government by dropping out and denying the existence of the authoritarian state. You don't bring change by seeding tiny utopias on ground controlled by the government. According to the Marxists the anarchists and antiauthoritarian Leftists simply deny social reality. "Have these gentlemen ever seen a revolution," asks Friedrich Engels. "A revolution is the most authoritarian thing there is; it is the act whereby one part of the population imposes its will on the other part by means of rifles, bayonets and cannon . . . and if the victorious party does not wish to have fought it in vain, it must maintain this rule by means of the terror which its arms inspire in the reactionaries."[20]

In keeping with John Reed's observation "that politics plays hell with your art," this struggle tore the press apart. "Talented underground staffers chafed under collectivity. . . . Staffers felt besieged . . . [as] alliances . . . formed, then . . . [blew] apart. . . . The 'Underground press' itself was bogged . . . down in formula, violence, negativity, cant . . . [and] uncritical reporting."[21] The staff of Boston's *Old Mole* lamented, in the paper's final editorial, that it

Seems . . . we all gave up what made us most human when we went into the movement. One of us feels she mustn't paint, it's bourgeois and not contributing directly to the process of making a revolution. Another would always go to a boring, pointless meeting. Rather than do something she really loves doing. Others, who get into the movement younger, have never even found out what they would be doing in a post-revolutionary society.[22]

Textbooks and Surveys

The problems I identified above, with the work of Glessing, Lewis, and Watson, are not unique to them. Instead, they are also found in the few survey histories of American newspapers and mass communication readers that acknowledge the existence of the underground press.

Given that survey histories of the American press published before 1965 ignored nonmainstream publications, the fact that the underground press was included in any of these texts reinforces my earlier observation that the underground press was treated as a fad. In keeping with this observation, as the Vietnam era recedes, the amount of space devoted to these publications diminishes with each consecutive edition.[23] Unfortunately, most of these survey histories repeat the assertion that the *Village Voice* and *Rolling Stone* were not only underground newspapers, but that they were also the only underground press successes.

This lack of attention is surprising in Lauren Kessler's 1984 history of alternative media in America. For her to delimit the Vietnam-era underground press to one and one-half paragraphs at the very end of the book is unacceptable. The situation is just as bleak in mass communication readers, where out of seventeen texts examined, only five discuss the underground press at any length, all reiterating the error that the first underground newspaper was the *Village Voice*.[24]

The Underground and Mainstream Press

The third body of literature I examine in this book consists of articles published in underground newspapers, mass-market magazines, popular journals, and commercial anthologies. Unsurprisingly, few of these authors are neutral or objective in their assessment of the underground press.

Some, such as John Sinclair and Richard Neville, as well as the many other underground press newsworkers, believed the underground press was a liberatory medium.[25] For example, the editor of *Capitalism Stinks* wrote that the underground press was committed "to the belief that each individual human being is necessary to society and must have the opportunity to realize his inherent, unlimited potential."[26] Likewise, the editor of *Scimitar* opined that

The underground press makes no pretense at providing 'objective' coverage of the news. None of these papers defines its mission as the strict presentation of verifiable facts, impartial reportage of empirical events. None among the underground aspires to be a *New York Times;* objectivity is implicitly viewed as impossible, or at least unachievable. . . . So the underground press has a point of view and no embarrassment about revealing it. But beyond this, methods vary. . . . Which is more effective depends on how the purpose of the underground press is defined, to liberate people by informing them, by convincing them, or maybe by just intriguing them, making them think. . . . Perhaps the numerous approaches attempted in the underground press reflect the simplest truth of all: it takes many ways to reach many people.[27]

Others, however, claimed these papers were the product of communists determined to subvert America's youth. For example, the cultural critic for the John Birch Society, Gary Allen, charged that

The Underground Press . . . is another in a series of revolutionary tactics which are part of a grand strategy to deliver America—decadent as crumbling Rome—into the lap of the far left. This time the revolutionaries are after our teenage sons and daughters.[28]

Likewise, the Chairman of the House Un-American Activities Committee, Joe Poole, insisted that

The purpose of these newspapers ... [is] to slander and libel everyone who opposes these traitors in their attempts to destroy the American government. . . . These smut sheets are today's molotov cocktails thrown at respectability and decency in our nation. . . . *The plan of this underground press syndicate is to take advantage of that part of the First Amendment which protects newspapers and gives them freedom of the press.* . . . They know the more obscene and dirty their newspapers are, the more they will attract the irresponsible readers whom they want to enlist in their attempts to destroy the country. . . . [Underground newspapers] *encourage depravity and irresponsibility, and they nurture a breakdown in the continued capacity of the government to conduct an orderly and constitutional society.* . . . [These newspapers] *make a mockery of decency* and respectability [emphasis mine].[29]

For Thorne Dreyer and Victoria Smith, these two positions were inextricably linked.[30] It was because of the all too often blinkered response of the mainstream media and those who believed the underground press was a communist threat that many of the papers had in fact become politically radicalized.[31] As the editor of Dallas underground newspaper—*Notes from the Underground*—pointed out:

Joe Poole calls us "subversives," the *Morning News* calls us "filth," the *Times Herald* calls us "hippies," the City Council calls us "radical college students," and SMU, which spawned us, refuses to recognize our existence at all. Bob Dylan, in the movie "Don't look back," told a *Time Magazine* reporter, "Time's got too much to lose by telling the truth." Maybe that's why we're hated. We tell the truth; we've got nothing to lose. We do have something to gain, however. It's our self-respect. Yeah, we tell the truth. It's about time some newspaper did.[32]

While there were some writers—including John Berks, Jacob Brackman, Joan Didion, and Jack Nelson[33]—who attempted to breach the gulf separating the mainstream and underground presses, most did not. Consequently, the bulk of these writings are broadly divisible into an internal discourse within, and an external critique of, the counterculture. Both helped define issues for the participants, yet both also tended to "feed upon one another, solidifying and intensifying unrest as it echoed back and forth among restless people."[34]

For Dreyer and Smith it was impossible to conceive of the counterculture without the underground press, or of the underground press without the counterculture. Each was central to the other, given the fact that "the people who made the underground papers were the same people who were in the streets."[35]

While these debates and discussions focused on the relationship between the underground press and its audience, they were, in part, responses to attempts by the mass media to transform the counterculture into "folk devils" worthy of "moral panic." While some of these descriptions attempted to be sympathetic, they more often than not treated this culture as deviant and deserving of restraint. This response, it should be emphasized, was not unique to the counterculture, but the consequence of journalists setting themselves up as "watchdogs, policing organizational life or deviations from their conceptions of the order of things."[36]

For example, in the first article explaining the underground press to a lay audience, published in *Time* on 29 July 1966, the author notes that "their subject matter is largely anti-establishment, they are typically against the war in Viet Nam, against the draft and against the police. President Johnson is their favorite whipping boy, and it is unlikely that he could win them over even if he changed his initials from L.B.J. to LSD."[37]

The differences in tone and content of the descriptions of the press result from the self-definitions of the underground press being articulations and the external descriptions being visualizations. Furthermore, these differences also result in large part from authors being committed to the political and journalistic norms of their respective media.

These articulations were written by underground newsworkers who believed they were providing, "information . . . [printing] news you can't get elsewhere, and in a way which cannot be gotten elsewhere. . . . We want to . . . [be] part of, and contribute . . . to a larger movement for social change in this country."[38] This commitment was underlined by the fact that most underground journalists worked for a pittance, or for what were euphemistically known as "movement wages."[39]

In contradistinction, most mainstream visualizations were written by staff and freelance journalists, who for financial and ideological reasons, were

Deeply marked by . . . impoverished spectacular thought [and] put [themselves] at the service of the established order right from the start, even though subjectively [they] may have had quite the opposite intention. . . . [They] essentially follow the language of the spectacle, for it is the only one he is familiar with; the one which he learned to speak.[40]

Consequently, they "present . . . only the falsified, official sense of words; in a manner of speaking, it forces them to carry a pass, determines their place in the production process . . . and gives them their paycheck."[41]

Unlike those journalists who wrote for the underground press, who "were happy to be amateurs in the original sense, doing the work for love," mainstream journalists were "the media's professionals bound by wages and other rewards."[42] It would be wrong to see this as a mutual relationship between the press as dependent on the status of the journalist and the journalist as dependent on the press for his or her status. Instead, the journalist is fully aware that what is provided by the spectacle can just as easily be revoked by the spectacle.

SEMIOTICS OF RESISTANCE

In *The Underground Press and Its Cave-in*, Gitlin writes that "without a mainstream journalism to inspire us,"[43] he and his fellow underground press journalists "turned, cockily and half-consciously to earlier generations of models, to Orwell, John Reed, [and] the pre-World War I *Masses* magazine."[44] In retrospect Gitlin might seem correct, but few underground press editors were either aware of or cared for the work of Reed, Eastman, or Orwell. As was noted by Tom Forçade: "Some people say [that] the underground press began with the socialist papers of the early 1900s, while others trace it either to the beatnik little magazines of the fifties or to the *Village Voice*. While it is certainly true that there are some similarities between these early efforts and the current underground press, the latter is a separate and unique phenomenon with a history of its own. That history began with the founding of the *Los Angeles Free Press* in 1964."[45]

While it is not my place to judge whether Forçade is correct, the confusion he alludes to was in large part the consequence of the inability of underground press newsworkers to develop a mutually acceptable frame of reference for their press. One finds editors referring to their publications as "underground,"[46] an "open forum,"[47] "progressive,"[48] a "free press,"[49] "subversive,"[50] an "opposition press,"[51] and, last but by no means least, a "fifth estate."[52]

While these papers belonged to the Underground Press Syndicate and subscribed to the Liberation News Service, many of the editors and staffs were unsure of what the term "underground" meant and whether it was applicable to their audience. For Greg Kern, the label "underground" was "a sloppy word and a lot of us are sorry we got stuck with it. Underground is meaningless, ambiguous, irrelevant, wildly imprecise, undefinitive, derivative, un-copyrighted, un-controllable, and used up."[53]

For John Sinclair, on the other hand, the label aptly embraced "our culture, our art, the music, newspapers, books, posters . . . clothing . . . homes, the way we walk and talk, the way our hair grows, the way we smoke dope and fuck and eat and sleep—it is all one message and the message is FREEDOM!"[54]

Still others argued that while the term "underground" did embrace these cultural activities, they were indivisible from and grounded in political struggle. For example, the editorial committee of *Black and Red* observed that the paper was

Subversive to the power structure, and thus it joins the . . . "underground press" as a vehicle through which the alienated, the oppressed, the exploited express themselves.[55]

Despite these variations, few underground press newsworkers would have taken issue with John Wilcock's claim that "There . . . [will] always . . . [be] an underground, whatever it happens to be called. I mean now you could technically say it was sub-underground, or something like that. And eventually somebody will get off into another definition. But there are always people who are undiscovered, relatively undiscovered, and so on. And people doing fantastic creative things."[56]

Although these editors seemed resigned to label their papers as underground, there was no such agreement on what an underground press was or what its focus should be. Thus one finds the papers being described as underground in terms of where the papers were produced, "First, the words 'underground newspaper.' We are literally underground because our office is in a basement."[57] Their politics: "We called *Connections* an underground newspaper: radical going to the root of things."[58] The papers aesthetics: "The editors of this newspaper, who are all working artists, poets, playwrights etc., have seen fit to expand the role of artist as Creator-Communicator into the sphere of journalism."[59] The paper's relationship with the counterculture:

The 'Underground press' is many things (Political freedom, human rights, protest, news, underground culture, revolutionary thought, etc.). Most of all, it is the thousands of people who, like you believe in a better world free of war, hate, injustice, poverty and ignorance.[60]

And in terms of its opposition to mass media:

We exist as a counter-medium standing against other media which purport to have all the answers and solutions to problems; against all other media which would give the impression that systems of knowledge exist and that blueprints exist based on those systems and that we should follow those blueprinted systems. We take issue in contrapunctual fashion, to those media which have a monopoly on right answers.[61]

It is important to note that these are ideal themes. However, variants of them can be found in feminist, high school, military, minority, movement, and countercultural underground newspapers. I have yet to find a genre of underground papers whose editors did not focus on the needs of their community and why their papers were ideally situated to serve them.

For Leamer, this lack of any set label or definition of the underground press meant underground newsworkers and their audiences could "look at it and see something of themselves. To the political radicals it conjured up images of those dangerous and noble undergrounds that have always existed in repressive societies—so what if this all seemed as foreign as suttee; there were those who saw another America being born. *Underground* pleased those . . . who thought of themselves as part of a cultural avant-garde."[62]

This observation contrasts starkly with talk by mainstream commentators and critics of the underground press. They had many reservations about labeling this press underground. For Ethel Romm, the fact that a majority of underground press editors accepted the label underground did not matter. For her, these papers did not deserve to be called underground because it trivialized the problems and consequences of publishing such a newspaper:

The word "underground" is unsatisfactory and will be avoided here. . . . A publication you can buy on a newsstand ought not to be called "underground", the term for the anti-Fascist resistance press of Europe. . . . No underground is permitted in Cuba. . . . [In] China . . . anti-Mao editors . . . [are] arrested. The underground in Russia consists either of typed "protests" circulated from hand to hand . . . or of literature used by writers for subtle political protest.[63]

Despite her stated purpose, "to provide information with which the . . . [underground press] may be better understood,"[64] her analysis is constrained by the Cold War dichotomy of totalitarianism versus freedom.

Such claims and reservations were rejected by underground press newsworkers as beside the point. For example, Greg Kern argued "with a combined circulation approaching 1,000,000 the underground press may not seem too underground, but it is. The ideas, the staffs, the papers, its readership is more underground (10$ to anyone who can come up with a better word than underground to describe what we're talking about) than when John-Paul Sartre edited *Combat* for the French Underground in W.W.II."[65]

Romm maintained that labeling the press underground obscured more than it revealed about these papers. Instead, the papers were broadly divisible into cultural or "street corner" papers on one hand and political or "movement publications" on the other. She notes:

To make some generalizations that do not always apply, a Movement or New Left paper covers "the struggle" for a "new society" soberly. It differs from a street-corner paper when it does not cover new record releases or rock concerts; does not publish obscenities stridently; rarely experiments with flamboyant layout or typography; prints no pornography; has no essays on oriental philosophies or astrology; accepts no sex ads; is not evangelical about drugs; is not hawked on the streets or distributed through regular newsstands.[66]

This claim might seem to echo Leamer's subdivision of the underground press, but Romm's division is different and fraught with problems. Her subdivision excludes those papers—such as *Oz Magazine, The Seed,* and *The Rat*—which artfully straddled the divide separating the movement from the counterculture. Her description of "Movement or New Left" papers suggests they were indistinguishable from publications produced by the Communist Party–USA (CP-USA) in the 1930s and 1940s. Such an unfortunate move would make it impossible to differentiate a publication such as *Anarchos*, which was published by a New York anarchist collective, from *The New Masses*, which had been the in-house publication of the CP-USA from 1926 to 1947.

Despite the fact there are token similarities between these two publications—both avoided obscenities and pornography, carried no advertising, and were sold through subscription—to equate *Anarchos* with *The New Masses* would fly in the face of too much history. For example, the editors of *The New Masses* had actively opposed such publications during the 1930s. Likewise they not only ignored the suppression of Trotskyists and anarchists in the Soviet Union and Spain, they, in fact, offered fallacious justifications for doing so.[67]

Her claim that the underground press was part of a genre of publications, whose roots go back as far as Benjamin Harrison's *Publick Occurrences*,[68] is also problematic. While I do accept the fact that there has been a long-standing tradition of dissident publishing in the United States, stretching back to the pre-Revolutionary period, I do not accept the fact that scholars should ignore the claims of those involved. Consequently, the fact that Thomas Forçade claimed 'the underground papers' of the 1960s "were in basic ways demonstrably different from all predecessors"[69] deserves to be respected.

Finally, Romm's declaration that "a publication you can buy on a newsstand ought not to be called 'underground' . . . the term for the anti-Fascist resistance press of Europe,"[70] is too close to conservative dogma for comfort. While she does not claim that these papers take "advantage of that part of the First Amendment that protects newspapers and gives them freedom of press,"[71] others have.

For example, Gary Allen claimed that "New periodicals following a newspaper tabloid format erupted like the pimples of their readers to serve as the voice of the 'youthquake.' . . . [These] newspapers form a Comintern of the 'youth revolution,' spreading the word nationwide and keeping the revolting faith. It is serious business and we had better take it seriously."[72]

For many underground press newsworkers, such claims could not stand the test of the harassment they faced each and every day. If it was the case that they were able to hide behind the protections afforded them by the First Amendment, why were so many of their papers subject to official harassment? As Lawrence Leamer noted, "Underground papers have . . . suffered from . . . repression. Editors have been arrested on trumped-up charges. Paper sellers have been pushed off the street. And printers have been warned not to take work from the underground press."[73]

Unfortunately, and all too often, mainstream journalists either ignored this repression or they concluded, "It has nothing to do with freedom of the press. For what these [underground news-workers] did they got what was coming to them."[74]

Claims such as these led underground press newsworkers to conclude the mainstream press was part of the problem, which then reinforced their prior opinion that the underground press was part of the solution. For example, Ed Sanders, the editor of *Fuck You: A Magazine of the Arts*, denounced mainstream media and, by implication, mainstream news-workers, as being controlled

... [By] the creeps. Establishment papers are demented; like a diplomatic mission in a foreign country—you have to ass kiss your way in. And who can they speak for? They've no idea what it means to live in the slum on the edge of a city. A paper and its audience need a living relationship, like an organism. . . . And you can get that now. . . . A cat from the village, say, can plug into a similar underground in cities all over.[75]

CONCLUSION

Given that the underground press has been ignored for most of the last quarter century, the extant historiography consists of a debate between underground press newsworkers and their critics. For some, including Gary Allen and Joe Poole, these underground press newsworkers exploited their First Amendment privileges to "encourage depravity and irresponsibility, and they nurture a breakdown in the continued capacity of the government to conduct an orderly and constitutional society."[76]

For underground press newsworkers, such claims were not only histrionic, they deliberately ignored the fact that they were "exercising the distinctly American right to offer alternatives to policies and activities which we feel are unjust or unconstitutional. There is nothing unpatriotic about that; Americans have been doing it for almost two centuries."[77]

While I have focused in this chapter on the claims and counterclaims that swirled around the underground press, the themes raised were not unique to the 1960s. Nonmainstream newsworkers have all too often been accused, by conservatives and supporters of the status-quo, of exploiting their constitutional privileges and freedoms. Likewise, nonmainstream newsworkers have always invoked "the truth" as their primary motivation for publishing. For example, the I. W. W. publication, *One Big Union*, consistently referred to the mainstream media as *The Daily Liar*. Likewise, as evidenced by the *Battle Hymn of the Republic*, abolitionists also argued that their struggle would "make men holy" because their "truth is marching on!"[78]

In the section of this chapter titled Semiotics of Resistance, I noted that I have yet to find a genre of underground papers whose editors did not focus on the needs of their community and on why their papers were ideally situated to serve them. In chapters 3 and 4 I test whether or not this was the case for the GI movement and its media.

NOTES

1. John Adams cited in Bernard Bailyn, *Ideological Origins of the American Revolution* (Cambridge, Mass.: The Belknap Press, 1967), v.

2. Abolitionist editors were—like their underground counterparts a century later—accused of taking advantage of that aspect of the First Amendment that guaranteed their right to publish such newspapers. For example "Judge Luke Lawless . . . [who claimed] he was in favor of freedom of the press . . . believed the law should protect society from abuses of the press such as printing sermons against slavery" (Louis Edward Ingelhart, *Press Freedoms* [New York: Greenwood Press, 1987], 184).

Likewise, Joe Poole—Chairman of the House un-American Activities Committee in 1967—claimed in a 6 November 1967 speech at Yale, that "the plan of this underground press . . . is to take advantage of that part of the First Amendment which protects them and gives them freedom of press." (Joe Poole cited in Marshall Bloom, "HUAC Confronts Underground Press," in *Notes from the Underground* 1, no. 20 [1–15 December 1967]: 6).

3. See, among others, Jack Angleman, *The Underground Press* (Las Vegas: Ram Classics, M-T Publishers, 1969); Joseph Berke, ed., *Counter Culture* (London: Peter Owen Ltd., 1969); Stephen Diamond, *What the Trees Said: Life on a New Age Farm* (New York: Delacorte Press, 1971); Marc Estrin, ed., *Recreation* (New York: Dell, 1971); Rev. Thomas. King Forçade, ed., *Underground Press Anthology* (New York: Ace Books, 1972); Mitchell Goodman, ed., *The Movement toward a New America, the Beginnings of a Long Revolution, (a Collage,) a What?* (Philadelphia: Knopf and Pilgrim Press, 1970); Abbie Hoffman, *Revolution for the Hell of It* (New York: Dial, 1968); Raymond Mungo, *Famous Long Ago: My Life and Hard Times with Liberation News Service* (Boston: Beacon Press, 1970); Richard Neville, *Play Power: Exploring the International Underground* (New York: Random House, 1970); Kirkpatrick Sale, *SDS* (New York: Random House, 1973); Peter Stansill and David Marovitz, eds., *BAMN: Outlaw Manifestos and Ephemera 1965–1970* (Harmondsworth, U.K.: Penguin Books, 1971); Massimo Teodori, ed., *The New Left: A Documentary History* (New York: The Bobbs-Merrill Company, 1969).

4. Francis M. Watson, *The Alternative Media, Dismantling Two Centuries of Progress* (Rockford, Ill.: The Rockford College Institute, 1979), 7.

5. Neville, *Play Power*, 155.

6. Roger Lewis, *Outlaws of America: The Underground Press and Its Context* (Harmondsworth, U.K.: Penguin Books, 1972), 59.

7. Lawrence Leamer, *The Paper Revolutionaries* (New York: Simon and Schuster, 1972), 58.

8. Ibid., 25.

9. Ibid., 25.

10. See Thorne Dreyer and Victoria Smith, "The Movement and the New Media," in *Liberation News Service News-packet* 144 (1 March 1969): 16; Tom Forçade, "Introduction," in *The Underground Reader*, eds. Mel Howard and

Thomas Forçade (New York: Plume Books, 1972): 1–4; John Wilcock, "How the UPS Papers Fill the Gap," in *Other Scenes* 4 (April 1967): 2.

For Dreyer and Smith the fact the *Voice* "could have cared less about the underground press . . . [was] probably something to be grateful for. The underground press escaped the danger of pollution from the *Voice*'s chickenshit liberalism." (Dreyer and Smith, "The Movement and the New Media," 16).

11. Robert Glessing, *The Underground Press in America* (Bloomington: Indiana University Press, 1970), 12–13.

12. Leamer, *The Paper Revolutionaries*, 162–66.

13. Glessing, *The Underground Press in America*, 107.

14. Watson, *The Alternative Media*, 18.

15. For Leamer, the most distinctive feature of these papers lay in the fact that "they operated . . . [under the] truism: 'Everything is all right as long as it doesn't hurt other people.' . . . [They] had no restraint in language or content. . . . In truth, EVO's slum goddess, the Oracle's romantic pictures of intertwined bodies, and the Barb's accounts of Sexual Freedom League activities weren't terribly titillating. The early undergrounds didn't intend that they should be, for the sensual aspects of the papers were simply counterparts of their other broad radical interests." (Leamer, *The Paper Revolutionaries*, 53).

Likewise, Abe Peck argues these papers were: "Radical or outré, not revolutionary. The half dozen were located in big cities and college towns. . . . To varying degrees, all were concerned with the emerging youth culture. . . . Most of the papers were owned but broke; the lack of materialism matched a prevailing anti materialism and minimized any fears of libel suits. Salaries were mostly minimal, but the work was uncompromised and had its counter-community perks and status. The small staffs were overwhelmingly white, male. Like the early S.D.S, they were at this time disproportionately Jewish. The new protest would be a white-hot but historical assault on a society that activist David McReynolds branded 'only rational but no longer sane.' But despite this thinness, even the goofiness, of some of its reporting, this fledgling press managed to give new communities a sense of identity. They offered criticism and debate. They had a sense of purpose and a sense of decency." (Abe Peck, *Uncovering the Sixties* [New York: Pantheon Books, 1985], 39).

16. See Leamer, *The Paper Revolutionaries*, chapters 3–9. Peck, in *Uncovering the Sixties*, draws the same conclusions as Leamer. This is not by accident, however, as Peck's book updates and extrapolates from *The Paper Revolutionaries*. As Peck notes in his introduction, his discussion was indebted to Leamer and adds nothing new to Leamer's work (Peck, *Uncovering the Sixties*, 10).

17. Rosa Borenstein and Alan Howard, *Liberation News Service: Bourgeois or Revolutionary Journalism* (New York: self-published, 1973), 61.

18. Lewis, *Outlaws of America*, 178.

19. This split, because it permeated the movement and counterculture at every level, can be ignored with difficulty.

20. Leamer, *The Paper Revolutionaries*, 50.

21. Peck, 258.

22. The staff of *Old Mole* cited in Leamer, *The Paper Revolutionaries*, 120.

23. For example, Emery devotes four pages to the underground press in the third edition of *The Press and America* (Englewood Cliffs: Prentice Hall, 1972). This diminishes to two pages in the fifth edition and one page in the seventh.

24. Ross K. Baker, "The Underground Press Has Fallen on Evil Days," in *The Media Reader,* eds. Joan Valdes and Jeanne Crow (Dayton, Ohio: Pflaum, 1975), 278–81; Thomas Elliott Berry, "The School Paper and the Underground Press," in *Journalism in America* (New York: Hastings House, 1976), 255–57; Joseph R. Conlin, ed., "Introduction," *The American Radical Press 1880–1960,* Vol. 1 (Westport, Conn.: Greenwood Press, 1974), 3–17; Everette E. Dennis, ed., "The Underground Press," in *Magic Writing Machine* (Eugene, Oreg.: School of Journalism, 1971), 7–8; Everette E. Dennis and William L. Rivers, *Other Voices: The New Journalism, in America* (San Francisco: Canfield Press, 1974), 136–72; Verne E. Edwards Jr., ed., "Promising Signs of Success," in *Journalism in a Free Society* (Dubuque, Iowa: William C. Brown and Company, 1970), 237–39; Michael Emery and Edwin Emery, *The Press and America,* 5th ed. (Englewood Cliffs, N.J.: Prentice Hall, 1984), 571–73; Michael Emery and Edwin Emery, *The Press and America,* 7th ed. (Englewood Cliffs, N.J.: Prentice Hall, 1993), 420–21; Michael Emery and Ted Curtis Smythe, eds., *Readings in Mass Communications* (Dubuque, Iowa: William C. Brown and Company, 1974), 127–28; Ronald Hicks, ed., "Underground Papers," in *A Survey of Mass Communication* (Gretna, La.: Pelican Publishing Co., 1977), 70–71; John L. Hulteng and Roy Paul Nelson, eds., "The Underground Press," in *The Fourth Estate* (New York: Harper and Row, 1982) 201–6; Ernest C. Hynds, ed., "Alternative Newspapers," in *American Newspapers in the 1970s* (Toronto: Saunders of Ontario, 1975), 119–23; Susan Johnson, "Bundles, Packets and How the News Gets Around Underground," in *Magic Writing Machine,* ed. Everette E. Dennis (Eugene, Oreg.: School of Journalism, 1971) 49–53; Timothy Kenny, "In the Land of the Blind the One-Eyed is King," in *Magic Writing Machine,* ed. Everette E. Dennis (Eugene, Oreg.: School of Journalism, 1971), 54–59; Jack A. Nelson, "The Underground Press," in *Readings in Mass Communications,* eds. Michael Emery and Ted Curtis Smythe (Dubuque, Iowa: William C. Brown and Company, 1979), 212–25; Don R. Pember, ed., "The Subterranean Mine Shaft beneath the Sod Press," in *Mass Media in America* (Chicago: Science Research Associates, 1974), 104–11.

25. Richard Neville suggested "if you want to know what's happening in the world, you have to read the underground press" (Neville, *Play Power* 151).

26. "Editorial" in *Capitalism Stinks* 1, no. 1 (25 June 1968): 1.

27. "Editorial" in *Scimitar* 1, no. 6 (ca. 1968): 1.

28. Gary Allen, "Underground for Adults Only," in *American Opinion* 10, no. 12 (December 1967): 2.

29. Joe Poole cited in Bloom, "HUAC Confronts Underground Press," 10.

30. See Dreyer and Smith, "The Movement and the New Media," 13–30.

31. For many underground press activists, the underground press's radicalism was not merely linked to the response of the authorities, it was in fact indebted to it. For example, the editor of the *Ann Arbor Argus* wrote that the " . . . kind of stupid suppression that says 'fuck' can't be printed is just as much an enemy as a police sensor" ("Credo," in *Ann Arbor Argus* 1 [January 1969]: 1).

32. Stoney Burns, "Notes Is a Year Old" in *Notes From the Underground* 2, no. 1 (March 1968): 1.

Joe Poole had a particular disliking for *Notes from the Underground* because it had published an exclusive about him in which they revealed he had been arrested for drunken driving and resisting arrest. He had then gotten the charges dropped and suppressed all news of it. Poole made it one of his political missions to get the newspaper crushed and enlisted the support of the Dallas police to do it. (See Geoffrey Rips, "The Campaign against the Underground Press," in *UnAmerican Activities*, eds. Anne Janowitz and Nancy J. Peters [San Francisco: City Lights, 1981], 37–158).

33. See John Berks, "The Underground Press," in *Rolling Stone* (10 April 1969): 11–32; Jacob Brackman, "The Underground Press," in *Playboy* (August 1967): 83, 96, 151–57; Joan Didion, "Alicia and the Underground Press," in *The Saturday Evening Post* (13 January 1968): 14; and Jack Nelson, "The Underground Press," 212–25.

34. Herbert Blumer, "Social Unrest and Collective Protest," in *Studies in Symbolic Interaction* 1, no. 1 (1978): 5.

35. Dreyer and Smith, "The Movement and the New Media," 18.

36. Richard Ericson, Patricia Baranek, and Janet Chan, Visualizing Deviance (Toronto: University of Toronto Press, 1987).

37. "Underground Alliance," *Time Magazine* 88, no. 5 (29 July 1966): 57.

38. "On What We Need to Be Doing," in *The Old Mole* 4 (November 1968): 12.

39. According to Gitlin, underground press newsworkers "were improvising without blueprints, trying out unconventional forms of writing, learning design and layout . . . [for] . . . $40 a week—when it came" (Todd Gitlin, "The Underground Press and Its Cave-in," in *Unamerican Activities*, eds. Anne Janowitz and Nancy J. Peters [San Francisco: City Lights, 1981], 21). See also note 15 above.

40. Guy Debord, *Comments on the Society of the Spectacle* (London: Verso, 1990), 31.

41. See "All the Kings Men," in *The Situationist Anthology*, trans. Ken Knabb (Berkeley: Bureau of Public Secrets, 1981).

42. Todd Gitlin, "The Underground Press and Its Cave-in," in *UnAmerican Activities*, eds. Anne Janowitz and Nancy Peters (San Francisco: City Lights Books, 1981), 21.

43. Ibid., 21.

44. Ibid., 21.

45. The Reverend Thomas King Forçade, "Introduction," in *The Underground Reader*, eds. Mel Howard and King Thomas Forçade (New York: Plume Books, 1972), 1.

46. "We have added the underground to our name, because we think it implies resistance to hypocritical officialdom, to empty politics, to deadening styles of living." ("The New Free Press," in *Free Press Underground* 3, no. 1 [October 1967]: 3).

47. "*The Aurora* in essence is an open forum, and as such, the opinions expressed in it are not necessarily those of the publishers or regular staff. Any literate opinion that is likely to interest our readers or arouse controversy (without being libelous) will be printed." ("Policy," in *Aurora* 1, no. 2 [2 August 1968]: 2).

48. "The editorial policy of this paper is progressive. It will support views and policies that are for the promotion of . . . the principles upon which this nation was founded." ("What is Alice?" in *Alice* 1, no. 1 [18 May 1968]: 1).

49. "We're the free press, as in freedom of and that's where we are at and would like to remain. This paper is not bound to any institution or special interest group, consequently we are free to put it down on paper exactly the way it reads in our heads." (Henry Aster, "And Other Works of Dogma," in *Miami Free Press* 1 [18 April 1969]: 2).

50. "*Black and Red* is an experiment. It is subversive to the power structure, and thus it joins the New Left's 'Underground Press' as a vehicle through which the alienated, the oppressed, the exploited express themselves. Its aim is to inform the world of the local movement, and the local population of the world movement." ("Editorial," in *Black and Red* 1 (September 1968): inside front cover).

51. "As a member of the Underground Press Syndicate—Liberation News Service, *The Blue Bus* is an integral part of a community of conscience, threat places a premium on the individual and his conscience. . . . We oppose any system or part of a system that destroys an individual's freedom." ("Apple Pie, Motherhood and the American Flag," in *The Blue Bus* 1, no. 3 [April 1968]:, 2).

52. "A 'fifth estate' has emerged over the past two years. . . . They are published by youthful artists . . . who have felt a need to struggle for a voice in the face of media conformity. The papers of the fifth estate . . . concern themselves with civil libertarian issues: the war in Vietnam, the freedom of pleasure . . . of religious choice . . . of privacy, and . . . to dissent. In a time where cynicism—the traditional frame of mind for the journalist—is lacking in the monied press. The fifth estate is fighting for cynicism's reinstatement." (Walter Bowart, "EMERGING: A Fifth Estate," in *The Paper* 2, no. 1 [29 September 1966]: 10).

53. Greg Kern, "The Underground Press," in *Haight Ashbury Maverick* 2, no. 7 [1968]: 8.

54. John Sinclair, "White Panther Statement," in *Underground Press Anthology*, ed. Tom Forçade (New York: Ace Books, 1972), 92.

55. "Black and Red Is an Experiment," in *Black and Red* 1 (September 1968): inside front cover.

56. Neil Hickey, "Publisher as Revolutionary. Neil Hickey and John Wilcock rap about the alternative press," in *Bitman* 3 (31 March 1971): n.p.

57. "Editorial," in *Counterpoint* 1, no. 4 (1968): 2.

58. "Editorial," in *Connections* 2, no. 5 (December 1967): 2.

59. Walter Bowart cited in Leamer, *The Paper Revolutionaries*, 36.

60. Advertisement for the *Voice of the 'Underground Press'* published in *Williamette Bridge* 1–20 (June 1968): n.p.

61. "Who is Counterpoint," in *Counterpoint* 2, no. 1 (undated 1969): 2.

62. Leamer, *The Paper Revolutionaries*, 41.

63. Ethel Romm, *The Open Conspiracy* (Harrisburg, Penn.: Stackpole, 1970), 17–19.

64. Ibid., 9.

65. Greg Kern, "What Does it Mean?" in *Countdown* 1 (1 February 1970): 183.

66. Romm, *The Open Conspiracy*, 23.

67. In keeping with the requirements of the Comintern, they published articles accusing the POUM and CNT/FIA of being fifth columnists and leveled unsupported claims they had evidence of Trotskyist sabotage throughout the Soviet Union.

68. This position, which is taken by Ethel Romm *(The Open Conspiracy)* and Lauren Kessler *(The Dissident Press: Alternative Journalism in American History* [Beverly Hills, Calif.: Sage Publications, 1984]), results in the press being further marginalized.

69. King Thomas Forçade, "Introduction," in *The Underground Reader*, eds. Mel Howard and Thomas Forçade (New York: Plume Books, 1972), 1.

70. Romm, *The Open Conspiracy*, 17.

71. Joe Poole cited in Dreyer and Smith, "The Movement and the New Media," 20.

72. Allen, "Underground for Adults Only," 4–5.

73. Leamer, *The Paper Revolutionaries*, 125.

74. Bill Thomas, City Editor of the *Los Angeles Times,* cited in Leamer, *The Paper Revolutionaries,* 125.

75. Ed Sanders cited in Jacob Brackman, "The Underground Press," in *Playboy* 8 (1967): 83.

76. Joe Poole cited in Bloom, "HUAC Confronts Underground Press," 10.

77. "The Patriotism of Protest," in *Bragg Briefs* 2, no. 3, 4.

78. From the final verse of "The Battle Hymn of the Republic." (Found at [http://www.choraegus.com/csm/csm0001.html].)

Chapter 3

The GI Movement

INTRODUCTION

After reading through most issues of the more than 130 different GI underground papers published between 1967 and 1971,[1] as well as trawling through the historiography of the GI movement, the following two claims can be made without fear of contradiction. The first GI underground paper published was *The Bond*,[2] and there were no GI underground papers published in South Vietnam.[3] There were, however, GI-run pirate radio stations in South Vietnam that broadcast nightly "under no [military] regulations on [the] FM dial."[4]

While some GI newsworkers claimed their papers filled a vacuum, most argued their papers were responding to the stultifying effects of the military's censorship of its own media. While I have not tried to locate the rules and regulations concerning what could be broadcast over Armed Forces Radio or printed in *Stars and Stripes*, former GI broadcasters claimed they had little choice but to broadcast and print what the brass deemed acceptable. GIs who bucked this were reassigned and in some instances threatened with court-martial. For example, the GI underground paper *Aerospaced* reported in January 1970 that

Another GI broadcaster in Vietnam has charged the American Forces Vietnam Network (AFVN) with news censorship, and is facing a court-martial for it.

The GI, Sp/5 Robert Lawrence, said . . . that newsmen with the network "are not free to tell the truth." . . . As a newsman, I am dedicated to giving the public news and events worldwide and on a local level I am pledged to tell the truth at all times, and I will always tell the truth either in the military or as a civilian.

"In the military in Vietnam, I have found that a newscaster at AFVN is not free to call the truth and in essence tell it like it is."[5]

The effect of this policy on those servicemen who worked as reporters, editors, information officers, and specialists was self-preservation through self-censorship. As was pointed out by Larry Craig,[6] to keep their jobs and avoid combat, these journalists and information specialists wrote "the kind of stories . . . the army wanted."[7] Such censorship, however, had nothing to do with military intelligence and everything to do with "keeping up morale."[8]

According to the *GI Press Service*, it was these policies that were responsible for the more than "58 GI antiwar newspapers published by and for GIs . . . on bases around the country and overseas. . . . [These] substantially [augmented] . . . the quality of news and analysis for GIs who previously had access only to . . . *Stars and Stripes*—the official mouthpiece of the brass and lifers.[9] Needless to say, [the brass were] not pleased."[10]

Unfortunately these GI underground newspapers have been treated in the historiography as a subset of the civilian press rather than on their own terms. Such a position is wrongheaded and debases those who worked for these newspapers.

Scholars should not forget that GIs, despite the fact that they swore an oath to protect the Constitution, had to conform to the rules and regulations of the *Uniform Code of Military Justice* (UCMJ). Despite the best intentions of its authors—who had attempted to bring military law in line with the Constitution—the UCMJ made the brass the arbiters of the Constitution. The practical result of this, according to the editor of *Anchorage Troop*, was the routine violation of GIs' First, Fourth, Fifth, and Eighth Amendment rights.

Despite the fact that these practices were unconstitutional, the Federal Courts ruled that GIs were no longer protected by the Constitution because they had "willingly [given] up their constitutional rights when they enlisted. Weighing the benefits, either consciously or subconsciously, the men in the armed forces [had chosen] the benefits of military service over those of the *Bill of Rights*."[11]

If the Vietnam-era military had been an all-volunteer force, the Court's position that GIs had willingly traded in their Constitutional privileges and protections would have been supportable. The Vietnam-era military, however, was not such an army. It was, in fact, peopled with draftees and enlisted men enticed to join up by the slogan "choose the army before the army chooses you."

In the latter half of the 1960s, GI activists seized on this issue and called on the military to quit paying lip service to the Constitution and restore its privileges and protections to all GIs. For example, the editor of *Graffitti* wrote that

The Bill of Rights guarantees Freedom of Speech, Freedom of the Press, and Freedom of Religion. Its [sic] time GI's moved up from second class citizenship and acquired their rights.[12]

Likewise, the editor of *Rough Draft* called on his fellow GIs to

> ... [B]egin asserting [our] rights. If you don't assert them you won't have them. Our own apathy stands in the way of our liberty. If we value our liberty we cannot afford to be apathetic.
>
> Discrimination in application of judicial and non-judicial punishment, shakedown inspections, mass punishment and limitations on the freedoms of speech and press, and many other daily occurrences [sic] are violations of the constitutional rights of individuals.
>
> Appealing your case thru military channels will usually be fruitless.... Take your appeal to the people. Put the pressure on the brass. Many have done so and won.
>
> So be strong. When the brass pushes, push back. And don't compromise your liberty.[13]

It is important to remember that these demands were not made in an institutional vacuum. They were influenced and effected by a number of different groupings, including the brass, GI movement activists, and their respective civilian supporters. While the brass were able, and did, use mainstream media outlets such as *Newsweek* and *Life*, GIs did not. To publicize their position, and their plight, GI activists became GI newsworkers and published their own newspapers.

SOME REMARKS ABOUT THE GI MOVEMENT

In 1969, the editor of *The American Exile in Canada*[14] claimed: "Soldier-edited underground newspapers are appearing on military bases this spring faster than the armed forces can keep track of them.... [These] antiwar GI newspapers are being taken to barbershops, smuggled into service clubs, post exchanges, company day rooms, laundries and even barrack latrines. For many GIs it is their first contact with the U.S. antiwar movement."[15]

These publications, however, were not merely "antiwar" publications. Instead, they were the products of an emergent antimilitarism among active duty personnel. By antimilitarism, I do not mean to imply that GI activists were opposed to all forms of military activity or to those involved in the military, however directly or tangentially. Instead, they opposed the synthesis of military action with the goals and needs of corporate imperialism.

Unfortunately, critics of the movement, including Terry Anderson and Robert Heinl, as well as some former GI activists, such as Andy Stapp and Larry Waterhouse, have retrofitted the GI movement to conform to their politics and biographies. For example, Stapp makes the claim that the GI movement was peopled with draftees and enlisted men who, like himself, had been antiwar activists before their induction.[16] It was not. Those GIs who enlisted while opposed to the war were not only a minority, they were well known to Army Intelligence at their time of enlistment and rarely sent to Vietnam.

Indeed, as was found by Hamid Molwana and Paul Geffert, most of the more than 2,0000 veterans attending the April 1971 Vietnam Veterans against the War protest in Washington, D.C., had either supported, or had no opinion about, the war before going to Vietnam. More than half, 61.7 percent, reported undergoing "a drastic change in . . . [their] views about U.S. involvement in Vietnam"[17] while serving in Vietnam.[18]

Similarly, claims by members of the Joint Chiefs of Staff—including Generals Westmoreland and Walt—that widespread desertion and dissent among active duty servicemen were unique to the Vietnam War also fly into the face of history. During the American Civil War, for instance, 260,399 soldiers deserted the Union Army, at a rate of 4,647 per month in 1863; 7,333 per month in 1864; and 4,368 per month in 1865. Of these, at least 10,000 were reportedly living in Canada.

Likewise, in 1917 and 1918—after the U.S. entered the First World War—30,000 to 60,000 U.S. citizens moved to Canada either to avoid being drafted or after they had deserted. Finally, more than 20,000 GIs were court-martialed for desertion during the Second World War. David Surrey (1982) argues these figures, coupled with evidence of widespread draft resistance, illustrate the fact that the Vietnam situation was by no means unique:

Resistance, while varied in form and . . . quantity, was apparent across our history of military conflicts. The destruction of draft board records dates back at least to the Revolution, was very significant in the Civil War, and was in evidence in World War 1. Draft evasion . . . was rampant during the Civil War, and widespread in World War 1. Desertions reached nearly epidemic proportions in both the Revolution and Civil War. . . . The use of Canada as a refuge also dates back to the Revolution, was very significant in the Civil War, and noticeable in World War 1.[19]

Claims that the GI movement was originally inspired, aided, or directed by the civilian movement are equally problematic and obscure the fact that few civilian activists had any time for, or paid any attention to, the military antiwar movement. For example, Fred Gardner, a pre-Vietnam veteran, approached movement activists in Berkeley and proposed setting up a network of "hip coffeehouses in army towns,"[20] but they rejected his overture. Among other things, these activists claimed GIs "were murderers, the enemy" and "no better than cops."[21]

There are other problems with the attempt to shift the locus of the GI movement from the military to the civilian sphere that need to be addressed. First, it voids the crucial issue of the GI movement's effect on the military as an institution as well as its ability to successfully prosecute

the war in Vietnam. While the question of its effect on the military's ability to prosecute the war in Vietnam lies outside the scope of this book, it
can be reported that GI activists believed the war would not end until
active duty servicemen refused to fight en masse. For the editor of *Aboveground:*

It is becoming more apparent everyday who is finally going to end the war in Vietnam. It is difficult for a soldier to oppose the war, this I know truly well. The fact
still remains that it is something we soldiers are going to have to do because of the
simple fact that nobody else can, half as effectively.[22]

Second, such claims either ignore or play down the legal and economic
ramifications facing GIs who chose to speak out. In spite of the fact that
the FBI,[23] CIA,[24] and local police departments sought to bypass the First
Amendment,[25] civilian newsworkers and antiwar demonstrators could
not be jailed for exercising their First Amendment rights.

This was not the case for GI activists and editors. In fact, between 1966
and 1969 the average sentence imposed on GI activists for their involvement in antiwar activities, by military court-martial, was five and one-
quarter years at hard labor.[26]

To ignore these differences, or maintain that the GI movement was
inspired and influenced by the civilian movement, supports and reinforces the claims of the movement's conservative critics. Chief among
these were the members and staff of the House Committee on Internal
Security, including Congressmen John Schmitz and Roger Zion, who
maintained that the GI movement was as follows:

A term used by the communist press . . . to describe that aspect of the antiwar
movement directed against the military. . . . It is a combination of . . . [a few] GIs
and civilians . . . whose antiwar efforts are directed toward organizing servicemen
against the war and the military system itself and linking that struggle with the
subsequent struggle for the takeover of political power in the United States.[27]

To support their position, the committee deliberately ignored the claims
and demands of GI activists, which, given the surveillance and infiltration
of the GI movement, had to be known to them. Instead, they pointed to
Lenin's *21 Conditions* (1919)[28] and the resolutions passed at the Sixth
World Congress of the Comintern (1928) as evidence of Communist control of both the civilian and military antiwar movements. These resolutions and conditions "contain . . . what many Soviet experts maintain is
the doctrinal framework of Communist-manipulated antimilitarism."[29]

One only need consider the grab bag of organizations, identified as
adhering to this "doctrinal framework," to see the bankruptcy of their
own intellectual leanings. Among other groups said to be using GIs were

"the Communist Party USA—CPUSA"[30] and their various unaffiliated New Left allies including "the SWP . . . and the . . . Progressive Labor Party."[31]

Unfortunately, not one of the "many Soviet experts" invoked by the Committee bothered to remind the congressmen that the "doctrinal framework" of the Communist Party since 1927 had identified Trotskyists as enemies of the Soviet Union. While the Soviets may have been fomenting antimilitarism abroad, they were in a virtual state of war with the People's Republic of China at home.

Given that the Socialist Workers Party (SWP) claimed to be Trotskyist and Progressive Labor Maoist, it does not take much to realize any alliance between these factions and the Communist Party would be polarized and tenuous at best. Among other problems, the movement's competing ideologies resulted in "agonizingly long meetings, sapped energies, frayed nerves, stalled planning and disillusionment."[32] Former Communist Party and SWP activists, such as Bettina Aptheker and Peter Canejo, now agree that their ideological blinkers caused them to "tear . . . each other apart,"[33] because "talking to each other as *humans* who want to end the war . . . was beyond us."[34]

If the GI movement were directed and influenced by these different organizations, as its critics claimed, then both the GI movement and its press should have been split asunder along the same ideological and political lines. This did not happen.

Ultimately, there was little difference between the accusations levied against the GI movement by the House Committee on Internal Security and those levied against supposed Communists by the FBI and the House un-American Activities Committee. What was different, however, was the response of these GIs, who not only refused to be intimidated by the trappings of power, but also dismissed their critics as "a racist-military clique," "pigs," "fascists," and "war criminals."[35] According to the editor of *Morning Report*, these critics were never ". . . concerned with the consequences of their actions. . . . [T]hey created and committed a war machine to fit their needs irregardless of cost in money or human suffering. They . . . used [us] as pawns in their giant games of imperialist expansion . . . to go fight and kill [their] enemies."[36]

It is important to note, however, that these activists were suitably equipped to confront their accusers. They had not only been socialized to believe that the Soviet Union was an "aggressive, godless empire intent on destroying freedom and subjugating the people of the world."[37] They had also been called on to "pay any price, bear any burden and meet any hardship"[38] in the defense of freedom (Figure 3.1).

Unlike those who had framed and propagandized this call to arms, most of whom were born before the Great Depression, these future GIs had internalized its broad ideological outlines in part through their edu-

Figure 3.1. Ask Not What Your Country Will Do to You.
Artist: unknown. *Source: Duck Power* 1, no. 7 (22 December
1969): 9.

cation and more importantly through their consumption of war comics
and movies. The latter had prepared the future GI for a lifetime of pop-
culture combat, which "only existed on celluloid, videotape and in
print. . . . [These] fed a generation a consistent diet of war images . . . giving symbolic form to a number of ideas which there upon achieved the
status of everyday knowledge."[39]

This is best illustrated by the fact that many GIs arrived in Vietnam
believing their war would be no different from the one fought by their
fathers and uncles in Western Europe. Unfortunately, they quickly discovered that they were not viewed as liberators. Instead, they were an occupation army to be resisted by any means necessary, including using
children as booby traps.

GIs quickly realized that they were fighting a war of attrition against an
enemy indistinguishable from the civilian population. Unprepared to
fight a guerrilla war, and unable to separate civilians from the enemy, GIs

began to exact a terrible revenge for their losses in battle on the local population.

Shocked by what they saw, and oftentimes did,[40] a number of veterans began to question whether Vietnam, with its corrupt authoritarian government, had been worth their burden and hardship. When they voiced these concerns, however, the brass accused them of introducing "divisiveness . . . into the army"[41] and causing fellow GIs to die needlessly.[42] They were then court-martialed, sentenced to years at hard labor without pay, and dishonorably discharged for exercising what they believed were their constitutionally protected First Amendment rights.

This flew in the face of what they had learned separated the United States from the Soviet Union. Among other things, the Soviet Union was a " 'police state' that hindered individual expression . . . and severely circumscribed public dialogue."[43] Consequently, when they were accused of being Communists for attempting to exercise their First Amendment rights, they reacted with understandable anger and scorn.

For example, the editor of *Anchorage Troop* suggested that it was typical of lifers to confuse the attempt to exercise those freedoms guaranteed under the Constitution with a Communist plot. "Ah yes, the Neanderthal minds of the lifers will probably attribute this paper to the work of the INTERNATIONAL COMMUNIST CONSPIRACY or at least give us the status of enemy."[44]

The editor of *Bragg Briefs* noted that "Freedom of thought is considered to be a communist plot by some of the babbling mentalities of our brass,"[45] and the editor of *Head-On!* claimed his paper was "not a Communist paper. It is not a Communist-controlled paper. We are not Communist-influenced or Communist inspired, and Russia does not send us weekly pay checks. So don't listen to the officers, lifers or weak-minded peons who talk through their dust covers."[46]

For the editors of *The Retaliation,* and *WE GOT THE brASS,*[47] the brass and lifers did not only misinterpret their actions, they were, in fact, responsible for those allegedly communist-inspired activities. "How did the movement start here? Well contrary to popular (lifer's) belief, it isn't a commie-inspired movement. Rather, it was inspired by the lifers themselves. The constant harassment and bullshit lifers subject us to has forced us up against the wall. We intend to reverse roles and put the lifers up against the wall. For only then will we gain the rights supposedly guaranteed us as American citizens."[48]

The importance of these rights, for GI newsworkers, can best be illustrated by the fact that out of the 710 articles examined for this book, 224 invoke the Constitution and the Bill of Rights. While only 18 of these specifically mentioned the Bill of Rights by name, 58 quoted the First Amendment in full, 33 invoked the GI's right to free assembly, 41 expressed their right to a free press, 92 mentioned their right of free speech, 24 included their right to petition the authorities for redress of their grievances, and 121 insisted their activities were sanctioned by the Constitution.

Some GI activists went beyond these appeals to the Constitution and Bill of Rights, arguing that the movement was engaged in the unfinished work of the American Revolution. For example, the editor of *Open Ranks* argued that GI activists, "like the revolutionaries who founded this country . . . believe that all men should possess certain inalienable rights. . . . Our newspaper . . . is run with the conviction that individual liberty really is the principle upon which this country was founded."[49] Similarly, editor of *Bragg Briefs* contended that he and his fellow activists were

. . . [E]xercising the distinctly American right to offer alternatives to policies and activities which we feel are unjust or unconstitutional. There is nothing unpatriotic about that; Americans have been doing it for almost two centuries.

When this Country was a world infant, its leaders established its first government according to Articles of Confederation; at the time, they judged such a form of government to be best. The people of the new nation proved them wrong. Dissent and even violence were prevalent throughout the 13 states. And so those leaders— the same men we have almost deified historically—admitted their mistake and sat down to reason out a new approach. The result was the Constitution of the United States. Similar events have been occurring ever since, and the nationwide upheaval the country is experiencing today is merely a reassertion of historical precedent.[50]

The Vietnam Veterans against the War referred to themselves as "Winter Soldiers," a term derived from the opening passage of Thomas Paine's first *Crisis Paper*.[51] The editor of *Fun Travel Adventure* likened the Fort Jackson 8 to the Founding Fathers, who "in 1776 . . . got together and petitioned the ruling authorities for their rights. They also held meetings to discuss the issues that were so important to them like free speech and the right to hold meetings and to present grievances. . . . At Ft. Jackson [South Carolina], a group of GIs are attempting to do the same thing, but it is unlikely that the Army will nominate them for the Medal of Honor."[52]

Still, other GI activists likened the military justice system to the British Star Chamber[53] and the trial of GI press activists to the trial of John Peter Zenger. They implied that the military and its corporate and political allies were the modern equivalent of the British colonial government. An anonymous artist in the *Fort Lewis Free Press* suggested that President Nixon should remember that the American people had already overthrown one tyrannical ruler (Figure 3.2).

Black GIs aligned with the Black Panther Party argued that the GI movement was, in fact, a continuation of the civil rights movement. For example, the editor of *As You Were* wrote that "the GI movement is similar to the older Black and Brown struggles, in that it was born out of oppression and fear. This Movement manifests itself in many ways and on many levels. It is revolutionary because new structures, attitudes, and possibili-

Figure 3.2. Advice for the Commander in Chief. Artist: unknown. *Source: Ft. Lewis Free Press* 1, no. 2 (September 1970): 4.

ties are either replacing old ones or are entirely unique to the scene the belief that ends and means are related is at the core of the Movement's revolutionary vitality."[54]

Still other GI activists argued their struggle was but one episode in the long and yet unfinished struggle of the American working class for economic and political justice. GI editors affiliated with the American Servicemen's Union (ASU)[55] claimed the Army was just a large factory where GIs were forced to work under sweatshop conditions with no recourse to representation. For example, the editor of the *Rap!* argued the following:

Well brothers good times have come. There is a way and a good, time-proven method to get your rights. This hope comes in the form of an organization formed by GIs to get their rights, it's called the American Serviceman's Union (ASU). . . . It is well organized and feared . . . by the brass. It is a successful organization. It is yours, if you are serious about wanting to be treated like a human being instead of a chunk of mobile meat. . . . The Union will help you organize against the pigs and will provide strong support for any . . . members in need of legal counsel. This Union is only as strong as the spirit and dedication that its members display, so don't join unless you are sincerely interested in obtaining your rights and making a *united* stand against the brass. Very few, if any, hot headed individuals have or can beat the pigs in a system that is set up for *pigs*. It's obvious then, that the ASU is the best course of action to follow to realize any significant results against the OD pigs.[56]

Finally, GI activists called on GIs to support the Women's Movement and Cesar Chavez's drive to unionize farm workers. Thus, the editor of *Rap!* demanded his fellow GIs boycott grapes in military messes:

Figure 3.3. Generals Gorge on Grapes. Artist: unknown. *Source: Aboveground* 1, no. 3 (October 1969): 2.

At a time when consumers all across America are rejecting the grapes of wrath and supermarkets are refusing to handle them, the Department of Defense has increased grape purchases over 350%. . . . The Defense Department is buying the scab grapes the growers cannot sell elsewhere. . . . Don't eat [these] grapes of wrath until the strike and boycott are over. . . . Let us show solid proof that we do not want to break the strike and boycott. Solidarity with the farm workers.[57]

This was accompanied by a cartoon (Figure 3.3), which graphically illustrated what activists believed were the consequences of the Pentagon's increased consumption of grapes.

THE INSTITUTIONAL LOCUS OF THE GI PRESS

By the fall of 1969, "every major base . . . [had] an activist group of soldiers . . . [who] bravely attempt to publish journals, organize rallies and establish peace centers. . . . Despite intimidation, harassment and imprisonment, large numbers of G.I.'s [sic] are speaking out against the war and are attempting to enlarge their efforts for peace."[58]

They were able to do so because the GI movement was no longer isolated from the larger civilian movement. While I do not have the time, or
space, to tease out the different ways in which GIs aided civilians and
vice-versa, I do need to note that some civilian activists did move to military towns to set up and run antiwar coffeehouses. These provided a
much needed refuge from "the violent, venal atmosphere of the . . . strips
of bars, whorehouses . . . and pawnshops"[59] that had sprung up in the
vicinity of every army base.

As the number of GIs opposed to the war increased, the GI movement
splintered into different groupings and alliances—including the American
Servicemen's Union, the GI Association, and the Movement for a Democratic Military—each of which claimed to represent all active duty GIs and
enlisted men. Among other demands, these and similar groups called for
the overhaul of the military justice system, an end to the military class system, and the immediate withdrawal of all U.S. forces from Southeast
Asia.[60]

While it is impossible, thirty years after the fact, to gauge the influence
and effect of these coffeehouses and antimilitarist organizations; they
were, in fact, subject to the whims of the local base commander.

Only the GI press could circumvent the restrictions imposed by the base
commander, who could not stop civilians from handing newspapers to
GIs outside the base. Nor could he, without a military policeman watching every nook and cranny on base, stop GI activists from leaving them in
"barbershops" and smuggling them "into service clubs, post exchanges,
company day rooms, laundries and even barrack latrines."[61]

These papers empowered their subscribers by drawing their attention
to the activities of other antiwar GIs in the military. The editor of The
AWOL Press, for example, argued that his paper kept its readers in contact
with the antiwar movement at bases throughout the United States and "in
touch with the ideas and actions of dissent everywhere."[62] Likewise, the
editor of Flag in Action insisted that his and other GI papers provided an
"information service which . . . seek[s] out and present[s] relevant information from across the country."[63] Lastly, the editor of The Ally argued
that these GI-produced papers not only provide a "means of communication among antiwar GIs," but break "down the isolation many GIs' [sic]
feel."[64]

These papers also helped link the GI and civilian movements and in the
process broke the barriers between GIs and civilians. As was pointed out
by the editor of Counterpoint in a letter to The Ally, "We GI's [sic] need the
civilians to defend us. If there weren't a civilian antiwar movement, there
wouldn't be a GI one. The civilians need us . . . to destroy that last bullshit
argument that opposing the war means you're not supporting the servicemen."[65]

CONCLUSION

In this chapter I have focused on the GI movement and its treatment in the historiography. In looking at this, I have sketched out a number of themes that will be explored at greater length in the following chapters. These include the relationship between the GI newsworkers and their publics, which I imply empowered both to continue with their struggle. I explore this at length in the next chapter.

I spent a good deal of time exploring the GI movement's own historicism, the central theme of which was best summed up by the editor of *Bragg Briefs*, who wrote that

If what we are doing is un-American, then that lauded ideal, the American Spirit, has undergone a number of degenerative changes since its inception. Have apathy, docility and intolerance been added to those patriotic qualities we have been taught to admire in our predecessors?

Being a patriot was not easy in 1776 and it is no easier today, for it demands sacrifice and a willingness to bear abuse and reprehension. We who have spoken out declare our willingness to be patriots in the true, historical sense of the word.[66]

Needless to say, the military did not only disagree with this GI, they in fact went out of their way to silence him and his fellow GI newsworkers. In the following chapters, I shall focus on the claims of these so-called patriots (chapter 4) and the lengths to which the military was willing to go in their effort to stifle them (chapter 5).

In chapter 6, I expand on the discussion above concerning the GI activist's response to claims that they were Communists and Fifth Columnists. This chapter focuses on how these GIs utilized their descriptions of those persons who effectively ruled their lives to fill out the movement's "maps of meaning."

Lastly, chapter 7 will expand upon my claim that the generation of servicemen who served in Vietnam had been uniquely prepared for a lifetime of pop-culture combat. In this chapter I pay special attention to both the environs in which the GI movement emerged and the communities these GI activists grew up in. Drawing on the work of Stuart Hall and his colleagues, I argue that the GI movement can most usefully be interpreted as a "spectacular subculture" and not as a subset or afterthought of the civilian movement.

NOTES

1. For a full list of GI publications produced between 1967 and 1973, see David Cortright, *Soldiers in Revolt: The American Military Today* (New York: Anchor Press, 1975), appendix 1. For a complete list of the GI publications, including the dates of each issue, used in this book, see Appendix 2: GI Publications, 1967–1970.

2. The first issue of *The Bond* was published on 23 June 1967.

3. Colonel Robert Heinl claimed that there was one GI newspaper, *GI Says*, published in South Vietnam. If this was true, then it was known to no GI activist outside South Vietnam. There is no record of it in any other GI newspaper, most of which actively sought out other GI publications to reinforce their claims that the U.S. military was seething with dissent. There was a Vietnamese edition of *WE GOT THE brASS*, but it was printed in Hong Kong. The only other newspaper to be printed in and around Southeast Asia was *The Whig*, which was published in Manila.

Furthermore, none of the principal archives of GI resistance materials, including the Special Collections department of Northwestern University Libraries, the State Historical Society of Wisconsin, Temple University's Contemporary Culture Archive, or Swarthmore College's Peace Collection have any record of this publication.

4. Radio First Termer ca. 1970. Radio First Termer was a Saigon-based radio station. Recordings of Radio First Termer broadcasts can be found at [http://www.earthstation1.com/1stermer.html].

5. "GI Broadcaster Tells the Truth," in *Aerospaced* 2, no. 1 (ca. January 1970): 1, 6.

6. Larry Craig served in Vietnam as a public information officer with the Twenty-fifth Infantry Division.

7. Larry Craig, in testimony before the Winter Soldier Hearings (Detroit), February 1971. (Downloaded from the Sixties Project web site at [http://lists.village.virginia.edu/sixties/HTML_docs/Scholar.html].)

8. Richard Perrin, "Blind Nationalism," in *Act* 1, no. 2 (ca. 1968): 1.

9. "Brass" and "lifer" were/are derogatory terms used to refer to career officers and noncommissioned officers. One's status as a brass or lifer was entirely dependent on rank.

10. "Distribution Denied (But Read All about It)," in *GI Press Service* 2, no. 3 (26 February 1970): 38.

11. T. C. Sinclair, "The Military and Freedom of Speech" (unpublished term paper, Austin: The University of Texas, 1967), 3–4.

12. "Editorial," in *Graffitti* 1 (June 1969): 4.

13. "From Apathy to Action," in *Rough Draft* 1 (March 1969): 3.

14. *The American Exile in Canada* was published by deserters and draft dodgers living in Montreal. According to its editor, the paper would assist deserters and draft dodgers adjust to their life in exile.

15. "Resistance in the Military," in *The American Exile in Canada* 1, no. 15 (May 1969): 8.

16. In Stapp and Waterhouse's case, this position was ideologically grounded because of their affiliation with the Socialist Workers Party (Waterhouse) and Youth Against War and Fascism (Stapp); they had been expected to enlist and try to radicalize the military from within.

17. In June 1971, Dr. Hamid Molwana and Paul Geffert published a "profile study of members of the Vietnam Veterans against the War." In contradistinction to the claims of the antiwar movement's conservative critics, most of these veterans had either supported—or had no opinion—about the war before going to Vietnam. Furthermore, when asked about their prewar political beliefs, 29.5 percent reported they had been conservative and 29.5 percent reported they had been moderates. Only 7 percent had reported being radicals. Finally, and most importantly, 61.7 percent reported seeing "a drastic change in . . . [their] views about U.S.

involvement in Vietnam [while serving in Vietnam]" (Hamid Molwana and Paul Geffert, "Vietnam Veterans against the War: A Profile Study of the Dissenters," in *The New Soldier,* eds. David Thorne and George Butler [New York: The MacMillan Company, 1971], 174).

18. David Surrey, *Choice of Conscience: Vietnam Era Military and Draft Resisters in Canada* (New York: Praeger, 1982), 20.

19. Ibid., 32.

20. Fred Gardner, "Hollywood Confidential: Part I," in *Viet Nam Generation Journal & Newsletter* 3, no. 3. (Found online at [http://lists.village.virginia.edu /sixties/HTML_docs/Scholar.html].)

21. Ibid., 5.

22. Curtis Stocker, "AG Unclassified," in *Aboveground* 1, no. 5 (December 1969): 2.

23. See Rev. Thomas King Forçade, "Obscenity, Who Really Cares?" in *The Underground Reader,* eds. Mel Howard and Thomas Forçade (New York: Plume Books, 1972) 159–72.

24. See Angus McKenzie, *Secrets: The CIA's War at Home* (Berkeley: University of California Press, 1997), 15–57.

25. See Geoffrey Rips, "The Campaign against the Underground Press," in *Unamerican Activities,* eds. Anne Janowitz and Nancy J. Peters (San Francisco: City Lights, 1981) 37–158.

26. See Table 6.1.

27. Alma Pfaff, "Testimony of Alma Pfaff," in House Committee on Internal Security, *Investigation of Attempts to Subvert the United States Armed Services,* 92nd Cong., 1st sess., 1971, Committee Print 6386.

28 Ibid., 6383.

29. Hon. Richard Ichord (D. Missouri), "Contributing Factors to the Morale Crisis in the Armed Services," in House Committee on Internal Security, *Investigation of Attempts to Subvert the United States Armed Services,* 92nd Cong., 1st Sess., 1971, Committee Print 6381–6395.

30. Ibid., 6383.

31. Ibid., 6383.

32. Tom Wells, *The War Within: America's Battle over Vietnam* (Berkeley: University of California Press, 1994), 54.

33. Bettina Aptheker cited in Wells, *The War Within,* 54.

34. Peter Canejo cited in Wells, *The War Within,* 55.

35. See "Editorial," in *A'bout Face* 1, no. 6 (12 September 1970): 1; "Check Us Out," in *Attitude Check* 2, no. 1 (1 February 1970): 5; "What We're About," in *Broken Arrow* 1, no. 1 (n.d.): 1; "Why This Newspaper," in *Demand for Freedom* 1 (7 October 1970): 1; Roger Priest, "The Great Disloyalty Trial," in *OM: Special Court-Martial Edition* (1970): 2.

36. "Editorial," in *Morning Report* 1, no. 1 (May 1970): 1.

37. Richard Stacewicz, *Winter Soldiers: An Oral History of the Vietnam Veterans against the War* (New York: Twayne Publishers, 1996), 24.

38. President Kennedy cited in Stacewicz, *Winter Soldiers,* 25.

39. Lloyd Lewis, *The Tainted War: Culture and Identity in Vietnam War Narratives* (Westport, Conn.: Greenwood Press, 1985), 22.

40. See Mark Lane, *Conversations with Americans* (New York: Simon and Schuster, 1970).

41. General Westmoreland cited in "Growth of GI Power," in *The Ally* 17 (June 1969): 3.

42. Ibid., 3.

43. Stacewicz, *Winter Soldiers*, 27.

44. Ibid., 1.

45. "The Birth of the Black Brigade," in *Bragg Briefs* 2, no. 5 (December 1969): 3.

46. "A Declaration," in *Head-On!* 1 (25 December 1968): 6.

47. *WE GOT THE brASS* was the only GI paper to appear in three editions, one produced in Germany, one in Japan, and one in Hong Kong. The latter listed itself as the Vietnamese edition.

48. "Editorial," in *WE GOT THE brASS* (German ed.) 3 (ca. 1969): 3.

49. "Statement of Purpose," in *Open Ranks* 1, no. 5 (February 1970): 3.

50. "The Patriotism of Protest," in *Bragg Briefs* 2, no. 3 (November 1969): 4.

51. See William Crandell's "Opening Statement" at the Winter Soldier Investigation hearings [http://lists.village.virginia.edu/sixties/HTML_docs/Resources /Primary/Winter_Soldier/WS_02_opening.html].

52. "Jackson's Doin It," in *Fun Travel Adventure* 8 (May 1969): 11.

53. See Roger Priest, "1st Amendment: "It's Crap," in *OM* 4 (October 1969): 2.

54. "As You Were—A Mirror Of Non-Violent Revolution In America," in *As You Were* 13 (April 1970): 1.

55. Among the publications edited by members of ASU were *Act, The Bond, Broken Arrow, Fed Up!, Fun Travel Adventure,* and *Rap!*

56. "ASU Power," in *Rap!* 10 (November 1970): 3.

57. "Farmworkers' Children Go Hungry as Generals Gorge on Grapes!" in *The Rap!* 2 (1969): 2–3.

58. David Cortright, untitled report prepared for the National Convention of the U.S. Antiwar Movement held in Chicago in December 1970, p. 1. (Found among the David Cortright Papers housed at the Swarthmore College Peace Collection.)

59. Fred Gardner, "Case Study in Opportunism: The GI Movement," in *Second Page Supplement* (October 1971): 5.

60. Among other things, the Movement for a Democratic Military demanded the right to collective bargaining, full constitutional protection for all servicemen and servicewomen, the immediate end to military censorship, the abolition of the present court-martial system, minimum wages, freedom for all political prisoners, the immediate withdrawal of U.S. forces from Southeast Asia, and an end to the draft.

61. "Resistance in the Military," in *The American Exile in Canada* 1, no. 15 (May 1969): 8.

62. "AWOL Needs You," in *The AWOL Press* 1, no. 11 (1969): 1.

63. "News from the Staff," in *Flag in Action* 1 (November 1968): n.p.

64. "Growth of GI Power," in *The Ally* 17 (June 1969): 3.

65. "We Disagree," in *The Ally* 16 (May 1969): 3.

66. "The Patriotism of Protest," in *Bragg Briefs* 2, no. 3 (November 1969): 4.

Chapter 4

The GI Underground Press

INTRODUCTION

A number of underground newsworkers—including Marshall Bloom, Thorne Dreyer, Ray Mungo, and Victoria Smith—argued that their papers filled a vacuum left by the collective failure of mainstream media to address the needs of the growing counterculture and anti–Vietnam War movements. This does not mean that the mainstream newsworkers ignored these communities. On the contrary, they actively visualized them as "folk devils" deserving "moral panic."[1]

In contradistinction to a biased and often distorted treatment, underground newsworkers "regularly . . . reported on the black revolt [the] GI . . . and . . . women's movement . . . police strategies and attacks, most of it news . . . not deemed *fit to print* in most respectable organs. They brought criticism of the war and sympathetic treatment of the antiwar movement to soldiers who had no other channels. They made public facts about the movement's growing net of community institutions. . . . They took the New Left seriously as something to write about, and at their best, probed deeper than did the movement's own organizational sheets."[2]

The breadth and depth of these concerns reflect well on the intellectual and political vitality of the counterculture/movement. The fact that these movements and activities were all covered in the underground press is indicative of the diversity of these papers and the special relationship between the underground press and its public.[3]

Underground newsworkers did not observe the counterculture and antiwar movement from the sidelines. They actively participated in both. Because they worked long hours for a pittance,[4] however, they depended on community activists to alert them to upcoming demonstrations and cultural events. Their treatment of these events provided a mirror for the community whose activities they publicized, yet it also emboldened the participants to continue organizing and agitating.[5]

As evidenced by the editorials and statements of purpose examined for this book, this interaction lies at the heart of the press relationship with its public and its differentiation from mainstream media. This was also the case for the GI press. To illustrate this, the chapter focuses on how GI newsworkers envisioned their relationship with those they claimed to speak for and how they differentiated their publications from the *New York Times*, *Time Magazine*, and *Stars and Stripes*.

THE GI PRESS AND ITS PUBLIC

I now turn my attention to the GI newsworkers' vision of their relationship with their public and how their papers served the needs of both. If these needs changed, the paper would either change its own focus to reflect new demands or simply close down. For example, the former editor of *Attitude Check* claimed his paper had

Closed down because it . . . [wasn't] getting the full support of the people. Third World people (black, brown, red, yellow) couldn't relate to it because they thought it was . . . white. White people . . . because they thought it was a black.[6]

These comments—made at a time when the military was being shaken by internal racial conflicts[7]—should not be interpreted as evidence that the GI movement was breaking down. Instead, the GI movement was spreading and growing. As this same GI newsworker noted, black and white GIs were "struggling to reach the same goals. Until all of us are free none will be free."[8]

As oft occurred, when some GI papers closed, others were founded to take their place. For instance, the closure of *Attitude Check* spawned two new papers, *All Ready on the Left* and *Black Unity*, which were neither carbon copies of each other nor of their predecessor.

All Ready on the Left was one of the few GI papers to publish record and film reviews, choosing as its logo a duck in a pith helmet with a raised clenched left fist. *Black Unity*, on the other hand, was unabashedly pro–Black Panther with no time for records or films. Despite these differences, both reported on movement activities—and the military's attempt to suppress these activities—at Camp Pendelton and other U.S. military installations across the United States, Europe, and Asia.

These reports served activists in a number of ways. First, they contradicted claims, made in the mainstream media by Gen. Lewis Walt and others, that the GI movement was nonmilitary, directed by communists, and, in effect, a GI movement in name only.[9]

Such accusations were dismissed as absurd by, among others, the editor of *Anchorage Troop,* who suggested they were made by Neanderthal minds. The editor of *Bragg Briefs* argued that the movement's critics considered "freedom of thought . . . a communist plot,"[10] and the editor of *Retaliation* roared: "This is not a Communist newspaper. It is not . . . Communist controlled . . . influenced . . . [or] inspired, and we receive no financial backing from any Communist regime. So don't listen to the officers and Pig lifers when they say this feeble minded shit to you."[11]

Second, they offered potential resistors concrete evidence that they were not alone in their opposition to, and alienation from, the war in Vietnam. The need for this was underscored by the editor of *Broken Arrow,* who wrote that

Our minds have not become warped and closed by twenty years of blind obedience to a corrupt, violent institution bent on not building, but destroying everything for which our country has stood these last two centuries. We as intelligent human beings are pressured to adopt these same standards with their moral and human wrongs. This we cannot, in all good conscience, do. As a result of this feeling, the GI Movement has become an important first step, one so unified and strong that for the last two years the brass have been faced with something they still don't fully understand. And it frightens them. They can no longer expect their impulsive moves to end our struggle. This has been proven many times in the past. . . . This has prevented much of the kangaroo court activity for which the military is infamous.[12]

Third, the fact that these papers existed at all, let alone were growing in size and number, offered concrete evidence to GIs—and civilians alike—that the military was seething with dissent and discontent. According to the editor of *The Underground Oak,* "We at Oak Knoll feel it imperative that other members of the armed forces and civilians become aware of dissent within the military. Therefore, we decided to promulgate our views, situations, conditions through this news paper."[13]

For the editor of *The Ally,* these papers were an important cornerstone and fulcrum of the GI movement. They provide a means of communication and break "down the isolation many GIs' [sic] feel." They also helped "morale, because they are a way of expressing criticism and anger, as well as poking fun at the military—which is pretty hard for a GI to do in the normal course of military life. They are a way of striking back at the guys who are standing on your stomach."[14]

GI PRESS RELATIONS WITH ITS AUDIENCE

In November 1969 the editor of *Attitude Check* detailed the interrelationship between the paper and its public. While it "was published . . . for the benefit of the common snuffy, grunt and EM,"[15] it was dependent on these same persons to write, assemble, type, edit and make "news for the paper. YOU ARE THE STAFF!"[16]

By highlighting "the injustices brought upon us by the pigs and [leading] the fight to destroy the racism that is working to divide us,"[17] the editor hoped the paper would engender the expansion of the movement on base. Simultaneously, "by providing a basis of communication between you . . . and other military men around the world,"[18] the paper would abet "unity, organization and solidarity among dissident Marines"[19] at both Camp Pendelton and around the world.

Attitude Check was not the first nor the only GI paper to envision a relationship with its audience as one where "the [GIs] who made the [GI] underground papers happen were the same"[20] GIs whose activities the paper propagandized. Likewise, it was not the only GI paper that claimed it would engender "unity, organization and solidarity," across the U.S. military. I shall deal with each issue separately.

You Are the Staff

Most GI newsworkers interpreted their relationship with their public in one of three ways. Some editors claimed that they and their subscribers were equivalent and interdependent. Others argued that their papers were molded by the subscribers' needs and interests. Still others claimed that they guided—and occasionally molded—their subscribers' demands and expectations.

Those GI newsworkers who envisioned this relationship as mutual couched their discussions in terms of shared goals and experiences. For them, the GI press provided an effective sounding board to "expound . . . and expand involvement in . . . the movement."[21] For instance, the editors of the *Coffee House News, Counterpoint,* and *GI Voice* argued that their papers broke through the anomie entrapping most GIs,[22] focused their attention, and provided a forum "to discuss the questions which so closely concern their well-being and life."[23] Most importantly, the papers ensured that "the story of the GI struggle . . . [reached] civilians and other GIs. Publicity is especially important in defending yourself against the vicious attacks of the brass."[24]

Of the GI underground papers examined for this book, twenty-two had editors who claimed "this is your paper,"[25] twenty-six suggested their papers were published "by GIs for GIs,"[26] two noted they were printing "in the interest of the enlisted man,"[27] and one confirmed that his paper was "set up as a means for you, the GI, to express your feelings and beliefs concerning your military experiences, the duty, the conscription, the war, the harassment, etc."[28] Lastly, the staff of the Ft. Sheridan GI underground paper, *The Logistic,* insisted that they would

Provide . . . what is lacking in the intellectual void of military service—what might be termed as an intellectual counterpart to military logistics.

Our "mental" logistics will be characterized by facts and ideas. Instead of moving troops, we will move minds. Instead of supplying troops, we will supply the facts-about the army, about the country, about the world. Instead of quartering troops, we vow to make our paper a forum for your ideas and viewpoints. Then and only then will this post have a paper which brings the true issues into light. We aren't interested in telling you what to think, but we do wish to inform you about what others are thinking so that you can make your own decisions and form your own opinions.[29]

While claims such as these suggest an open-ended and essentially democratic relationship between these papers and their subscribers, most editors subscribed to an organizational model that differentiated between journalists and audiences. I found a number of examples, however, where these distinctions were erased.

The editor of *The Last Harass* wrote that his paper would not become a "success . . . [until] it becomes the press of the GI here at Fort Gordon, we need your participation and . . . your criticism."[30] Likewise, the editor of *Up Front* called on his readers to send "in some of your short works on war and freedom. . . . [Now] is your chance. We need as many GIs as possible to work together to make *UP FRONT* a success."[31]

In my sample I found forty-three GI papers whose editors envisioned their papers as dependent on their subscribers for contributions and money.[32] Typical of these was the following from the editor of *Aerospaced*, who wrote that his paper needed "News leads, articles, letters, and though we hate to bring the subject up, money. . . . The funds came out of our own pockets and being GIs like you, we aren't rich. We want this paper to be yours as much as it is ours."[33] While many editors argued their needs for money and contributions were not mutually exclusive,[34] I found three that focused on their need for staff,[35] nineteen on their need for contributions,[36] and seven on their need for funds.[37]

For the editor of *All Hands Abandon Ship,* the paper's need for staff was caused by the fact that "over the last couple of months many of the staff have been transferred, or have gotten out and gone away for awhile to get their heads together. So we're getting a little short on people."[38] The editor of *As You Were* suggested if GIs at Ft. Ord wanted an on-base paper they should get involved in its production. Lastly, the editor of *Rap!* petitioned GIs to become involved and "make this a bigger and better paper."[39]

Unfortunately for these and other GI editors, surveillance and infiltration were an unavoidable fact of life. This put many GI editors in a catch-22. On the one hand, bitter experience had taught them to "be careful about admitting new people on the staff (discretion being the better part of paranoia?)."[40] On the other hand, they constantly needed new people to submit "letters, articles, cartoons, artwork, jokes, poetry, photographs: anything in [their] bag."[41]

The importance of these letters, articles, cartoons, and so forth cannot be overemphasized. In fact, as was noted by the editors of *A'bout Face*, *Fall in at Ease*, *GAF*, and *The Graffitti*, these were needed because, without them, their papers could not claim to "express . . . [their contributors] opinion to the utmost."[42]

The editor of *The Green Machine* wrote, "We can't print the news unless you tell us what's happening (anything that goes on in your unit, no matter how small)."[43]

The editor of *Flag in Action* argued, "If you have any interest at all in us for Christ's sake write to us and criticize our format, articles, or anything. What we would really dig is articles and information on what's going on in your units."[44]

Lastly, the editor of *USAF* claimed that his paper was "set up as a means for you, the GI, to express your feelings and beliefs concerning your military experiences, the duty, the conscription, the war, the harassment, etc. Whatever you wish to express, and in any form that you see fit, we welcome."[45]

For a number of editors, the importance of these contributions went beyond merely expressing their contributors' "opinion to the utmost."[46] They, in fact, kept them "in touch with the ideas and actions of dissent everywhere."[47] This was necessary, because

One of the favorite weapons of the Army is the news blackout—a protest by guys at Baumholder will go unheard of by guys at Munich, etc. That makes it much easier to silence protesters—without the public exposure brothers at the Presidio would be serving 15 year sentences. *WE GOT THE brASS* can help smash that blackout. Whenever anything happens in your division, write to us and we'll print it. Likewise, we'll see to it that all news you send us gets to the press in the States.[48]

A number of GI newsworkers concentrated on their papers' needs for money rather than on submissions from subscribers. For example, the editor of *B Troop News* wrote "the fact is . . . it costs money to put out *B Troop News*. . . . It's your paper, so help keep it going."[49]

The editor of *Huachuca Hard Times* noted—with apparent regret—"This issue cost the staff over $40.00 to publish. All from our own pockets. But this much of a financial load is impossible to bear on Army Pay. Unless we can get contributions from GIs . . . we may be forced to fold our operation."[50]

The editor of *About Face!* wrote "this is your newspaper, & to keep it coming to you, we need your help. Please send us a piastre—or its U.S. counterpart—so that you can help keep *ABOUT FACE: the E.M. News* appearing regularly."[51] The editor of *Gigline* remarked that "It should be obvious . . . the newspaper you are holding in your hands costs money to produce. In addition, GI's [sic] for Peace urgently needs funds for other projects such as press releases, legal defense for GI's [sic], etc. Eventually we hope to rent office space here in El Paso. GI's for Peace can only function if it receives GI support, your support."[52]

I argued above that GI newsworkers envisioned their interrelationship with their subscribers in three ways. Having dealt with the first two, I turn to the claims of those GI newsworkers who contended that their papers were not only independent of their subscribers, they in effect guided and, on occasion, molded their subscriber's demands and expectations. For these activists, their relationship with their readers was educational rather than symbiotic.

For example, the editor of *Anchorage Troop* argued that while most GIs were "perceptive enough to know the Army is fucked-up,"[53] it was up to the GI press to "develop this knowledge toward a comprehensive awareness that the military is an oppressive, exploitative, fascist, imperialistic, neo-fascist and organizationally insane system."[54] The editor of *Flag in Action* likened the paper to an "information service which will seek out and present relevant information from across the country which concerns the GI."[55]

The staff of *A Four Year Bummer*, in conjunction with the local antiwar coffeehouse, organized a lending library, a lecture series, and discussion groups. Likewise, the editor of *Reveille* claimed the paper's purpose was to increase his readers' awareness of relevant "religious, political, sociological . . . [and] philosophical"[56] arguments against military service in general and the Vietnam War in particular.

Still other GI newsworkers argued they could best serve and aid their fellow activists by alerting them to similar struggles throughout the U.S. military. For example, the editor of *GI Alliance* claimed the paper

Will seek to exchange information and ideas and success and failures between bases so that all will gain a better sense of where others are, of what problems and repression others are encountering, of what difficulty in organizing groups are finding, of what is needed to further this movement, of where it is going, of where it can go.[57]

This Is Not Your Newspaper

While I have concentrated on the GI movement and its media over these last two chapters, it is important to note that GI newsworkers were not the only military journalists. Likewise, the GI press was not the only available printed source of information for GIs. They could listen to Armed Forces Radio and/or read mainstream military publications, such as *Stars and Stripes* and *Army Times*.

For GI newsworkers, however, the choice between mainstream military media and the GI press was in fact a no-brainer. As was noted by the editor of *Graffitti:*

There seem to be two sides—two truths. . . . Generally when one side is terrified of the other side's truth it's a natural reaction to try to suppress this other side. . . . When one side is glad to logically present it's truth opposite the other, it has no fear. Which side seems more reliable to you? *Graffitti* is not afraid of *The Stars and Stripes.* But I've been trying to bring *Graffitti* to soldiers for months now, and I can assure you the Army is afraid of underground newspapers.[58]

For the editors of the *GI Press Service, Where It's At,* and *The Whig,* the *Stars and Stripes* and other official military publications were hamstrung and could only publish news the brass considered fit to print. The editor of the GI paper *ACT,* Richard Perrin, argued that their sole function was to keep up morale, question nothing, and "indoctrinate you with pro-war ideas. They must make you believe that U.S. policies in Vietnam are just."[59]

The editors of *Duck Power, Dull Brass, The Last Harass,* and *Open Ranks* each claimed the sole function of mainstream military media was to bootlick the brass. Lastly, the editors of *Confinee Says* and the *First Amendment* not only compared *Stars and Stripes* to a fourth-grade cowboy book, but they recommended that officers and lifers "who are hungry for reading material [read] *The Army Times, The Three Little Pigs,* and other 'clean' literature."[60]

Like their civilian press counterparts, who argued "if there is to be any truth . . . found in today's American Press, it is going to be up to us . . . to print it, and keep printing it till we win or fold,"[61] GI newsworkers claimed their various publications had "one thing in common: they [told] the truth."[62]

The importance of "truth" for these press activists is indicated by the fact that 45 of 116 GI newspaper articles exploring the role and function of the GI press claimed their publications "tell the truth."[63]

GI newsworkers use the truth in a number of ways. Some employed it for the purposes of parody. For example, the editor of *Fun Travel Adventure* wrote that "the truth encourages unrest and disloyalty among the members of the Armed Forces,"[64] and the editor of *PEACE* claimed that he and his fellow GI newsworkers were

Wanted For Printing The Truth About The Military, The Establishment, And The War. These Men Are Dangerous Because They Know The Establishment's Are Screwing The People. They Must Be Stopped Before Too Many People Find Out The Truth.[65]

Some used "truth" to compare and contrast what GIs could read in the GI press with the counterclaims of the movement's critics:

The people who are unfortunately in temporary custody of your nervous system are telling each other in all sorts of notices and memorandums to watch out for *The Bond*. . . . Their only "argument" is that The Bond is "communist propaganda" and therefore not to be considered with an open mind. Let's drag that argument out in the open and look at it:

We say that you are the best judge of what you are living through. Is that the truth or is that "communist propaganda?" YOU decide.

We say that you are being treated like shit. Is that the truth or is that "communist propaganda?" YOU decide.

We say that no Vietnamese ever attacked you as a human being. Is that the truth or is that "communist propaganda?" YOU decide.

We say that the same people who are treating you like shit are feeding you into the war against the Vietnamese. Is that the truth or is that "communist propaganda?" YOU decide.

The truth is that any ray of light and truth, and especially any suggestion that you decide for yourself what is true will be called "communist propaganda," and while they're throwing word-dust in your face they're doing their thing, which is stamping out life by force.[66]

Still others utilized "truth" to draw hard and fast boundaries between the GI and mainstream press. For example, the editor of *Bragg Briefs* argued his paper had "unfurled its banner for the purpose of establishing responsible alternatives to the current military system by publishing the news of truth."[67] The editor of the *Obligore* insisted that his paper was the GI's "voice for dignity & truth," and the editor of *Up against the Bulkhead* suggested that his paper was "armed with the truth, and . . . not kidding around."[68]

Given these claims and their underlying assumptions, it comes as no surprise that GI newsworkers would argue that the GI press was "the only . . . [media] which could conceivably represent or serve . . . GIs."[69]

The editor of *The Ally* proposed that his and other GI underground papers would fill the information gap left by mainstream military media regarding "what purpose Americans are giving their lives. To what end must Vietnam be tortured and destroyed? What does it mean to die for "national security"? How many young men must die before some "peaceful settlement" is eventually found? Are you required to defend a policy not of your making? Whose interests are you really defending?"[70]

Finally, the editor of *The Whig* wrote that he—and his fellow GIs—had started the paper because he was "tired of reading only what the military wants you to read in the news as in the *Stars and Stripes* newspaper. I'm tired of listening to the news on the radio and t.v. knowing that it is censored."[71]

CONCLUSION

In my preliminary definition of the underground press, I make the claim that the underground presses of the 1960s were countercultural community newspapers whose staffs were active participants in the events they covered. As I have shown in the last two chapters, this was also the case with the GI press.

Believing—like their civilian counterparts—that "Facts [were] less important than truth and [that] the two are far from equivalent,"[72] GI newsworkers savaged the work of their mainstream colleagues for never writing anything "controversial, relevant, or interesting."[73] Likewise, they insisted that GIs could not depend on *"Army Times* or the *Stars and Stripes* . . . to tell the truth . . . [or] keep GIs informed about what's going on in other parts of the [world]."[74]

In spite of the fact that as artifacts, these GI papers seemed to have been modeled on pre-WWI leftist pamphlets and newspapers rather than the underground press, their staffs were not. Instead, GI news-workers, like their civilian counterparts, understood themselves to be intimately connected to their public. They did not see themselves as gatekeepers who used the press to provide prorated and preselected facts. Instead they envisioned themselves as abetters providing a forum that not only expressed their contributors' "opinion to the utmost,"[75] but kept them "in touch with the ideas and actions of dissent every-where."[76]

The fact that both civilian and GI newsworkers understood their relationship with their public in this way is made most clear in their use of "you" and "your" when addressing their audiences. For example, the editor of Chicago's *Kaleidoscope* claimed that to "continue to exist, to function, to grow" his paper "needs your support."[77] Likewise, the editor of *Flag in Action*, wrote that "Your response will determine" the paper's "success or failure. Please help us make this project a success. SUPPORT YOUR LOCAL UNDERGROUND PAPER!!!"[78]

In spite of these similarities there was very real difference between the civilian and military press. Importantly, however, this had nothing to do with the paper's content and everything to do with the consequences of becoming involved with the movement and its media. As I noted in the last chapter, no civilian was ever arrested for working on or possessing an underground paper. This was not the case for GIs. Consequently, GI newsworkers consistently reminded their public that they should be careful to cover their asses by putting "a fake return address (or none at all) on the envelope to save yourself intimidation and harassment by your company rulers."[79] In the next chapter I focus on why such warn-ings were needed.

NOTES

1. See Todd Gitlin, *The Whole World Is Watching* (Berkeley: University of California Press, 1980) and Melvin Small, *Covering Dissent: The Media and the Anti-Vietnam War Movement* (New Brunswick: Rutgers University Press, 1994).

2. Todd Gitlin, "The Underground Press and Its Cave-in," in *Unamerican Activities*, eds. Anne Janowitz and Nancy Peters (San Francisco: City Lights Books, 1981), 22.

3. Lawrence Leamer argues the underground press was "an amorphous, variegated clan whose only common link is allegiance to the heady pastiche of pot, peace Panthers, rock, anti-war, anti-imperialism, anarchism and Marxism that is the contemporary 'Movement.' . . . Only in the pages of the underground press, with its melange of stories, articles, events, hunches, graphics, fantasies, exposés and theories can one find the Movement. To do this the underground press has had to create a revolutionary medium that interweaves personal life, journalism and activism." (Lawrence Leamer, *The Paper Revolutionaries* [New York: Simon and Schuster, 1972], 13–14).

4. Gitlin recalls that while he and his fellow underground press newsworkers "worked eight or nine days a week . . . it was a marvelous adventure, full of infectious enthusiasm. With little money, less professional help or experience, we were improvising without blueprints, trying out unconventional forms of writing, learning design and layout and distribution as we went. On $40 a week—when it came—writers were staying up all night to do layout and set type." (Gitlin, "The Underground Press and Its Cave-in," 20–21.)

5. This complex interrelationship between press and community could be seen most clearly in events such as Gentle Thursday in Austin and the First Human Be-In in San Francisco, which though only advertised through the underground press, attracted thousands.

6. "All Ready on the Left," in *All Ready on the Left* 1, no. 1 (August 1970): 6.

7. For a discussion of these tensions and their effects on the U.S. military in Vietnam, see Ronald H. Spector, *After Tet* (New York: Vintage Books, 1993), 242–59.

8. "Untitled Note," in *All Ready on the Left* 1 (August 1970): 8.

9. For the editor of *The Ally*, these accusations evidenced the fact that "Under the guise of discipline and saving lives the brass want to blame the anti-war GI when it is they that are to blame. At the same time they want to suppress the rights that GIs are pledged to defend. The anti-war base papers represent a grasp for these rights and for the freedom of GIs to think. We believe that when GIs think, they conclude that this war is not in their interest. This brings them in conflict with the system. The brass, of course, wants to avoid this kind of conflict. In the long run, they can't avoid it" ("The Growth of GI Power," in *The Ally* 17 [June 1969]:, 3).

10. "The Birth of the Black Brigade," in *Bragg Briefs* 2, no. 5 (December 1969): 3.

11. "Editorial," in *The Retaliation* 1 (September 1969): 2.

12. "Call for GI Awareness," in *Broken Arrow* 2, no. 2 (15 October 1970): 7.

13. "An Explanation," in *The Underground Oak* 1 (22 December 1968): 1.

14. "The Growth of GI Power," in *The Ally* 17 (June 1969): 3.

15. "Check Us Out," in *Attitude Check* 1, no. 1 (1 November 1969): 3.

16. Ibid., 3.

17. Ibid., 3.

18. "Check Us Out," in *Attitude Check* 1, no. 2 (1 December 1969): 5.

19. Ibid., 5.

20. Thorne Dreyer and Victoria Smith, *Liberation News Service Newsletter* 144 (March 1969): 18.

21. "Editorial," in *Up Front* 1, no. 1 (May 1969): 4.

22. The editor of *Last Harass* commented this anomie resulted in "a great deal of injustice which exists wholly because of ignorance; ignorance of the individual soldiers rights, ignorance of victories by other soldiers against the brass in other units, and ignorance of support from other soldiers who know what's up. This ignorance is no accidental thing. . . . By keeping us separated from each other and silent through intimidation we are kept in ignorance of what goes on in other companies." ("The Army Is Out to Get You," in *The Last Harass* 1 [October 1968]: 3–4).

23. "Our Position," in *GI Voice* 1 (February 1969): 2.

24. "Ft. Jackson GIs Win Victory," in *Dull Brass* 1, no. 2 (15 May 1969): 2–3.

25. The papers whose editors claimed "this is your paper" were *Aerospaced, All Hands Abandon Ship, The Ally, As You Were, B Troop News, Broken Arrow, The Destroyer, Dull Brass, Flag in Action, The Graffitti, The Green Machine, Huachuca Hard Times, The Last Harass, My Knot, Peace, Rap!, Rough Draft, Shakedown, Up Against the Bulkhead, Up Front, Venceremos, WE GOT THE brASS* (German ed.).

26. The papers claiming to be published by GIs for GIs were *A'bout Face, Aboveground, Anchorage Troop, As You Were, Attitude Check, Broken Arrow, Counterpoint, The Destroyer, Dull Brass, Flag in Action, Ft. Polk GI Voice, The Graffitti, New Salute, Our Thing, Out Now, Peace, P.O.W., Short Times, Twin Cities Protester, Unity Now, Up from the Bottom, Up Front, Venceremos, WE GOT THE brASS* (German ed.), and *Xpress.*

27. These were *About Face!* and *Duck Power.*

28. "Editorial," in *USAF* 1, no. 1 (1 April 1969): 3.

29. "Editorial," in *The Logistic* 1 (ca. 1968): 1.

30. "Need GI Participation," in *The Last Harass* 1 (October 1968): 2–3.

31. "Editorial," in *Up Front* 1 (May 1969): 1.

32. These were *Aboveground, Aerospaced, All Hands Abandon Ship, The Ally, American Exile in Britain, As You Were, The AWOL Press, The Bond, Bragg Briefs, Broken Arrow, Catharsis, the Chessman, Counter-Attack, Counterpoint, Dull Brass, Eyes Left, Fed Up!, Flag in Action, Fun Travel Adventure, GAF, GI Alliance, The GI Organizer, GI Voice, Gigline, The Graffitti, The Green Machine, Huachuca Hard Times, the Last Harass, The Morning Report, Napalm, Navy Times Are Changing, The Obligore, Out Now, The Pawn, Reservists Committee To Stop The War Newsletter, Rough Draft, the Short Times, Star Spangled Bummer, The Ultimate Weapon, Up Against the Bulkhead, Up Front, USAF,* and *Xpress.*

33. "Help *Aerospaced*—The Best Peace at GAFB," in *Aerospaced* 1 (ca. 1969): 3.

34. This interdependence is summed up in the following editorial, published in the GI underground paper *AWOL:* "*AWOL* needs you, Only with your consistent help and continued cooperation can *AWOL* live up to its maximum possibilities as the voice of dissent, You can help in many ways. First by SUBSCRIBING. Subscriptions are free to GIs; and a subscription guarantees your contact with the antiwar movement at military bases around the nation. It helps you keep in touch with the ideas and actions of dissent everywhere. And it keeps you armed with useful

information. Second, you can help by CONTRIBUTING to the paper. Letters and articles are always needed to bring the news right home to Ft. Riley. Also clippings from other newspapers help to extend AWOL's scope, accuracy and interest. Third, you can help *AWOL* by DISTRIBUTING. Make sure your copy gets around the unit; or have *AWOL* send you several copies. If you can't spread the paper, SPREAD THE WORD. Let others know that *AWOL* is here. Fourth, send MONEY, which is desperately needed just to cover basic expenses and postage costs. Build political consciousness—build *AWOL*. Build the GI movement—build *AWOL*" ("AWOL Needs You," in *The AWOL Press* 1, no. 11 [ca. 1969] : 1).

35. These were *All Hands Abandon Ship, Attitude Check, Lewis McChord Free Press,* and *Spartacus.*

36. These were *Antibrass, Attitude Check, Coffee House News, Dare to Struggle, The Destroyer, Fall in at Ease, A Four Year Bummer, GI Press Service, Lewis McChord Free Press, The Logistic, Open Sights, Peace, Peace Exchange, Rap! Reveille, Stars n' Bars, Up from the Bottom,* and *Venceremos.*

37. The papers that focused on their need for money were *About Face!, B Troop News, COM Newsletter, The Next Step, Our Thing, Stuffed Puffin,* and *WE GOT THE brASS.*

38. "Untitled Appeal," in *All Hands Abandon Ship* 7 (ca. 1971): 2.

39. "Help!" in *Rap!* 1, no. 9 (August 1970): 11.

40. "Untitled," in *Flag in Action* 1, no. 3 (November 1968): 3.

41. Ibid., 5.

42. "Editorial," in *A'bout Face* 1, no. 6 (12 September 1970): 1.

43. "Untitled," in *The Green Machine* 1 (ca. 1969): 4.

44. Notes from the Staff in *Flag in Action* 1, no. 1 (November 1968): n.p.

45. "Untitled," in *USAF* 1, no. 1 (1 April 1969): 3.

46. "Editorial," in *A'bout Face* 1, no. 6 (12 September 1970): 1.

47. "Untitled," in *AWOL* 1, no. 11 (undated): 1.

48. "Untitled," in *WE GOT THE brASS* (German ed.) 1 (ca. 1969): 11.

49. "Just the Facts Man," in *B Troop News* 3 (May 1970): 3.

50. "Untitled," in *Huachuca Hard Times* 1 (April 1969): 6.

51. "Untitled," in *About Face!* 4 (June 1969): 6.

52. "Help," in *Gigline* 2, no. 5 (April 1970): 2.

53. Ed Jurenas, "Statement of Policy, Purpose and Scope," in *Anchorage Troop* 1, no. 1 (January 1970): 1.

54. Ibid., 1.

55. "Notes from the Staff," in *Flag in Action* 1 (November 1968): n.p.

56. "Subversive Propositions about Ethical Action," in *Reveille* 1, no. 1 (April 1968): 2.

57. "Untitled," in *GI Alliance* 1 (3 June 1970): 1.

58. "Dissident' Views," in *The Graffitti* 4 (ca. 1970): 5–6.

59. Richard Perrin, "Blind Nationalism," in *ACT* 1, no. 2 (1968): 1.

60. "Untitled," in *The First Amendment* 2 (ca. 1970): 1.

61. Liberation News Service Collective, "Dear Friends" (15 November 1967): 1.

62. "Editorial," in *Fun Travel Adventure* 8 (May 1969): 9.

63. These were *A'bout Face, Act, Aerospaced, Attitude Check, The Awol Press, Black Unity, The Bond, Bragg Briefs, Broken Arrow, COM Newsletter, Confinee Says, Counterpoint, Dare to Struggle, Demand for Freedom, Dull Brass, Fall in at Ease, Fed Up!, Flag*

in Action, Fun Travel Adventure, The Graffitti, The Green Machine, Kill for Peace, The Last Harass, Left Face, The Logistic, The Obligore, OM, Out Now, Peace, Rap!, The Right-On-Post, sNorton Bird, Spartacus, Task Force, Top Secret, The Ultimate Weapon, Unity Now, Up Against the Bulkhead, Up Against the Wall, Up Front, USAF, Venceremos, WE GOT THE brASS, XPRESS, and *Your Military Left.*

64. "Pfc. Dennis L. Davis (15 and a Wake Up) Gets an Early Out!!!," in *Fun Travel Adventure* 8 (May 1969): 6.

65. "Wanted for Freedom of Speech," in *PEACE* 3 (1 October 1970): 1.

66. "Keep The Pressure On!" in *The Bond* 1, no. 10 (16 October 1967): 3.

67. "Subscribe," in *Bragg Briefs* 2, no. 5 (December 1969): 8.

68. "Bulkhead Editorial," in *Up against the Bulkhead* 1, no. 3 (15 June 1970): 2.

69. "Distribution Denied," in *Aerospaced* 2, no. 1 (ca. 1970): 6.

70. "Editorial," in *The Ally* 1 (February 1968): 3.

71. "Editorial," in *The Whig* 1 (4 July 1970): 1.

72. Raymond Mungo, *Famous Long Ago: My Life and Hard Times with Liberation News Service* (Boston: Beacon Press, 1970), 69–70.

73. "Lies and Half-Truths?" in *Broken Arrow* 2, no. 3 (17 November 1970): 8.

74. "Ft. Jackson GIs Win Victory!!!" in *Dull Brass* 1, no. 2 (15 May 1969): 3.

75. "Editorial," in *A'bout Face* 1, no. 6 (12 September 1970): 1.

76. "Untitled," in *AWOL* 1, no. 11 (undated): 1.

77. "Editorial," in *Kaleidoscope* 1, no. 1 (6 October 1967), 1.

78. "Notes from the Staff," in *Flag in Action* 1, no. 1 (1968): n.p.

79. "We Could Be So Good Together," in *The Last Harass* 6 (May 1970): 2.

Chapter 5

Response and Repression

INTRODUCTION

Today, nearly thirty years after my primary source material was first published, it is impossible to identify an author for most of the articles cited in this study. This is not because of sloppy scholarship on my part, nor was it the consequence of sloppy editing by GI newsworkers. It was, in fact, the result of these GIs not wanting to draw attention to themselves and incur the wrath of the lifers and brass whose actions and motivations they regularly pilloried. With few exceptions, readers were encouraged to

Cover your ass! When you write us, don't put *The Ally* on the envelope, just P.O. Box 9276, Berkeley, Calif. 94749. If possible, don't put your name on the envelope's return address—this protects you.[1]

To avoid leaving the impression that these GI newsworkers were cautious to the point of being paranoid, I begin this chapter looking at the Pentagon's prosecution of Roger Priest, who was the publisher and editor of, and oftentimes the sole contributor to, the GI paper *OM*. Having outlined the specifics of the Priest case, I broaden my focus to an analysis of the various strategies that the brass devised to quarantine the GI press. These were, I argue, belated attempts to regain control of a situation that had, in effect, gotten out of hand.

THE CASE OF ROGER PRIEST

Roger Priest—an apprentice seaman stationed at the Pentagon—never tried to hide the fact he was the editor/publisher of *OM* and he listed his

DON'T JUST STAND THERE

Help in the liberation of this
country from those power pigs
that have their hands in our
pockets and around our throats.
If you would like to help write
to: Roger Priest, U.S. Navy
      P.O. Box 1033
      Washington, D.C. 10013

Figure 5.1. Advertisement for *OM*. Artist: unknown. *Source: OM* 3 (June 1969): 12.

name and address in every issue. As indicated by Figure 5.1 if Priest had
wanted to avoid the brass's attention—as most GI newsworkers tried to
do—he was going the wrong way about it.

He had nothing but contempt for those he considered responsible for
the undeclared war in Vietnam. For example, in an article entitled "Do
You Believe in Their Madness," he wrote that "The Brass keep telling us
how those GIs who oppose the war are just a few kooks. We think it's just
the opposite. When you find a [serviceman] who loves the military and
thinks the war is great you know you're either talking to a lifer or a nut.
It's damn clear that a majority of servicemen hate the military and think
the Vietnam war stinks."[2]

He charged that the U.S. Government was legally liable for violating
Article VI of the Constitution, the Nuremberg Principles, the United
Nations Charter, and complicity in war crimes. For these violations alone,
he claimed, the "United States actions in Vietnam . . . [could] only be
viewed as aggressive and criminal."[3]

His descriptions of the military high command and its political allies
were deliberately insolent and uncompromising (Figures 5.2, 5.3, and 5.4).
For example, he accused the chairman of the Joint Chiefs of Staff, General
Earle Wheeler, of being "ready to fight to the last drop of your blood."[4] He
described the Secretary of Defense Melvyn Laird as a pig who was "proud
of his war monger haircut"[5] and a "practicing prostitute and pimp for the
military industrial complex."[6]

He referred to J. Edgar Hoover as grass, who would be easily cut down
when the "revolution comes."[7] The chairman of the House Armed Services Committee—Congressman Mendell Rivers—was likened to a pig

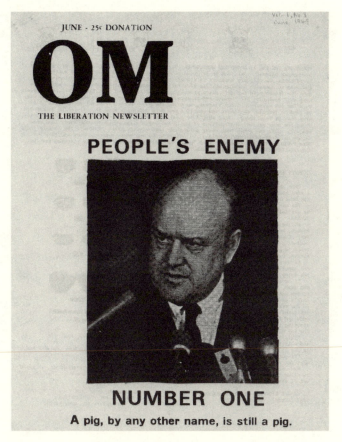

Figure 5.2. Melvyn Laird. Artist: unknown. *Source: OM* 3 (June 1969): front cover.

that was pissing and shitting on the country. And he apologized to his readers for the "obscenities which are frequently used in *OM*, such as: army, brass, lifer, war, kill, gun, stockade or brig, barracks, 'duty' and capitalism. These gross terms have to be used in order to describe the obscene situation we are in."[8]

The chairman of the House Armed Services Committee did not appreciate Priest's brand of political humor, instead he "decided it was a 'gross abuse of the constitutional right of free speech'"[9] and demanded that the Pentagon investigate Priest. In response, the Pentagon enlisted the help of the FBI and AT&T to tap his phone, the U.S. Post Office to intercept his mail, and the Washington, D.C., Sanitation Department to collect Priest's garbage and deliver it to the Pentagon.[10]

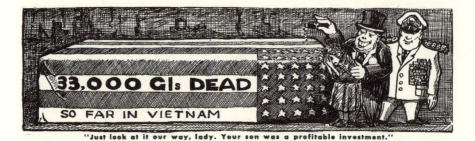

Figure 5.3. Your Son Was a Profitable Investment. Artist: unknown. *Source: The Bond* 3, no. 4 (17 June 1969): 1.

Figure 5.4. The Military Machine. Author: unknown. *Source: The Bond* 2, no. 8 (15 August 1968): 1.

Finally, twenty-five military intelligence agents were detailed to follow him at all times. Their duties included looking through his garbage, opening his mail, and listening to his telephone conversations.[11] They were also supposed to impersonate "ordinary GIs," approach him while on duty, and offer to help publish and distribute *OM*. Had he accepted their help, he would have been charged with violating the military's sanction against distributing an "underground newspaper . . . while on duty."[12]

Following a two-day investigative hearing in July 1969, which Priest described as "an elaborate ritual, very similar to a Star Chamber proceeding,"[13] the navy announced plans to proceed with a general court-martial the following November. If the Pentagon and its political allies had hoped these proceedings would gag or at least restrain him, they were wrong. What they did was turn him into a cause célèbre and a poster boy for GI repression, a position that Priest was more than happy to milk and satirize. For example, Roger Priest raised money for his legal defense by offering souvenirs of his trial for sale (Figure 5.5) and invited his readers to

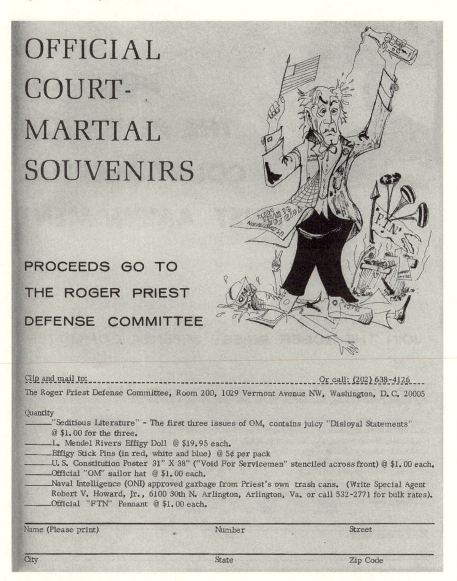

OFFICIAL
COURT-
MARTIAL
SOUVENIRS

PROCEEDS GO TO
THE ROGER PRIEST
DEFENSE COMMITTEE

Clip and mail to: Or call: (202) 638-4126
The Roger Priest Defense Committee, Room 200, 1029 Vermont Avenue NW, Washington, D. C. 20005

Quantity
_____"Seditious Literature" - The first three issues of OM, contains juicy "Disloyal Statements"
        @ $1.00 for the three.
_____L. Mendel Rivers Effigy Doll @ $19.95 each.
_____Effigy Stick Pins (in red, white and blue) @ 5¢ per pack
_____U. S. Constitution Poster 31" X 38" ("Void For Servicemen" stenciled across front) @ $1.00 each.
_____Official "OM" sailor hat @ $1.00 each.
_____Naval Intelligence (ONI) approved garbage from Priest's own trash cans. (Write Special Agent
        Robert V. Howard, Jr., 6100 30th N. Arlington, Arlington, Va. or call 532-2771 for bulk rates).
_____Official "FTN" Pennant @ $1.00 each.

Name (Please print)   Number   Street

City   State   Zip Code

Figure 5.5. Fundraiser for Roger Priest's Defense Committee. Artist: unknown.
Source: OM 7 (ca. 1970): 16.

come to his trial by printing up a mock invitation to a "Command Perfor-
mance of the Uniform Code of Military Injustice Players" (Figure 5.6).

The editor of *Fun Travel Adventure* reported that Priest had been accused
of soliciting men to desert, showing disrespect toward General Earl
Wheeler, J. Edgar Hoover, and Melvin Laird, and intending to interfere

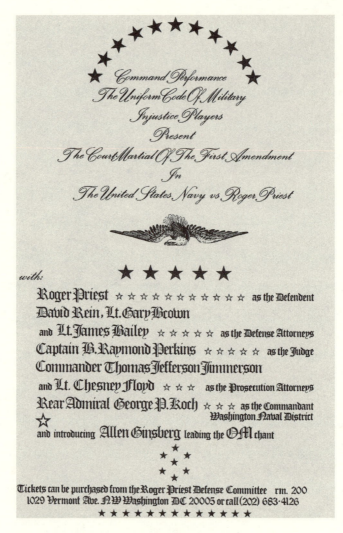

Figure 5.6. Court of Military Injustice. Author: unknown.
Source: OM 7 (ca. 1970): unpaginated insert.

with, impair, and influence the loyalty, morale, and discipline of the military. The editor then noted that "the best one of all is that . . . Roger Lee Priest . . . did . . . on or about 1 June 1969 in the June issue of a pamphlet entitled *OM The Liberation Newsletter* wrongfully use . . . contemptuous words against the chairman of the Armed Services Committee to the House of Representatives, L. Mendell Rivers."[14] Having outlined the charges against him, the editor noted that Priest faced a possible thirty-nine years at hard labor and a dishonorable discharge.[15]

In a speech that was reprinted in the Fort Ord underground newspaper, *Right-On-Post!*, Priest argued he was persecuted for "speaking the truth about the Amerikan [sic] war in Vietnam. . . . I never minced words about my disgust and contempt for the lying politicians in Washington and the . . . war criminals in the Pentagon who give the orders, make the policies, gain the promotions, the medals and the money while our blood and the Vietnamese blood is shed to make profits for a few and poverty for the many. . . . The military, the government, and the war industries need the big lies to survive. How else do you think they can get us to fight their wars and die for them?"[16]

ENVISIONING REPRESSION

While the effect—on GI newsworkers and their publics—of the military's harassment of Roger Priest is difficult to assess, it should not be underestimated. Although GIs had always been warned by press activists to remain incognito, the fact that Priest could have been sentenced to thirty-nine years at hard labor for legally publishing a newspaper on his own time and with his own money had to have forced some GI press newsworkers to reevaluate their own involvement. While some may have quit, the fact that no GI underground paper suspended publication suggests that most decided to follow his example. For example, the editors of *The Whig* commented in their first editorial:

The reason for this paper is because we care about us, you, and America. Do you think we would risk jail, and that's what will happen when Uncle finds out who we are, if this was not important not only to us but for you also? Many of us have many plans for when we get out of the military such as college, getting married, etc. and being jailed solely for publishing this newspaper would greatly upset these plans, but we're still doing it.[17]

By focusing on the military's treatment of Roger Priest, I do not mean to suggest his was an isolated case. It was not. Priest's arrest and subsequent court-martial was just one among many incidents of intimidation, harassment, and court-martial. To illustrate this, the editor of *The Ally* reported that while Priest was clearly the "best example of the brass' reaction to GI papers . . . many other examples of harassment, intimidation and courts-martial could be cited."[18] Among the papers whose staffs had been so harassed were *The Last Harass*, the *Broken Arrow*, *Head-On*, *The Fatigue Press*, *Shakedown*, and *Short Times*.

Despite their own problems, these and many other GI papers covered Priest's case in depth. In a random selection of newspapers published after August 1969, the incident was treated at length in twenty publications, including *Attitude Check*, *Duck Power*, *Fun Travel Adventure*, *The GI Press Service*, *Left Face*, and *Right-on-Post*. In these articles, the various authors focused on the military's legal machinations and duplicity or the suppression and denial of Priest's constitutionally protected First Amendment rights.

Regarding the military's duplicity, *Attitude Check* reported that, although the navy realized it could not sustain the case, it was forced to reinstate the proceedings by the chairman of the House Armed Services Committee who was smarting over Priest's description of him as a defecating fat pig. The fact Mendell Rivers was out to "make an example out of Priest"[19] was made clear in a reported exchange between the chairman and a reporter from *Link News:*[20]

Rogers: What about servicemen who have published papers, like Seaman Roger Priest?

Rivers: They ought to be in jail.

Rogers: Are you familiar with Seaman Priest's publication?

Rivers: I, I've seen some of them. He ought to be in jail in my opinion.

Rogers: Is it your view then that this is not a question of constitutional rights, or free speech, or, a matter of servicemen being allowed to speak their views?

Rivers: No, I don't think so, I, I can't elaborate on that now, you know, there's something that's very close to—ah, you know you've got to distinguish between dissent and treason.[21]

By so forcing the military's hand, Mendell Rivers' did more for the GI movement than the collected writings of Roger Priest could have ever done had the military simply ignored him. He not only enabled GI activists to argue that "the court-martial system is not a system of justice, but merely an instrument of military discipline."[22] He provided them with more than enough fodder to claim that the Pentagon, and its political supporters, could not care less about trampling "the *Bill of Rights,* that historic document which is supposed to protect us from the government. . . . [In] fact, our rights have already been trampled and are not worth the paper they are written on as long as the Pentagon Brass have the power to arbitrarily decide and interpret in what manner and form those rights may be exercised."[23]

In a similar vein, the editor of the *Last Harass* claimed that the navy had "conveniently [forgotten that] freedom of the press is a guaranteed right. Roger must be aghast. After all, he always was taught that there was freedom of the press, freedom of etc. etc. Sad but true, the navy, an organization, 'supposedly' protecting his right, has violated the very right itself. Kiss the Constitution goodbye. Hello 1984 a little early."[24]

THE GUIDANCE ON DISSENT

Had the military followed its own institutional directives, Priest would never have been charged. He not only followed military regulations to the letter, he did so despite the efforts of agent provocateurs to entice him into distributing his publication on base and on duty.

This would have contravened the military's supposedly liberalized *Guidance on Dissent*, which was distributed in May 1969 to instruct base commanders on how to deal better with dissidents and dissenters. Prior to this, GI newsworkers and other activists were subject to the whim and volition of their local commanders and were as likely to be given an early out, or a transfer to another base, as they were to being court-martialed.

In 1969 and 1970, the U.S. armed services experienced a dramatic increase in the levels of disaffection and dissent. For example, in 1967 and 1968 there were 2,216 in-service applications for conscientious objection, and in 1969 and 1970 there were 5,752.[25] Likewise, in 1967 and 1968 there were forty-one incidents of unauthorized absence (AWOL) per 1,000 servicemen, and in 1969 and 1970 this rose to fifty-eight. Lastly, in 1967 and 1968 there were fourteen incidents of desertion per 1,000 men, and in 1969 and 1970 there were twenty-four.

In August 1968 the commanding general of the United States Continental Army Command asked the Department of the Army to furnish him with "guidance . . . as to the proper manner of dealing with . . . requests and/or proposals"[26] from active duty GIs claiming to belong to GI unions and other organizations. In this letter, he also requested guidance on how best to "control . . . subversive publications disseminated at military installations."[27]

In one of the many coincidences, which seem to mark the late 1960s, the *Guidance on Dissent* was distributed in the immediate aftermath of the Peoples' Park events in Berkeley[28] and the bloody fiasco of Hamburger Hill[29] in May 1969. While I do not have the time or room to expand on these two events, the fact that GI and civilian activists believed the two were intimately connected is clearly illustrated by Figure 5.7. The fact that it was distributed at this time suggests to me that the military was indeed bracing for waves of internal protest. In fact, as was noted by its authors, the "following guidelines are provided to cover . . . manifestations of dissent which the Army . . . [may] encounter"[30] (Figure 5.7).

Such a concern was not unfounded. For example, in the six months preceding Hamburger Hill, from November 1968 to April 1969, there were only six incidents of on-base rioting, no GI-organized antiwar demonstrations, and no GI antiwar organizations formed. In the six months following Hamburger Hill, from June to November 1969, there were twelve on-base riots, eight GI organized antiwar demonstrations, and six GI antiwar organizations formed.

After the guidelines were distributed, GI newsworkers focused on the fact "that . . . [they laid] out guidelines regarding possession and distribution of political materials, coffeehouses, servicemen's unions, publication

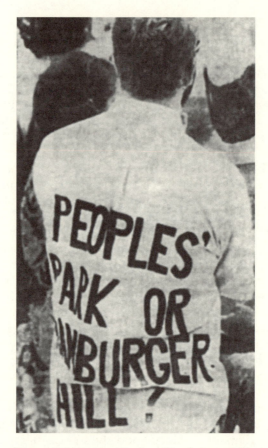

Figure 5.7. Peoples' Park or Hamburger Hill.
Artist: unknown. *Source: The Ally* 17 (June
1969): 4.

of underground newspapers, on-post demonstrations by civilians,
off–post demonstrations by soldiers, and grievances."[31]

Specifically, base commanders were instructed that they could only
place an antiwar coffeehouse "off limits" if they determined that the pro-
prietors, or any of their staffs and civilian patrons, were engaged in the following:

Counseling soldiers to refuse to perform duty or to desert or otherwise involve
illegal acts with a significant adverse effect on soldier health, morale or welfare[32]

Likewise, commanders were instructed that they could not stop the men
under their command from participating in an antiwar demonstration or
rally, unless they were

. . . On duty . . . in a foreign country, or when their activities constitute a breach of law and order, or when violence is likely to result, or when . . . in uniform.[33]

Lastly, base commanders were also instructed as to what kinds of publications GIs could read, publish, and under what conditions these publications could be distributed on base. In so doing, the *Guidance on Dissent*'s authors differentiated between the civilian press, which the authors defined as political newspapers, and the GI press, which they labeled as underground newspapers. Although this distinction is one of my own making, it is based on the author's failure to discuss under what conditions, and where, political publications could be produced. This is not the case, however, for underground newspapers. In discussing these, the *Guidance on Dissent* specified when, where, how, and under what conditions they could be produced.

Regarding political—or civilian—publications, the guidelines stated that "a commander may not prevent distribution of a publication simply because he does not like the contents. . . . [He] may prohibit distribution of publications which are obscene or otherwise unlawful. . . . In any event, [he] must have cogent reasons, with supporting evidence, for any denial of distribution privileges. The fact that a publication is critical—even unfairly critical—of government policies or officials is not in itself a grounds for denial."[34]

Given the distribution problems facing civilian underground papers in nonarmy towns,[35] coupled with the political conservatism of most army towns and the almost omnipotent status of base commanders in these communities, it is hard to imagine civilian underground newspapers were readily available to GIs.

Having effectively empowered these commanders to ban most underground newspapers, the authors of the *Guidance on Dissent* turned their attention to the GI press. Noting, as they do throughout the document, that servicemen's First Amendment "right[s] of expression should be preserved to the maximum extent possible,"[36] commanders were instructed that GIs could not be disciplined for "personal literary efforts" so long as they do it "off-post, on their own time; with their own money and equipment."[37]

While they could not veto the production of these papers, they could, and did, delimit its distribution on and around the base. This was because GI newsworkers had to submit a copy to their commander for prior approval. If he determined the publication contained "language the utterance of which is punishable under Federal law . . . of the Uniform Code of Military Justice [UCMJ],"[38] the authors could be disciplined and on-post distribution privileges could be refused. Unfortunately, a number of GI newsworkers ignored this proviso and submitted their papers for prior approval. Unsurprisingly, they were all turned down.

Among the publications found wanting was *Aboveground.* The editors, without receiving any explanation, were told that their request had been turned down. *Aerospaced* was refused on the grounds it was obscene;[39] *Bragg Briefs* and *Left Face* endangered the loyalty, discipline, and morale of their fellow GIs, and the editor of *Left Face* was warned that "distribution of this publication on this installation without permission . . . is in violation of existing regulations."[40]

The editors of *Head-On, Huachuca Hard Times,* and *Last Harass* were discharged early following their requests for distribution. The editor of *Huachuca Hard Times* had actually obtained permission to distribute his paper on base. However, the day before he was supposed to distribute the paper he was honorably discharged and banned from the base.

THE UCMJ AS A TOOL FOR CONTROL

Few GI newsworkers operated under the illusion that the "arbitrary" and almost omnipotent powers invested in base commanders would not be used to suppress their First Amendment rights. They knew that they could, and probably would, be sentenced to hard labor, transferred without warning to a less conducive base hundreds—if not thousands—of miles away, or dishonorably discharged for publishing a newspaper.

If it had not been for the diligence of GI newsworkers and their sources on army bases in Asia, the United States, and Europe, many GIs who had fallen into the hands of military justice would have languished in isolation and obscurity, without the support of family and friends. To illustrate this, the GI Press Service published the following report about the GI paper *Last Harass:*

In a series of flagrantly illegal actions, Fort Gordon brass have moved to try to destroy the *Last Harass,* an antiwar paper produced by GIs at the base. The attack centered on the Headquarters Detachment of the 3rd AIT Brigade.

When issue number 4 of the *Last Harass* appeared July 14, a shakedown inspection was held the next day and all copies found were confiscated. Pfc. Thomas Sampson, who was found with a copy and who had been restricted to the company area while awaiting court martial for being AWOL, was thrown into the stockade. Others were interrogated by Military Intelligence.

Then on July 24, a second shakedown took place. This time the brass illegally confiscated articles which were being written for the next issue, along with letters addressed to the *Last Harass.*

As a result of this shakedown, Pfc. Gary King was placed in the stockade in maximum security on the pretext that he had refused to guard Sampson. Pfc. Tim Johnson was given orders for Vietnam and Pvt Jeff Budd and Pfc. Boyce Brunson were told they would "be off Fort Gordon by the 30th of July." These last three GIs were restricted to the company area and required to sign in every hour.[41]

So long as these GIs were forced to depend on the Judge Advocates Division for redress of their grievances, the brass could deal with them in whatever manner it deemed fit. This did not mean, however, that the brass could act with absolute impunity. Instead, its response was limited by the degree of support the GIs had on and off base.

Between 1965 and 1968, with few GIs willing to come out against the military and with no support from the civilian movement, GI activists were "hung out to dry." The brass was able to prosecute and sentence GIs whose behavior was deemed to be "inconsistent with the requirements of military discipline."[42]

In fact, as indicated in Table 5.1, between 1965 and 1968 GIs who were so accused received an average of four years at hard labor, the harshest known sentence being ten years and the lightest being one year. The editor of *The Ally* argued these sentences had been imposed by military courts "to suppress any antiwar sentiments that GI's [sic] may have. In short, they're trying to make an example of . . . [activists] to quiet or dissuade anyone else from ever attempting to say anything."[43] While I have not seen any official documents outlining such a policy, the fact that each of the GIs and officers listed in Table 5.1 were arrested and court-martialed for politically motivated "speech crimes"[44] supports *The Ally*'s position.

For example, Pvt. George Daniels and Cpl. William Harvey were "convicted for taking part in barracks discussion and saying that black men should not be fighting in a white man's war against Vietnam."[45] Captain Howard Levy was jailed for "talking against the war" to his patients. Pvt. Ken Stolte and Pfc. Dan Amick were sentenced for distributing a leaflet, and Lt. Henry Howe was arrested for attending an antiwar rally in El Paso out of uniform and off duty.

According to the editor of *Rap!,* these, and similar, arrests reinforced their supposition that, "Freedom of speech is guaranteed only to those GI's [sic] whose opinion is in agreement with official military policy. This is certainly true of expressed opinions relating to the war in Indochina. At least one GI has been arrested for distributing subversive material when he passed out copies of the *Bill of Rights*.[46] GIs are regularly harassed, intimidated, or arrested for having a perfectly legal 'underground' newspaper in their possession. Unpopular opinions (especially political ones) often result in job reclassification, sudden shipment orders, harassment, additional details promotion pass-over."[47] (See Appendix 1: Partial Chronology of Dissent, 1965–1970.)

While the army attempted to deflect attention away from the political nature of these charges by obscuring them behind the seemingly neutral text of the UCMJ, occasionally its guard slipped. For example, Air Force General Estes admitted that there could be a "highly undesirable impact

Table 5.1
Court-Martials 1965–1968

Date	Persons	Charges	Yrs. at hard labor
12.65	2nd Lt. Henry Howe	Guilty of violating Art. 88 and 133.	2
9.66	Pfc. J.Johnson,	Found guilty of violating Art. 134.	3
9.66	Pvt. D. Moras,	Found guilty of violating Art. 134.	3
9.66	Pfc. D Samas	Found guilty of violating Art. 134.	5
6.67	Dr. Howard Levy	5 counts of willful disobedience, and talking against the war to his patients.	3
8. 67	Pfc. George Daniels	Found guilty of "advising, counseling, urging, causing insubordination, disloyalty and refusal of duty by members of armed forces."	10
8. 67	L.Cpl William Harvey	Found guilty of "advising, counseling, urging, causing insubordination, disloyalty and refusal of duty by members of armed forces."	6
11. 67	Robert Lockman	Refusing orders to Vietnam.	2.1/2
03. 68	Cpt. Dale Noyd	Refusing to train pilots for Vietnam.	1
04. 68	D. Ciesielski	Refusal of orders to Vietnam.	1
05. 1968	John Perry	Refusal of orders to Vietnam.	3
05. 68	George Edwards	Refusal of orders to Vietnam.	1
05. 68	Pvt. Ken Stolte	Violation of Art. 134.	4
5.22.68	Pfc. Dan Amick	Violation of Art. 134.	4
11.05. 68	Pfc. Bruce Petersen	Guilty of 2 counts of possession of marijuana in a general court martial.	8

Source: Assorted GI underground newspapers published between 1968 and 1970.

on military discipline if armed forces personnel [were] permitted to demonstrate against national defense policies with impunity."[48] When the staff of the GI underground paper *Your Military Left* was arrested for distributing its publication on base, "a military spokesman was quoted in the September issue (no. 16) of the *San Antonio Light* as saying 'the paper contained primarily political opinions which were contrary to army regulation.'"[49]

Between 1968 and 1971—as illustrated by Table 5.2[50] and Charts 5.1–5.3—incidents of GI opposition increased, while the length and severity of the average sentence decreased. One only need contrast the case of

Table 5.2
Court-Martials 1969–1970

Date	Persons	Charges	Yrs at Hard Labor
01.11.69	Lt. Susan Schnall	Guilty of a felony.	6 Months
03.15.69	Ed Horvath	Guilty of distributing antiwar literature.	3 Months
04.__.69	Kent Morris,	Possession of antiwar literature.	Restricted to post
04.__.69	Danny Ward	Possession of antiwar literature.	Restricted to post
04.21.69	R. Bisson	Distribution of underground newspaper.	Ordered to desist
06.23.69	Pvt. J. Miles	Convicted of being AWOL.	1.5 months pay
07.14.69	Pvt. K. Cross	Distribution of antiwar flyers on base.	3 months
07.18.69	Pvt. Joe Cole	Antiwar activities.	Undesirable discharged
07.18.69	Pvt..Edwin Glover	Antiwar activities.	Undesirable discharged
07.28.69	Pfc Jorge Caputo	General courtmartial for showing disrespect to a senior NCO.	6 months
08.09.69	Sp4c Hal Muskat	"For distributing antiwar literature and contemptuous utterings to the court."	71/2 months
09.__.69	Lt Mike Szpak	Transferred from Ft. Sam Huston to other bases around the country.	
09.01.69	Pvt L Svirchev	Transferred to Ft Lewis in chains at an hours notice.	
11.13.69	Pfc J. Nies, Pfc E. Barresi & Pfc R. Lund	Transferred without notice to Ft. Ord and Ft. Polk.	
07.__.70	Sp4c David Cortright	Transferred from Ft. Hamilton (NY) to Ft. Bliss.	

Source: Assorted GI underground newspapers published between 1968 and 1970.

Pvt. Ken Cross with that of Pvt. Dan Amick and Pfc. Ken Stolte, each of whom were court-martialed for distributing antiwar leaflets on their respective bases. Unlike Amick and Stolte, whose arrest and trail only became an issue after they had been sentenced four years at hard labor in Leavenworth, Ken Cross's arrest and trial was covered by civilian and GI newsworkers, who called on their readers to support him. Ken Cross was sentenced to three months at hard labor in the Fort Jackson stockade.

Perhaps the most famous example of the influence and effect of such pressure on the military was the Presidio 27 case.[51] These men, who had

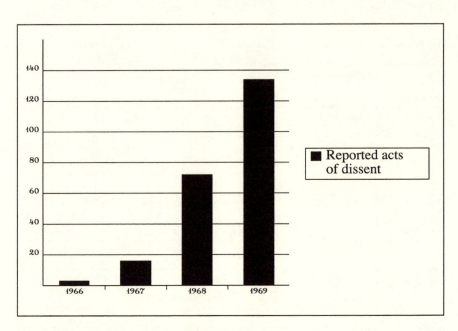

Chart 5.1. Reported Incidents of GI Dissent. *Source:* Assorted GI underground
newspapers published between 1968 and 1970.

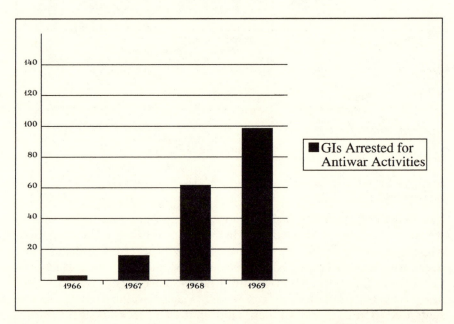

Chart 5.2. Military Antiwar Activists Arrested. *Source:* Assorted GI underground
newspapers published between 1968 and 1970.

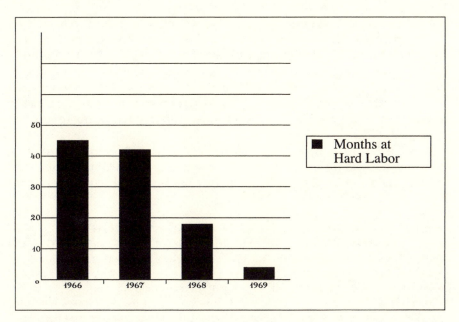

Chart 5.3. Average Sentence per GI Activist. *Source:* Assorted GI underground
newspapers published between 1968 and 1970.

been charged with mutiny for holding a sit-in to protest the killing of a fellow inmate by a guard, could have drawn life sentences in Leavenworth.
Instead, the first three were sentenced to sixteen, fifteen, and fourteen
years, respectively, at hard labor, and the remaining twenty-four had no
reason to believe they would be treated any less harshly.

Given the fact that the brass had been free to deal with dissidents, it was
not prepared for the "storm of [public] protest against the [sentences]. . . .
The antiwar movement responded magnificently."[52] Over the next six
months, protest rallies and fundraisers were organized, petitions were
passed around, and the Pentagon was barraged with a firestorm of articles
and opinions from GI and civilian papers. By the time the issue percolated
into the mainstream press, the army had reduced the sentences from fifteen to two years and from sixteen to four years.

Similar attention forced the army to reduce the sentences of the Fort
Hood forty-seven, who had their average sentence dropped from five
years to six months, and the Fort Dix thirty-eight. Finally, the Fort Jackson
eight—who had been busted on charges of "inciting to riot: and disturb-
ing the peace" because they had organized an on-base teach-in that had
attracted 150 GIs—had all charges dropped.

For GI newsworkers, these reductions and acquittals, which coincided
with the upsurge in GI newspapers, were no accident. Indeed, they would

not have occurred without the active participation of their publications. As was pointed out by editor of *Fall in at Ease*, it was "the massive outcry caused by the publication of the facts about the 'Presidio 27' "[53] in his and other GI papers that was responsible for the reduction in their sentences. Likewise, the editor of *Huachuca Hard Times* noted that it was "publicity from underground newspapers . . . and GI papers such as this one [which] brought enough pressure—in the form of public outrage, to reduce"[54] these sentences.

When the Pentagon realized that it could no longer suppress the GI movement by jailing or dishonorably discharging every GI dissenter, the military tried curbing potential dissent by transferring GI activists to what were considered safe bases:

Two Fort Sam Houston soldiers . . . were arrested . . . by military police . . . for allegedly distributing copies of *Your Military Left*. Sp./4 Tom Connell, Pfc. Damon Ruttenburg . . . were taken to the post MP station where they were interrogated by CID agents. Tom and Damon were told they were under "suspicion of intent to solicit" and were released to the custody of their commanding officers. . . . [O]n September 28 Ruttenburg and Connell were transferred to other bases without any charges having been brought against them. Ruttenburg was sent to Fort Bliss. Connell was transferred to Fort Sill, and less than 24 hours later transferred again, this time to Fort Chaffee, Arkansas, a de-activated base with only 22 men assigned to it.[55]

Finally, in December 1971, the Pentagon decided to just be rid of known dissenters and "announced that overseas returnees and troops with less than six months service need only ask to receive an immediate honorable discharge. For many disgruntled soldiers the offer was like a dream come true, and tens of thousands rushed to take advantage of the program."[56]

THE UCMJ AS A DOUBLE-EDGED SWORD

These shifts in the military's response to dissent resulted from the fact that its legal system was fraught with several potential problems, which oftentimes only became clear when it was too late to avoid them. For example, while the punishments meted out between 1965 and 1969 for politically motivated behaviors "inconsistent with the requirements of military discipline" may have quarantined the individual dissenter, they did not limit dissent. Instead, the severity of the sentences reinforced the GI activists' claim that

The UCMJ . . . is an instrument of ignorance . . . it openly violates a number of constitutional freedoms and gives the soldier an illusion of legal protection which . . . doesn't exist. . . . [I]t is so vague . . . an officer who wants to bust a low-ranking EM can twist . . . regulation[s] to fit the circumstances. Finally the GI is faced with a corrupt courts martial system which gives complete power to the same officer who brought charges in the first place. He can pack the court, ignore evidence and generally get the kind of vote he wants whether you are guilty or not.

All this is called military "justice." When mindless harassment can't stop soldiers who stick by their rights as human beings, the lifers hide behind what is really a legal system opposed to all the principle's that soldiers are dying to protect.[57]

Earlier I noted that the brass had traditionally dealt with dissent in three ways. First, they could make an example of the dissident GI and sentence him to years at hard labor. Because of the efforts of individual civilian activists, such as Alice Lynd, as well as civilian-run support groups, including the GI Civil Liberties Defense Committee, the plight of jailed GI activists was brought to the attention of the civilian antiwar movement, and this ceased to be a viable option. The importance and effect of this was highlighted by the editor of *Broken Arrow,* who noted that

This vocal, mass support has had a very influential roll in the outcome of court martial attempts in that the brass have been forced to abide by the rules of the Constitutional judiciary system, and not their own. This has prevented much of the kangaroo court activity for which the military is infamous. Through coordination with the local civilian peace movement, we have been able to build and carry through actions such as the May 30 Picnic for Peace with a minimum of trouble. The brass would have liked nothing better than to hang us, but, since everything had been completely legal, they had no grounds on which to base their accusations. As a result their plan of attack was from the rear (commonplace in their species).[58]

Second, the brass could quarantine dissident GIs by reassigning them to bases thousands of miles away. Unfortunately for the Pentagon, not only did this do nothing to stem the GI movement, it oftentimes resulted in the movement's expansion to as yet untapped additional bases. For example, Joe Miles, who had helped found the group GIs United at Fort Jackson, was transferred from Fort Jackson to Fort Bragg in an effort to quarantine him from the organization and vice versa. Unfortunately for the military, this attempt failed, and Miles "successfully formed a second chapter of GIs United. . . . Miles was once again shipped out in highly unusual circumstances—this time to Fort Richardson, Alaska, the US Army's equivalent of Siberia. . . . Joe then helped form another GIs United group at Fort Richardson."[59]

Third, the brass could wash their hands of a dissident GI and discharge him. This too was fraught with problems and pitfalls. Because they were no longer subject to the UCMJ, veterans could attend demonstrations in whatever uniform they wanted. They could leaflet former comrades and aid in the distribution of GI underground newspapers. As evidenced by the following editorial from *The Ally,* once released from military service, GIs were free to question assumptions and raise issues largely off limits to most soldiers on active duty:

We are preoccupied with nagging questions about the war. . . . [These] cannot be answered all at once, but they must be faced. *The Ally* will try to answer them in this and future issues by reporting the facts of the war and the anti-war movement. We will get beyond the nonsense which the government feeds servicemen and the general public. We will supply information that the government tries to keep from servicemen.

Newspaper reports show that at least one-third of those Americans fighting in Vietnam oppose the war, *The Ally* supports these men and seeks to enlist their support in informing others. *The Ally* offers its assistance to those who refuse to serve in this war. We want to open a new channel of communication to servicemen. We hope that you will write to us about your ideas on the war and your responses to this paper.[60]

CONCLUSION

In this chapter, I focus on how the interplay among four different groupings—the brass, their political supporters, GI antiwar activists, and the civilian antiwar movement—influenced and effected the military's treatment of GI newsworkers and antiwar activists.

Between 1965 and 1968, this interplay was limited to a few GIs who dared speak out against the war and the brass who moved swiftly to quarantine these dissenters in Leavenworth. For example, Pfc. George Daniels and Cpl. William Harvey were sentenced to ten and six years, respectively, at hard labor in Leavenworth for "counseling, urging, causing insubordination, disloyalty and refusal of duty by members of armed forces."[61]

Following the Tet Offensive, however, as more civilians and servicemen began to oppose the war, the military was forced to take the potential public reaction to their treatment of antiwar activists into account. The effect of this is clearly shown in Charts 5.3 and 5.4.

Once GI newsworkers were aware that the military could be so restrained, command and control began to collapse. When the brass attempted to restore their control through the *Guidance on Dissent*, the fact that Roger Priest was arrested in spite of his abiding by these new rules and regulations convinced many GIs that these new regulations were not worth the paper they were printed on.

This loss of legitimacy can be seen most clearly in the cartoons that were published in this period as well as the GI newsworkers descriptions of the lifers and brass that ruled their lives. I examine both in the next chapter.

NOTES

1. "To Our Readers," in *The Ally* 1, no. 12 (1968), 3.
2. Roger Priest, "Do You Believe in Their Madness?" in *OM* 2 (May 1969): 7.
3. Roger Priest, "A Call to Resist Illegitimate Authority," in *OM* 2 (May 1969): 2.

4. Roger Priest, "Does This Pig Speak for You," in *OM* 3 (June 1969): 5.

5. Roger Priest, "Remember the Pig Is Armed and Dangerous," in *OM* 3 (June 1969): 2.

6. Ibid., 2.

7. Roger Priest, "Superpig," in *OM* 3 (June 1969): 5.

8. Roger Priest, "Bring the War Home," in *OM* 3 (June 1969): 8.

9. David Cortright, *Soldiers in Revolt: The American Military Today* (New York: Anchor Press, 1975), 107.

10. See Roger Priest, "The Great Disloyalty Trial," in *OM: Special Court-Martial Edition* (1970): 2.

11. Ibid., 2.

12. This is taken from the Pentagon's 1969 "Guidance on Dissent" (cited in *Dull Brass* 1, no. 4 [ca. 1969]: 4–5). In a review of Priest's predicament, the editor of *Fun Travel Adventure* argued the "tactics that the Navy used are truly unbelievable. Besides following him, tapping his phone and other traditional tactics, the brass actually went rummaging through Roger's garbage in the hope of finding something that they could use against him. This is surprising since Roger has always made it clear that he was publishing the paper and there could be no question of his connection with it." ("Roger Priest—OM," in *Fun Travel Adventure* 1 [September 1969]: 7).

13. Roger Priest, "1st Amendment: 'It's Crap,'" in *OM* 4 (October 1969): 2.

14. "Roger Priest—OM," in *Fun Travel Adventure* 11 (September 1969): 7.

15. His court-martial was moved to April 1970, by which time his lawyers had successfully gotten most charges dismissed. Despite the prosecution's attempt to get at least six years at hard labor, Priest walked out with a reprimand and a bad conduct discharge.

16. Roger Priest cited in "Write on Roger," in *The Right on Post* 1 (ca. 1970): 3.

17. "Editorial," in *The Whig* 1 (4 July 1970): 1.

18. "Freedom of the GI Press," in *The Ally* 19 (September 1969): 3.

19. "Editorial," in *Attitude Check* 2, no. 3 (1 April 1970): 5.

20. Unbeknownst to Rivers, *Link News* was the newsletter of the organization Servicemen's Link to Peace. This was the organization that was coordinating Roger Priest's defense at this time.

21. Carl Rogers, "Interview with Mendell Rivers," in *Link News* 1 (November 1969): 2.

22. "The Priest," in *Left Face* 2, no. 1 (April 1970): 6.

23. Roger Priest, "Up against the Pentagon," in *Up against the Bulkhead* 1 (ca. 1970): 3.

24. "Save the Priest," in *Last Harass* 6 (May 1970): 6.

25. These figures are taken from David Cortright, *Soldiers in Revolt*, 16.

26. Letter to the Department of the Army, in "Secret Document Bares Army's Fear of ASU," in *The Bond* 3, no. 4 (15 April 1969): 1, 4.

27. Ibid., 3.

28. For a description of the events in and around Berkeley during the People's Park crisis, see Frank Bardacke, "Who Owns the Park?" in *The Movement toward a New America*, ed. Mithchell Goodman (Philadephia: Knopf Pilgrim Press, 1970), 505; Todd Gitlin, "The Meaning of People's Park," in *The Movement toward a New*

America, 506–7; Michael Rossman, "Claiming Turf in Berkeley," in *The Movement toward a New America,* 502–3.

29. Despite the fact that Hamburger Hill seems to mark a watershed in the war, scholars—with the exception of Christian Appy—have ignored it. This is unfortunate and needs to be revised. According to the editor of *The Ally,* the battle for Dong Ap Bia "indicated that" after five years of failing to achieve any kind of breakthrough in Vietnam, "the tactics of the brass in Saigon have not changed ... Though tactics of the brass have not changed, GI attitudes toward the war are changing ... GIs are accusing the brass of using World War II tactics of storming an entrenched position—a standard infantry maneuver. When the Vietnamese do this we call them suicide attacks. One 19-year-old Sergeant, when asked what it was like, was reported to have said, 'Have you ever been inside a hamburger machine?' Another reportedly said, 'It was the most ridiculous tactical boob I have ever seen.' ... One bitter GI scrawled on a burned tree stump: 'Hamburger Hill—was it worth it?' The answer, of course, is NO!" ("Hamburger Hill, Was It Worth It?" in *The Ally* [June 1969]: 1).

30. Department of the Army, "Guidance on Dissent," section 5, cited in *Dull Brass* 1, no. 4 (ca. 1969): 4–5.

31. "Editorial," in *Rough Draft* 5 (August 1969): 6.

32. Department of the Army, "Guidance on Dissent," section 5b, cited in *Up against the Bulkhead* 1 (1970): 3.

33. "DOD Document Attempts to Handle 'Dissent,'" in *GI Press Service* 1, no. 8 (2 October 1969): 116.

34. Department of the Army, "Guidance on Dissent," section 5a, cited in *Dull Brass* 1, no. 4 (ca. 1969): 4–5.

35. See Rev. Thomas King Forçade, "Obscenity, Who Really Cares?" in *The Underground Reader,* eds. Mel Howard and Rev. Thomas King Forçade (New York: Plume Books, 1972).

36. "DOD Document Attempts to Handle 'Dissent,'" in *GI Press Service* 1, no. 8 (2 October 1969): 116.

37. Department of the Army, "Guidance on Dissent," section 5d, cited in *Dull Brass* 1, no. 4 (ca. 1969): 4–5.

38. "Know Your Rights," in *Aboveground* 1, no. 5 (December 1969): 4.

39. See "Distribution Denied," in *Aerospaced* 2, no. 1 (ca. 1970): 1.

40. "War Ft. McClellan," in *Left Face* 1, no. 5 (January 1970): 2.

41. "Gordon Brass Attack *Last Harass,*" in *GI Press Service* 1, no. 4 (7 August 1969): 61.

42. "Guidance on Dissent," in *Dull Brass* 1, no. 4 (ca. 1969): 4.

43. "Stolte, Amick Get Four Years for Free Speech," in *The Ally* 5 (June 1968): 1.

44. This phrase is adapted from Roger Priest, who had picketed the Pentagon with a sign claiming he was being charged with speech crimes.

45. "GIs Continue to Oppose Vietnam War," in *The Ally* 1, no. 6 (July 1968): 1.

46. See "Brass Fink Out," in *Counterpoint* 2, no. 12 (2 June 1969): 3.

47. "Untitled," in *Rap!* 9 (August 1970): 8.

48. General Estes cited in *Fact Sheet on GI Dissent* (Washington, D.C.: The Serviceman's Link To Peace, ca. 1970), 3.

49. "Two GI's [sic] Busted for 'Distributing' Paper at Ft. Sam," in *GI Press Service* 1, no. 9 (16 October 1969): 137.

50. For a chronology of GI resistance see Appendix 1: Partial Chronology of Dissent, 1965–1970.

51. For a detailed description of the Presidio 27 protest, their arrest, and their court-martial, see Corey Miller, "The Lost Mutiny," in *As You Were* 3 (June 1969): 1.

52. "Pressure Wins Big Presidio 27 Victory," in *Task Force* 1, no. 4 (25 March 1969): 8.

53. "GI Mov't Spreads," in *Fall in at Ease* 1 (1970): 1.

54. "There Is No Turn-in," in *Huachuca Hard Times* 1 (April 1969): 2.

55. "Two GI's [sic] Busted for 'Distributing' Paper at Fort Sam," in *GI Press Service* 1, no. 9 (16 October 1969): 137.

56. David Cortright, *Soldiers in Revolt,* 91.

57. "GI Rights," in *Green Machine* 1 (ca. 1969): 1.

58. "Call for GI Awareness," in *Broken Arrow* 2, no. 1 (12 July 1970): 6.

59. David Cortright, *Soldiers in Revolt,* 60.

60. "Editorial," in *The Ally* 1 (February 1968): 3.

61. Department of Defense, "Article 134," *Uniform Code of Military Justice,* 1951.

Chapter 6

Envisioning Resistance

INTRODUCTION

This chapter addresses the GI newsworkers' vision of those who effectively ruled their lives. While few of them were as openly confrontational as Roger Priest, his descriptions of Nixon, his cabinet, and the Joint Chiefs of Staff as secondhand warmongers[1] "ready to fight for the last drop of YOUR blood"[2] were standard fare for these papers. In fact, the GI press was filled with articles and announcements leveling similar charges and accusations. For example, the editor of *Attitude Check* claimed that he and his fellow newsworkers had to "expose the injustices brought upon us by the pigs and lead the fight to destroy the racism, that is working to divide us in our common fight against the brass and their bosses."[3]

These claims were given added weight by the graphics and cartoons published in these newspapers. For example, the staff of *A Four Year Bummer* responded to charges that they were communists by visualizing their critics as demonic pigs (Figure 6.1). In the same issue, they represented Nixon as a deranged figurehead (Figure 6.2) and suggested the President should do servicemen a favor by fragging himself (Figure 6.3). Likewise, the *GI Press Service* accused Nixon and his cabinet of being war criminals (Figure 6.4). *Out Now* compared the military's rigid hierarchy to a two-story outhouse (Figure 6.5). The editors of the *Ft. Lewis Free Press* and *Gigline* compared the United States to a rampaging mechanical behemoth (Figures 6.6 and 6.7), and the editor of *Bragg Briefs* claimed the military considered GIs as worthless as tobacco (Figure 6.8).

In keeping with Stuart Hall's claim that a subculture's maps of meaning make its "systems of belief . . . mores and customs . . . uses of objects and

Figure 6.1. This Is Commie Propaganda. Artist: unknown. *Source: A Four Year Bummer* 2, no. 8 (October 1970): 11.

Figure 6.2. The Commander in Chief. Artist: unknown. *Source: A Four Year Bummer* 2, no. 8 (October 1970): 11.

Figure 6.3. Do It. Artist: J. Baldwin. *Source: Duck Power* 2,
no. 7 (10 July 1970): 5.

WAR CRIMINALS

Figure 6.4. War Criminals. Artist: unknown. *Source: GI Press Service* 1, no. 13
(December 1969): 193.

material life . . . intelligible to its members,"[4] I interpret the visions and representations, published in the GI underground press, as serving to center
and focus the movement. Consequently, they gave substance and form to
"the patterns of social organization and relationships through which"[5] GIs
were empowered to break with the army and come out against the war.

Figure 6.5. The Military Is an Outhouse. Artist: unknown. *Source: Out Now* 1, no. 4 (August 1970): 7.

Figure 6.6. Behemoth Amerika. Artist: Rutledge. *Source: P.E.A.C.E.* 1, no. 2 (1 September 1970): 5.

Figure 6.7. The Military as an Insane Mechanized Monster. Artist: Gary Vistupré
Source: Gigline 2, no. 5 (May 1970): 2.

DEPICTIONS OF POWER AND AUTHORITY

Lifers

In spite of the best efforts of the GI movement's critics to prove it was
directed by and peopled with Communists, the GI movement was neither
the realization of a plot hatched by the Comintern in 1928, nor were its
members communists. Few in the GI movement had heard of Karl Marx,
and those who had may well have been exposed to his ideas through the
publications of the John Birch Society and the books of J. Edgar Hoover.[6]

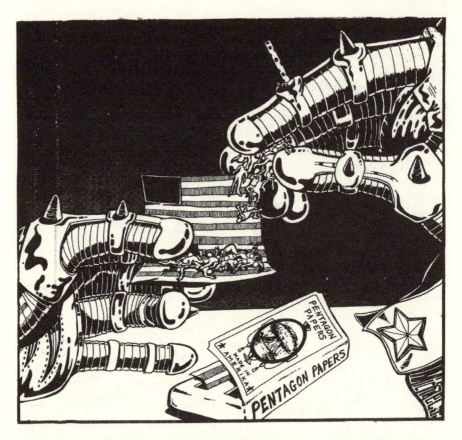

Figure 6.8. Why Do You Think They Call It Dope? Artist: unknown. *Source: Bragg Briefs* 5, no. 1 (February 1972): 1.

While there is no evidence to support the following observation, it is difficult to imagine that the GI movement was any better "read in Marxism or . . . radical literature"[7] than the membership of Students for a Democratic Society, who according to Jack Newfield

Had . . . [never] read Rosa Luxemburg, Max Weber, Eduard Bernstein, John Dewey, Peter Kropotkin or John Stuart Mill. Less than five had actually read Lenin or Trotsky, and only a few more had ever read Marx. . . . Almost all of them had read C. Wright Mills and Camus . . . more had read *The Realist* than Mill's "Essay on Liberty."[8]

Despite a lack of formal education, GI newsworkers were not only politically radical, they interpreted their place within the military—and by association—their living conditions exclusively as a consequence of class.

For example, an anonymous contributor to *Out Now,* described conditions aboard a U.S. navy vessel:

On a navy ship the officers' spacious quarters take up a giant share of the best and safest part of the ship topside. They have . . . private state rooms with daylight streaming in the portholes where there is fresh air and the freedom to get off in a hurry if you have to. The men live below in the bowels of the ship, crammed in layers of racks hung one under the other by chains where daylight never reaches, and even the air has to be sucked down from above, and where you'd have a hell of a time getting out if trouble came. Meanwhile, up above the officers enjoy the comforts of home. . . . Wall to wall carpeting softens the footsteps of EM waiters who have to serve them with special officers food on china plates with sterling silver utensil's then clean up after them and bring them champagne.[9]

For these GIs, the military was irrevocably split between GI/EM and their families on the one side, and lifers, brass, and their corporate/political allies on the other. Since I examined their vision of GI/EMs at some length in chapter 4, I will limit my remarks to their descriptions of the latter. These descriptions, coupled with the cartoons reprinted in this chapter, bounded and framed the GI movement. Although these remarks were often aimed at individual commissioned and noncommissioned officers, taken together they form an ideal type that the GI movement was desperate to get out from under.

Importantly, and in spite of the fact that GI newsworkers blamed both the lifers and the brass for what the editors of *Fun Travel Adventure*[10] claimed was "the obscene situation we are in,"[11] they did not hold them to be equally culpable. On the contrary, as was noted by the editor of *The Ally,* the lifer was entrapped in a paradox of power.

On the one hand, it was the lifer who was expected "under the guise of discipline . . . [to] suppress the rights that GIs are pledged to defend."[12] On the other hand, "it is not just the bastard sergeant handing out shit. It is the guy dumping on him and so on up the ladder. And at the top of the ladder are those who profit from the war—the brass, the businessmen and some politicians in whose interest GIs are being asked to fight and die, while they get rich and fat."[13]

The Ally was not alone in pointing out that lifers were also victims of the military establishment. For example, the editor of *Anchorage Troop* wrote "If a man desires to grovel before his wardens, crouch under the veil of scrutiny, and indulge his drooping ego by being a 'tough guy' and giving orders we aren't going to deny him his demented, vile life so long as he doesn't force people to participate in his sadomasochistic desires."[14] In a similar vein, the editor of *Bragg Briefs* suggested that "the lifer" was the desired product of "a training program laced with nationalistic propaganda" that instills "a mechanical like obedience to the point of actually substituting his normal behavior."[15]

As is made clear in Figures 6.9 and 6.10, every GI faced a choice. On the one hand, they could conform, internalize, and enthusiastically enforce the brass's rules and regulations. On the other hand, they could refuse and actively resist the military's petty rules and regulations.

If they conformed (Figure 6.11), GIs would lose their identity as individuals and be subsumed into the rank hierarchy that marked the U.S. military. If they refused, they would not only face the full weight of military discipline, they would also be subjected to the wrath of those who had been subsumed. This situation would not change until the military had been radically transformed.

Despite their general consensus that the lifer was the product and consequence of military resocialization, GI activists were at odds as to how best to respond to his wrath and harassment. For some, the lifer—because he had internalized his own repression to the point where he believed in those regulations that effectively ensured his subordinate status—was pitiful and should, whenever possible, be ignored and avoided. For example, *The Ally* advised its readers to never "leave *The Ally* laying around where the lifers can find it. *The less they know about it* the better [emphasis mine]."[16]

While most GI newsworkers were aware that avoiding, or keeping their publications out of the hands of, lifers was impossible, they advised their readers to give them as wide a berth as possible. This did not mean, however, that GIs were stranded without any legal protection.

Among other things, once the Pentagon had distributed the *Guidance on Dissent*, there was nothing lifers could legally do to limit a GI's access to antiwar materials. As was noted by the editor of *Aerospaced*, "lifers can't do one fugging thing to you for having '*Aerospaced*.' Your right to possess it is protected by DOD Directive 1325.6."[17]

Likewise, the editor of *Attitude Check* advised his readers, "any lifer, officer, etc., who tries to bust you for having a copy of *Attitude Check* can be charged with Article 92a of the UCMJ—violation or failure to obey a Lawful general order."[18]

For some GI newsworkers, the lifer's subservience was akin to a medical condition brought on by "twenty years of blind obedience to a corrupt, violent institution,"[19] which could, under the right circumstances, be treated and the lifer brought back to his senses. This was possible because lifers were still GIs, albeit GIs once removed:

If actual freedom of speech, press and assembly existed in this country the lifers' numbers would dwindle. Without constant reinforcement these diseased people could begin to realize their pathology and start on the road to recovery. The lifer is, in reality, his own worst enemy.[20]

There were other GIs who vehemently disagreed with any such claim. For them the lifer had long since ceased to have any connection or fruitful

Figure 6.9. The Evolution of a Lifer. Artist: Lisa Lyons/LNS. *Source: Gigline* 2, no. 4 (April 1970): 12.

Figure 6.10. Re-Up. Artist: unknown. *Source: Rap* 1, no. 1 (November 1969): 8.

Figure 6.11. Eat Shit for Four Years. Artist: unknown. *Source: Duck Power* 1, no. 4 (4 October 1969): 3.

relationship with GIs. For example, the editor of *Fun Travel Adventure* argued that the differences between GI activists and lifers were all too apparent. GI activists intended "to be destructive and detrimental to the interests of the big businessmen, the wealthy, the corrupt politicians and pentagon officials who don't mind starting and maintaining wars as long as it means more money and power for them."[21] Lifers, on the other hand, supported the interests of "a war economy where the rich get richer and the working man gets taxed."[22]

For instance, the editor of *Aerospaced* accused lifers of using Nazi scare tactics. The editor of *Anchorage Troop* claimed they were system lackeys with Neanderthal minds. For the editor of *Bragg Briefs*, lifers were "military minded brainwashed Uncle Toms" who possessed a "mechanical like obedience to the point of actually substituting his normal behavior."[23] For the editors of *Counter-Attack, Demand For Freedom, Peace,* and *Rap!*, all lifers were pigs, who enthusiastically enforced the dictatorship of the oppressed. In a similar vein, the editors of *Black Unity* and *Pay Back* claimed "lifers are the same pigs who murder our brothers and sisters on the street, only they hide and cover up their racist policies."[24]

The Brass and Their Corporate Allies

Despite these genuine feelings of hostility, GI activists understood that it was "not just the bastard sergeant handing out shit. It is the guy dumping on him and so on up the ladder. And at the top of the ladder are those who profit from the war—the brass, the businessmen and some politicians."[25] For them, these persons (collectively labeled the brass), and not the lifers, were responsible not only for the suppression of their constitutional rights and freedoms, but also for the war in Vietnam.[26]

Their distinction between the brass and lifers should not be interpreted as trivial. At their worst, lifers could only effect the lives of those GIs directly under their command. The brass, on the other hand, under the guise of promoting freedom and democracy and defending the free world from communism, enforced the needs of American multinationals at the expense of indigenous populations (Figures 6.12–6.14). Likewise, and in

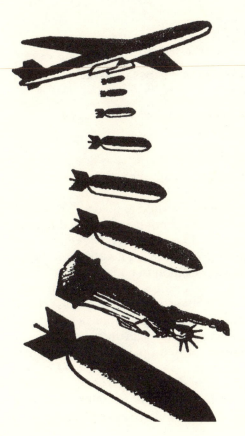

Figure 6.12. Foreign Aid I. Artist: LNS. *Source: Aboveground* 9 (May 1970): 4.

GIVE ME YOUR TIRED, YOUR POOR
YOUR HUDDLED MASSES YEARNING TO BREATHE FREE.
THE WRETCHED REFUSE OF YOUR TEEMING SHORE,
SEND THESE, THE HOMELESS, TEMPEST TOSSED TO ME:
I LIFT MY LAMP BESIDE THE GOLDEN DOOR.

Figure 6.13. Foreign Aid II. Artist: unknown. *Source: P.E.A.C.E.* 4
(1 October 1970): cover.

spite of pledging to uphold and defend the Constitution, the brass actively
suspended these rights for GIs (Figures 6.15–6.17).

Many GI newsworkers linked their being required to defend "freedom"
and "democracy" in South Vietnam with their not being allowed to vote
because of their age or to exercise their supposed unalienable rights. Furthermore, their presence in the military, their enforced involvement in the
South Vietnamese civil war, and their opposition to both had everything
to do with class and their opposition to oppression and exploitation.
According to the editor of *About Face!*, "You . . . the ruling class, have
closed the doors of protest and frank discussion of your policies."[27]

While GI activists blamed the local brass for this closure and absence of
frank discussions, the officers were caught in a quandary of the Pentagon's own making. As was made clear in a directive distributed by the
Department of the Army, if they agreed to engage activists in any frank
discussions, they would have been replaced and charged with disrupting
"the system of military indoctrination . . . and military discipline."[28]

Figure 6.14. Foreign Aid III. Artist: Vilpin. *Source: The Ally* 9 (September 1968): 7.

On the other hand, if they enforced the military's rules and regulations they played into the hands of GI activists, who visualized each and every such incident as proof that the military actively suppressed a GI's constitutional rights and privileges. For example, the editors of *Aboveground* pointed out that "'Congress shall make no law ... abridging the freedom of speech or of the press' means exactly that. ... We see, however ... this is not at all the case. There is an organization in the United States that has made laws and regulations governing the freedoms of speech and press. The United States Army has done this under the guise of protecting the rights of the citizen. How is it possible for the Army to protect the rights of a citizen by disenfranchising him of these very rights?"[29]

Figure 6.15. Freedom of the Press? Artist: unknown. *Source: Aboveground* 5 (December 1969): cover.

The brass's refusal to debate the question of how and why the United States was involved in Southeast Asia effectively gave GI activists unchallenged space to claim the war fit the needs of the military industrial complex. For the editor of *The Ally*, these persons had more than a passing stake in continuing the war because "GIs are being asked to fight and die, while they get rich and fat."[30] Likewise, *Broken Arrow* accused them of being responsible for "tens of thousands of GI dead, and the genocide of Vietnam is the direct result of the greed, and the drive for wealth and power, of big American businessmen and the Pentagon generals."[31]

The editor of *Out Now* claimed, "A fortunate few get fat off the profits they compel us to create for them. How do we create these profits? By

Figure 6.16. Freedom of Speech and Assembly? Artist:
unknown. *Source: Rap!* 1, no. 4 (March 1970): 4.

going to war creating thereby a market in which vast manufacturing
resources are spent, lives are spent, and from which we see no gain. Who
orders the war? Men in government. Who controls the government?
Those who have the money to buy men into office? Who are they? Those
who manufacture the weapons of war."[32]

For some GI newsworkers, including the editors of *Broken Arrow, Fed
Up!, Fun Travel Adventure, Morning Report,* and *Up Front,* GIs were not only
being trained to fight in Southeast Asia, they were being readied to fight
in the American inner city (Figure 6.18). To support this charge, the editor
of *Fight Back* pointed out that GIs were "used to bust strikes,[33] quell
domestic riots, and vamp on our brothers and sisters."[34] In a similar vein,
the editor of *Rap!* predicted the following:

**"Constitutional rights? I'll decide
who's got Constitutional rights on
this base!"**

Figure 6.17. The Oath of Enlistment. Artist: unknown.
Source: Your Military Left 8 (15 March 1970): 3.

Now that the U.S. role in Indochina has changed from the blatantly obvious
aggressor to the discrete aggressor . . . then let us examine the future in light of the-
aters of operations in which U.S. troops . . . are most apt to be concerned.

First, the Middle East is undoubtedly of major interest presently, and promises
to be more important in the coming years. . . . The second theater of operations
will be the "trouble spots' in the free world.

The third theater of operations will be centered here at home. The Awakening
spirit of American people to the type of government that is controlling them will
witness government's attempt to smash the spirit wherever it manifests itself.
Incidents such as Kent State, Jackson State, Augusta, Detroit, Berkeley, New
Orleans . . . [and] Philadelphia will keep occurring. Highly sophisticated methods
of surveillance and repression, such as exist already, will increase.[35]

To counter this development, GI newsworkers argued they and their
fellow GIs should turn and openly confront those who effectively ruled
their lives. While there seems to have been a critical consensus regarding
the need for such a response, GI activists differed on what form this con-
frontation should take. For some this could be most effectively accom-

Figure 6.18. Bringing the War Home. Artist: unknown. *Source: Fun Travel Adventure* 2, no. 8 (May 1970): cover.

plished through "the most powerful weapon of the GI peace effort,"[36] the GI underground newspaper. To do so, the editor of *Attitude Check* argued, GI papers "must provide a reliable forum of communication for all men on base. We will try to print only what the staff believes to be true, in a way that helps develop insight into the nature of our problems. We must expose the injustices brought upon us by the pigs and lead the fight to destroy the racism, that is working to divide us in our common fight against the brass and their bosses."[37] For the editor of *Gigline*, this was possible, because in effect the GI press "was mightier than the M-16."[38]

Other GI newsworkers—especially those GI activists aligned with the Black Panther Party—argued their papers could only "expose the racist-military clique for what they are."[39] If GIs wanted to change things, however, they should be prepared to turn their guns around and join with civilian militants in armed rebellion.[40] As was claimed by the editor of *The ASH*, GI militants were "born from the cleansing fires of Hate, Prejudice and Ignorance, *ASH* is the beginning of the destruction of the very reasons, which gave it birth. For years have the ashes lain smoldering but now they are growing warmer, now will they be recognized."[41] Likewise, the editor of *Counter-Attack* called on his fellow GIs to "join with representatives of change of the anti-military breed. . . . The time is now for you to be part of the 'change heard round the world.'"[42]

Alternately, the editor of *Black Unity* argued that GIs were left with no choice but to abandon the military en masse and "help in the struggle of freedom for our people, and for all people who are being deprived of what is rightfully theirs by the pigs of this nation. The only way to do this is through the unification of our people and through self-education, self-development, and by arming ourselves so that when you leave here you can help unite the people of your own communities. VICTORY TO THE PEOPLE'S WAR."[43]

Lastly, a minority of GI newsworkers argued that they should be prepared to work with mainstream, as opposed to militant or radical, civilian peace organizations. In a long letter, sent to *The Ally* by the editor of *Counterpoint*, the author argued as follows:

GIs should certainly do on-post organizing, but we don't think that excludes working with civilians. . . . In fact . . . we GI's need the civilians to defend us. If there weren't a civilian antiwar movement, there wouldn't be a GI one. The civilians need us to prove to the American people that GI's are against the war, to destroy that last bullshit argument that opposing the war means you're not supporting the servicemen. They can use us to help build the civilian movement. At least we'd better hope they can, because if the civilian antiwar movement dies then there will be no one to support us, no one to make it to hot for the army when they try to victimize us.[44]

CONCLUSION

In this chapter I explore how the loss of legitimacy implied at the end of the previous chapter was played out in the GI newsworkers descriptions of those who ruled their lives. This can be seen most clearly in their depictions of President Nixon as someone who should assassinate himself (Figure 6.2), as a maniac (Figure 6.3), as a pathetic figure who has fantasies about being important and ruling the world in the toilet (Figure 6.19) as Frankenstein's monster (Figure 6.20), and as the creature from the Black Lagoon (Figure 6.21).

Given Nixon's status as both president and commander in chief, the insubordinate nature of the representations of him reproduced in this

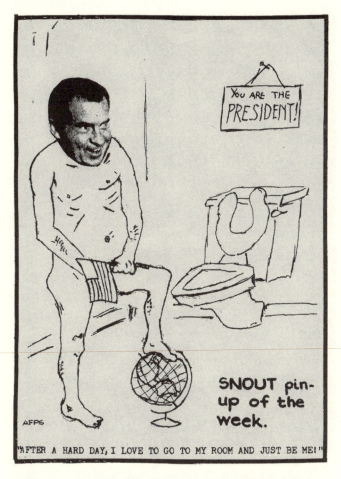

Figure 6.19. A War a Day, Helps Me Work, Rest and Play.
Artist: AFP6. *Source: All Ready on the Left* 1 (December
1970): 3.

chapter encapsulate the dilemma of the Pentagon's own making that the
brass was caught in. Each and every one of these cartoons, because of their
contents, violated Article 88[45] of the UCMJ. For the brass to have ignored
this and simply allowed GIs to suggest that the President should consider
fragging/assassinating himself opened a can of worms they would have
rather left shut. On the other hand, if they moved against the GI responsible, they were opening themselves up to charges that they were sup-
pressing the GIs constitutional rights. As I show in this chapter, GI
newsworkers happily exploited the brass's dilemma.

Figure 6.20. Nixonstein. Artist: unknown. *Source: Up Against the Bulkhead* 1, no. 5 (December 1970): 4.

At the start of this chapter I argue that the visions and representations, published in the GI underground press, served to center and focus the movement. Consequently, they gave substance and form to "the patterns of social organization and relationships through which"[46] GIs were empowered to break with the army and come out against the war.

These patterns of social relations were not invented by the GI movement; instead they were rooted in the GIs' common experience of growing up as working class. In the next chapter I focus on this experience through the prism of the Birmingham School's discussion of the relationship

Figure 6.21. Nixon from the Black Lagoon. Artist: unknown.
Source: Underwood 1, no. 3 (May 1970): 9.

among spectacular subcultures, their parent culture, and the dominant culture, which had channeled them into the armed forces.

NOTES

1. Roger Priest, "Slogan," in *OM* 2 (May 1969): 8.
2. Roger Priest, "Does This Pig Speak for You," in *OM* 3 (June 1969): 5.
3. "Check Us Out," in *Attitude Check* 3 (February 1970): 5.
4. John Clarke, Stuart Hall, Tony Jefferson, and Brian Roberts, "Subcultures, Cultures and Class," in *Resistance through Rituals: Youth Subcultures in Post-War Britain,* eds. Tony Jefferson and Stuart Hall (London: Hutchinson, 1986), 10.
5. Ibid., 10.

6. While a number of VVAW activists claim to have read some Marx in high school, prior to their enlistment, they wryly observe this was through materials sent to them, or their schools, by the John Birch Society.

7. Paul Jacobs and Saul Landau, *The New Radicals: A Report with Documents* (New York: Vintage Books, 1966), 29.

8. Jack Newfield cited in Abe Peck, *Uncovering the Sixties: The Life and Times of the Underground Press* (New York: Pantheon Books, 1985), 38–39.

9. "Unfair," in *Out Now* 4 (August 1970): 4.

10. *Fun Travel Adventure* was more often known by the acronym FTA, which also stood for "fuck the army."

11. "Obscenities," in *Fun Travel Adventure* 8 (May 1969): 7.

12. "Growth of GI Power," in *The Ally* 17 (June 1969): 3.

13. Ibid., 3.

14. "Life in the Military," in *Anchorage Troop* 1, no. 1 (January 1970): 2.

15. "The Black Brigade," in *Bragg Briefs* 2, no. 5 (December 1969): 3.

16. "Editorial," in *The Ally* 12 (December 1968): 3.

17. "Lifers React," in *Aerospaced* 1, no. 2 (ca. 1969): 5.

18. "Brass Harass, Harass the Brass," in *Attitude Check*, special issue (May 1970): n.p.

19. "Call for GI Awareness," in *Broken Arrow* 2, no. 1 (12 July 1970): 6.

20. "Death to Lifers?" in *Anchorage Troop* 1, no. 1 (January 1970): 5.

21. "The Right-Wing Responds," in *Fun Travel Adventure* 10 (August 1969): 6.

22. Ibid., 6.

23. "The Black Brigade," in *Bragg Briefs* 2, no. 5 (December 1969): 3.

24. "From a Black Brother," in *Pay Back* 1, no. 1 (ca. 1970): 5.

25. Ibid., 3.

26. To support this position they need look no further than the public statements of Mendel Rivers, who, when asked about GI opposition to the war in general and about GI underground newspapers in particular, responded that not only were they exploiting the First Amendment but they were traitors.

27. "One Reason for *About Face!*" in *About Face!* 2 (April 1969): 1.

28. "Growth of GI Power," in *The Ally* 17 (June 1969): 3.

29. Curt Stocker, "AG Unclassifed," in *Aboveground* 1, no. 1 (August 1969): 2.

30. Ibid., 3.

31. "G.I.V.A.W.V.," in *Broken Arrow* 1, no. 7 (23 September 1969): 4.

32. "In General," in *Out Now* 1 (May 1970): 2.

33. In March 1970, during the New York mail strike, U.S. troops were "used as strikebreakers [for the first time] in over fifty years." (*Reservists Committee to Stop the War Newsletter* 2 [April 1970]: 1).

34. "Editorial," in *Fight Back* (undated and unnumbered issue): 1.

35. "Vietnam and the Next Victim," in *Rap!* 1, no. 11 (February 1971): 2.

36. "The Pen Is Mightier than the M-16," in *Gigline* 2, no. 3 (March 1970): 2.

37. "Check Us Out," in *Attitude Check* 2, no. 1 (1 February 1970): 5.

38. "The Pen is Mightier than the M-16," in *Gigline* 2, no. 3 (March 1970): 2.

39. "Editorial," in *A'bout Face* 6 (12 September 1970): 1.

40. In 1970, Wallace Terry III found that 36.3 percent of black combat troops and 30.6 percent of all black enlisted men that were currently serving in South Vietnam planned on joining "a militant group like the Black Panthers when . . . [they]

returned . . . home" (Wallace Terry III, "The Angry Blacks in the Army," in *Two, Three . . . Many Vietnams: a Radical Reader on the Wars in Southeast Asia and the Conflicts at Home,* eds. Banning Garrett and Katherine Barkeley [San Francisco: Canfield Press, 1971], 227). Even more alarming was his finding that 44.6 percent of all black enlisted men "would . . . use weapons to secure . . . [their] rights back home" (Ibid., 227).

41. "Editorial," from *The Ash,* reprinted in *WE GOT THE brASS* (German ed.) 2 (ca. 1969): 8.

42. "Editorial," in *Counter-Attack* 3 (ca. 1970): 11.

43. "Unity," in *Black Unity* 1 (August 1970): 3.

44. "We Disagree," in *The Ally* 16 (May 1969): 3.

45. Article 88 prohibits the use of "contemptuous words against the President, the Vice President, Congress, the Secretary of Defense, the Secretary of a military department, the Secretary of Transportation, or the Governor or legislature of any State, Territory, Commonwealth, or possession." (Department of Defense, *Uniform Code of Military Justice.* Found at gopher://wiretap.Spies.COM:70/11/Gov / UCMJ, Article 88.)

46. Ibid., 10.

Chapter 7

Situating the GI Movement

INTRODUCTION

In chapter 1 I discuss how Stuart Hall and his colleagues—including Iain Chambers, Phil Cohen, Dick Hebdige, and Angela McRobbie—broke the "massive dependence" of postwar British social sciences "on American theories and models."[1] In this chapter I focus on a specific aspect of their work, namely how—given the unequal relations of power in society—ruling ideas were challenged by subcultural groupings. And, how, if at all, these ruling ideas were actually transformed.

Regarding the second of these questions, Hall and his colleagues ruefully noted that subcultural activists "continue to exist within, and coexist with, the more inclusive class from which they spring. Members of a [subculture] may *walk, talk, act, look* 'different' from their parents and . . . some of their peers: but they belong to the same families, go to the same schools, work at much the same jobs, live down the same 'mean streets' as their peers and parents."[2]

Despite the fact that most subcultural activists eventually come to terms with their subordinate status, they do challenge the status quo by walking, talking, acting, and looking different from their parents and class cohorts. For Cohen, these behaviors were not empty gestures produced by a "vacu[ous] . . . shoddy, stereotyped 'with-it' . . . generation enslaved by a commercial machine,"[3] as subcultural critics had claimed.[4]

Instead, these were attempts "to work out through a system of transformations, the basic problematic or contradiction which is inserted in the [subculture] by the parent culture."[5] Because of the disconnect between the pop-culture combat they had internalized as children and young adults and the real thing, as well as between their fathers' war and Vietnam, many GI movement activists struggled with an equivalent set of contradictions. To test this observation, I shall treat the GI movement as a spectacular subculture.

Drawing on Althusser and Gramsci, Hall and his colleagues differentiate between the material terrain on which subcultures form up and the cultural superstructure where "social groups develop distinct patterns of life, and give *expressive form* to their social and material life-experience."[6]

In this chapter I interpret this material terrain to consist of architectural environments[7] that, "despite the apparent neutrality of the materials from which they are constructed . . . carry within themselves implicit ideological assumptions [that] are literally structured into the architecture itself."[8]

Despite the best efforts of the ruling elite to represent these environments as natural, they cannot obscure the fact these "have *nothing* to do with [nature]. They are . . . [imposed] on the vast majority of men. They are perceived—accepted—suffered cultural objects and they act functionally on men via a process that escapes them."[9]

In the essay *Ideology and Ideological State Apparatuses*, Althusser argued that the ruling ideas in society are imposed through an array of institutional structures, including the family, the media, and the educational system. While most of these "function massively and predominantly *by ideology*"[10] to facilitate the internalization of the "ruling ideas in society," there are some that "function with maximum efficacy and ruthlessness"[11] to resocialize persons who come under their control and strip them of prior socialization. The U.S. military is one such institution. It "provides the [recruit] with a wholly circumscribed social universe whose parameters are clearly drawn with gates, barbed wire and armed guards."[12]

As evidenced by Figure 7.1, to ensure that recruits do not resist this resocialization, the military provided written instructions.[13] Given that the U.S. military can turn most recruits into soldiers in six weeks, this resocialization obviously works. One only need reflect on how, even today, most ROTC students stand out from the mass of the student body to gain some insight into the distance between these soldiers and most college freshmen.

It is my contention that this distance not only accounts for the sociocultural and ideological differences between students and soldiers, but also why it would have been impossible for civilian activists to have "introduce[d] the divisiveness found in our society into the army."[14]

THE GI MOVEMENT AS A SPECTACULAR SUBCULTURE

If one compares and contrasts behaviors characteristic of spectacular subcultures with the restrictions imposed on GIs by the *Guidance on Dissent* and the UCMJ, my recasting of the GI movement seems far-fetched.

Figure 7.1. Fort Dix Stockade. Artist: Steve Gilbert/LNS.
Source: The Rat Subterranean News 2, no. 10 (23–29 May
1969): 3.

For example, the provision of the *Guidance on Dissent* that forbade GIs
from attending any demonstration "when their activities constitute a
breach of law and order . . . violence is likely [or] they are in uniform,"[15]
effectively precluded their commanding "the stage of public attention for
a time."[16] Likewise, the fact that the UCMJ empowered the brass to man-
date what GIs could wear, and where they could wear it, makes it hard to
envision or understand how GIs could have developed any one of the
symbolic subsystems that Cohen, Hall, and Hebdige argued were characteristic of spectacular subcultures.

This seeming distance between the GI movement and spectacular sub-cultures can also be found if one compares the environs where they emerge. Unlike spectacular subcultures—which "form up on the terrain of [the] social and cultural life" of their parent culture—the GI movement emerged away from home on bases and in army towns, which were hardly conducive to the formation of social movements.

Finally, Hall and his colleagues insist that because of class differences, spectacular subcultures have little in common with middle-class subcul-tures. Without such shared interests, middle- and working-class subcul-tures viewed each other with mutual hostility.

Given the fact that the GI movement allied itself with and was advised and assisted by middle-class activists may suggest that the GI movement was something other than a spectacular subculture. It is my contention, however, this is not the case.

While it is the case that the GIs got involved with the movement after they had moved away from their immediate parent culture, the parent culture of the communities they were stationed in was essentially the same as the towns they grew up in. The GI movement was by and large a working-class movement. And while GI activists sought out alliances with an overwhelmingly middle-class antiwar movement, they did not feel that civilians had any real effect on the conduct of the war. In fact, as was noted by the editor of *Top Secret*, "We are forced to recognize that we must organize among ourselves so that we can exert pressure on the gov-ernment to serve us as it should. If we are serious about ending the war, there is no other choice."[17]

Also, GI activism even more so than membership in a spectacular sub-culture was a career choice without a future. As attested to by the editor of *The Whig*,[18] GI newsworkers knew they could, and most likely would, be dishonorably discharged. Once saddled with such a discharge, a veteran was not only stripped of all veteran benefits, including his pension, he had become unemployable in all but the most menial jobs.

With no money and/or career prospects, activists would have little choice but to return home and attempt to "exist within, and coexist with, the more inclusive culture of the class from which they spring. . . . [Mem-bership] of a subculture cannot protect them from the determining matrix of experiences and conditions which shape the life of their class as a whole."[19]

This determining matrix was reinforced during the Vietnam War through education and denied opportunities. Consequently, between 1965 and 1971, the bulk of draftees and enlisted men had been preselected by the state, which had channeled "the working-class toward the military and the middle and upper classes toward college."[20]

For instance, drawing on statistics gathered by the Veterans Adminis-tration, Christian Appy observed that the Vietnam-era military was comprised of 25 percent poor, 55 percent working-class, and 20 percent middle-class representatives. In fact, he claimed that "most Americans in Vietnam were nineteen-year-old high school graduates. They grew up in the white, working-class enclaves of South Boston and Cleveland's West Side; in the black ghettos of Detroit and Birmingham; in the small rural towns of Oklahoma and Iowa; and in the housing developments of working-class suburbs."[21]

These young men were entrapped in the political economy of the draft. Those who did not graduate from high school were scooped up on leaving school. Those who qualified for college but could not afford to go full time found they were ineligible for any in-school deferment and were available to be drafted. Finally, those who had graduated from high school, but chose to work instead of going to college, were unable to secure "stable, well-paying jobs. Even when good blue-collar jobs were open, many employers were reluctant to hire draft-vulnerable men."[22]

Given the effects and consequences of the political economy of the draft, it comes as no surprise that "Vietnam *more than any other American war* in the twentieth century, perhaps in our history, was a working-class war. . . . America's most unpopular war was fought . . . by the . . . children of waitresses, factory workers, truck drivers, secretaries, firefighters, carpenters, custodians, police officers, salespeople, clerks, mechanics, miners and farm-workers: people whose work lives are not only physically demanding but in many cases physically dangerous."[23]

This channeling of working-class youth toward the military—while catering to the needs of the military industrial complex—did not emerge in a sociocultural vacuum. On the contrary, many Vietnam-era draftees and enlisted men had grown up in families and communities where the parent—and the popular—culture fed off of, and reinforced, one another.

As Lloyd Lewis and Christian Appy have observed, many Vietnam-era servicemen grew up with fathers who "served in WWII, and the conversation about war was conducted exclusively in terms engendered by that conflict. War, so the fathers recounted and the movies bore dramatic witness . . . was a stage, on which heroism could be displayed . . . [and] manhood could be proved. . . . Indeed manhood could only finally be verified in combat, and thus war was more than just another activity; it was a basic rite-of-passage from boy to man."[24]

In fact, their fathers' war stories—combined with a steady diet of war films and war games to play out what they imagined had been their fathers' war—had effectively socialized them for war long before the requirements of the corporate state channeled them toward military service.[25]

As Todd Dasher reported to Christian Appy, "our little town had a Legion Post and a VFW Post and a DAV Post and this kind of post and that kind of post. We were just swamped with it all our adolescent years. My father was in the service with all his brothers. His father and all his uncles were in the service. . . . [They] talked about World War II and Korea and how "this one was there" and that one was there and . . . it was the right thing to do. It [was] part of life."[26]

The strength, influence, and effect of this premilitary socialization for war was felt most acutely by those GIs who were either considering desertion or going AWOL as a way of avoiding combat. GI newsworkers considered both options more trouble than they were worth for themselves, their readers, and the GI movement, in general. For example, the editor of *The Ally* advised the following to his readers:

The question of AWOL is becoming a problem of greater magnitude than ever before. Military brigs are overflowing with soldiers who abhor the gross inequities between American ideologies and American activities. Individual protest is one way the GI can regain a personal integrity that national policies have forced him to abandon. But singular activity does not stop a war.[27]

Likewise, GIs considering desertion were warned that they would be plunging alone into a life on the run—hunted by the FBI, local and military police—and would have to stay in hiding until they had gotten safely out of the United States. If they chose to desert, they should be prepared to never return home and sever all contact with their parents, girlfriends/wives, and/or longtime friends. To do otherwise would result in arrest and incarceration.[28]

This was made all the more difficult—as evidenced by the long passage from Gloria Emerson's *Winners and Losers* below—by the treatment of their families in their local communities, which more often than not ostracized them. Given their parents' treatment, most deserters understood that contacting them was not an option, as it would have made an uncomfortable and untenable situation worse:

Rennie Perrin, a middle-aged Vermont barber, was sound asleep when his wife, a nurse, came home from her shift at the Veterans Administration Hospital, so she thought it wiser to wait until morning to tell him their son, Richard, had deserted. Mrs. Perrin heard it on the radio at the hospital where she had night duty. The next day—it was in September 1967—Mr. Perrin had to be told, for there was a story on their son, a nineteen-year-old private, in the local paper. . . . Mr. Perrin, a veteran of World War II . . . listened to his wife Betty. Then he began to cry. . . .

"We had a terrible time for a long time," Mr. Perrin said. "As long as he is in Canada, it will never really be over for us." . . .

Mr. Perrin was still a member of the American Legion because he paid his dues, but he had stopped going to their meetings. Mrs. Perrin was a member of the Daughters of the American Revolution.

"I've never been back because I know how they would feel. It would be hard for me to listen to them talk—oh, I know how they talk . . . You know they all went to war, and anybody who doesn't do that—well I feel I'm just as good a legionnaire as they are. I believe in this country. I love this country. Even if Dick did desert, he said himself he loved this country. There was the time they asked him if he wanted to become C.O. and he said no. He wasn't against all wars, just this one. If someone came to attack this country, he'd fight for the defense of it . . .

"In the beginning it was terrible for us. I was very patriotic, like most men are. I used to make statements like those I've heard people say in front of me since Dick deserted. People saying 'Anyone who deserts should be shot.' It's awful hard for people to understand. When this first happened we didn't go along with Dick because we didn't understand it. Like most people don't. But when you're involved in it you start asking yourself questions, why all this happened. Now that we know, we feel a lot better. In the beginning it was terrible."[29]

While the Perrin family eventually came to understand their son's actions, many parents did not. For example, one of the Vietnam-era conscientious objectors, interviewed for *The Strength Not to Fight*, remarks the following of his father: "[He] cut me off completely. He literally cut me out of his will. When my children were born, he refused to recognize them as his grandchildren. I no longer have much contact with my parents. Twenty-five years after I refused to fight in Vietnam."[30]

Like their spectacular subcultural counterparts, who had been socialized within counterschool cultures where "working-class themes . . . [were] mediated to individuals and groups in their own determinate context and where working-class kids creatively develop, transform and finally reproduce aspects of the larger culture in their own praxis,"[31] future GI newsworkers were socialized for war by the mass media, which fed them a constant diet of war films and war comics that emphasized how "in the real world the only certainty of justice came from . . . [American] power."[32]

The influence and effect of this diet on the generation that served in the Vietnam-era military has been addressed at length by Lloyd Lewis, Christian Appy, and Fred Turner, among others.[33] Picking up on Michael Herr's observation that "you don't know what a media freak is until you've seen the way a few of those grunts would run around during a fight . . . they were actually making war movies in their heads."[34] Lewis argues that many GIs arrived in Vietnam half expecting to become movie stars.

Furthermore, like their British working-class counterparts, these GI activists not only attempted to mediate the contradictions between their expectations, as Americans, and their everyday lives, as grunts. They coalesced around seemingly mundane objects, which they then transformed into "signs of forbidden identity, sources of value."[35]

For example, Black GIs opposed to the war began referring to each other as "bloods," wearing "afro-style haircuts and using black power signs and banners."[36] They wore homemade bracelets called "Black Unity Bands." As with Genet's tube of Vaseline,[37] these became objects of defiance.

The Black Unity Band, also called Slave Bracelet and Bondage Band, was invented by our Black Brothers in Viet Nam. . . . They wore the Unity Band to protest the war in Viet Nam . . . to say that our war is inside the U.S. . . . [It] brought them more together and let them show their unity with one another and with us. . . . This is a time of trouble for the Black Man. Not only for the civilian but, for us in the military. Dig it. The Black man in the military . . . wear the Unity Band to show that their Black minds are united to the Black Struggle for FREEDOM![38]

While it is true that these unity bracelets were "humble objects . . . [designed] to exasperate all the . . . [brass] in the world,"[39] there was nothing oblique, covert, and/or anonymous about wearing them. These Black GIs defiantly violated the military's dress code, which explicitly banned all "external adornments [except] watches and metallic identification bracelets."[40] For the brass to ignore this code would have meant that the military tacitly accepted the right of GIs to "show the pigs and their followers that we are opposed to their racism . . . oppression, and to their war in Viet Nam."[41]

THE BASE AND THE CAMPUS

Christian Appy, in *Working Class War,* notes that "class . . . was the crucial factor in determining which Americans fought in Vietnam."[42] Consequently, it comes as no surprise that for many GIs, especially those who had served in Vietnam, "all protest seemed like yet another class privilege enjoyed by wealthier peers, and even moderate objections to the war, if made by draft-immune college students, were often read as personal attacks."[43]

In spite of the fact that dissident GIs and civilian activists were wary of one another, and in the face of an obvious class conflict, the Pentagon and its conservative allies in Congress argued that GI opposition to the war was inspired and directed by civilian antiwar activists. This was not the case. As I show in the following pages, the structural and institutional differences between military installations and universities coupled with their influence and effect of their institutional culture on the surrounding community deterred any such intervention.

Among other things, American campuses, which Herbert Marcuse once described as "enclaves of relatively critical thought,"[44] are open to the surrounding communities. They situate the students and faculty within an unfolding history of intellectual investigation and discourse by reproducing

The categorization of knowledge into arts and sciences . . . in the faculty system which houses different disciplines in different buildings, and most colleges maintain the traditional divisions by devoting a separate floor to each subject.[45]

In some instances, this is reinforced by carving the names of significant intellectuals in the field into the facade of the building itself.

The layout of military bases, on the other hand, while paying homage to the base's own history by preserving its past,[46] are not intended to stimulate either investigation or inquiry. Instead, as can be seen in Figure 7.1, these bases are laid out in such a way as to reinforce the fact that "restrictions on a soldier's civil liberties are nearly absolute."[47]

Most are fenced off and closed to surrounding communities. They can be locked down and declared off limits to all nonmilitary personnel. As was pointed out to Bill Ehrhart, and all other Marine Corps recruits upon their arrival at Parris Island, the boundary was nonnegotiable and could only be crossed without permission at the recruit's own risk:

This is Parris Island. . . . It's surrounded by swamps, and the swamps are filled with poisonous snakes. The snakes work for the Marine Corps. The causeway you came in on is guarded day and night, so you can't get out that way. If you can get through the swamps, you have to swim a two mile channel against some of the strongest currents in the world. And if you don't drown, the MPs will be waiting to pick you up when you get to the mainland.[48]

Even bases that were not fenced off and open to the general public strictly maintained these boundaries. And while nonmilitary personnel could drive across these bases, they could not step outside the confines of their cars without permission.

While both campuses and military bases have their own police forces, there is a world of difference between them. With few exceptions, university police are not regular police officers, but private employees; they are never armed and have only limited jurisdiction beyond the campus. Military police, on the other hand, are armed, and their jurisdiction is not confined to the boundaries of the base.

Finally, the legal power and authority of university presidents has always been restricted. While the office may endow its occupant with a high degree of prestige and status on campus and in the local community; a university president cannot arbitrarily limit the formation of or deny university funds to political and cultural organizations among their student populations, nor can they outlaw any public demonstrations.

Base commanders, on the other hand, have almost unlimited power over those under their command.[49] Before 1969—in part because the military had never faced the kind of widespread and sustained dissent that marked the latter years of the Vietnam War—these powers had never been clarified, and commanders had the freedom to suppress dissent as they saw fit.

With the upsurge of dissent in 1968 and 1969, and in response to repeated requests from various base commanders, the Pentagon codified their control over the activities of soldiers under their command.

For instance, commanders were advised that they could prohibit any publication they believed posed "a clear danger to the loyalty, discipline, or morale of military personnel, or if the distribution of the publication would materially interfere with the accomplishment of a military mission."[50] Once prohibited, the commander could impound any and all copies of the publication.

Likewise, they had "the authority to place" civilian "establishments 'off-limits' . . . when . . . the activities taking place there . . . involve acts with a significant adverse effect on members' health, morale, or welfare."[51]

In spite of the First Amendment, commanders could prohibit any civilian "demonstration or activity [on base] which could result in interference with or prevention of orderly accomplishment of the mission of the installation, or present a clear danger to loyalty, discipline, or morale of the troops."[52] And while they could not prohibit civilian demonstrations outside the base, they could prohibit any servicemen from "participating in off post demonstrations when they are on duty, or in a foreign country, or when their activities constitute a breach of law and order, or when violence is likely to result, or when they are in uniform."[53] For example, on 28 August 1968, General Estes sent the following message to General McConnell in San Francisco:

SUB. 2nd Lieutenant Hugh F. Smith. . . . Smith is organizing a 'Peace in Vietnam' demonstration for men in uniform to take place in San Francisco. He applied for and received a permit for a demonstration to be held on . . . 12 October. Strongly believe this demonstration should be *quashed* if possible because of . . . *the highly undesirable impact on military discipline if armed forces personnel are permitted to demonstrate in uniform against national defense policies with impunity* [emphasis mine].[54]

Lastly, they did not have to recognize, and could not bargain with, any organization or union that included, or claimed to represent, GIs under their command.

Universities and military bases shape the character and identity of their surrounding communities to such a degree that their influence and effect are literally written into the community's physical infrastructure. For example, Columbia, South Carolina, which services Fort Jackson, has "many streets and a park are named after obscure generals."[55] Likewise, Swarthmore, Pennsylvania, which services Swarthmore College, has many streets named after other universities.

Both Fort Jackson and Swarthmore College are "a good source of income for the local businessmen,"[56] many of whom are veterans or alumni. In each case, while these persons chose to settle in these communities because they find them comfortable and conducive, they reinforce the institution's effect on the character of the town. Consequently, "'Columbia . . . is a good Army town.' Officers seem to agree. Many . . . settle there upon retirement, the . . . relationship between them and the brass naturally gives the place a hawkish flavor."[57] Swarthmore, on the other hand, is comfortable and bookish.

Civilian activists who moved to military towns to "help staff the coffee-houses and movement centers"[58] were warned that "Life on a project is not easy, and a commitment to do this kind of work should not be taken lightly."[59] They were told they would "have to cope with periods of low activity and downright boredom"[60] and should "expect hostility from the civilian communit[y]. . . . Projects have been shot up and firebombed."[61] Lastly, they would be "subject to harassment and surveillance by civilian and military pigs."[62]

THE INFLUENCE AND EFFECT OF THE UNIVERSITY

While scholars have explored the evolution of the anti–Vietnam war movement on and off campus, they continue to focus on the more spectacular moments of this period.[63] For example, Terry Anderson argues that this era was marked by "an endless pageant of political and cultural protests, from sit-ins at lunch counters to gunfire at Wounded Knee. [These] *relentless demonstrations,* [these] fires in the street forced neighbors to take a stand and decide publicly about policies concerning a legion of new topics."[64] Unfortunately, too little attention has been paid to how this movement was shaped and effected by the institutional culture and affiliations of the American University.

This has had a debilitating effect on scholarship and has given rise to competing claims as to who stabbed whom in the back during this period. On the one hand, scholars and historians such as David Halberstam and Michael Hunt argue that the American people were, in effect, stabbed in the back by political, military, and intellectual elites in Washington, D.C. Blinkered by their anticommunism, they had deliberately deceived the American people about the depth, duration, and cost of U.S. involvement in Vietnam.

Still other scholars, critics, and former cold-war warriors—including William Buckley, Norman Podhoretz, Richard Nixon, and General West-moreland—argue that it was the military and their South Vietnamese allies who were stabbed in the back by a Washington-based coalition of liberal politicians, journalists, intellectuals, and anti-American students posing as pacifists. In contradistinction to Halberstam, these former cold-war warriors maintain that the Vietnam War was a noble effort that needed the full support of universities and defense corporations.

Consequently, they dismiss on-campus protests against university involvement in the war effort as misdirected and wrongheaded at best and treasonous at worst. For example, Terry Anderson argues that protesters forgot that

Producing weapons . . . *was patriotic*—it constituted legitimate corporate behavior . . . . By 1967 Dow was the only company producing napalm, and to activists it became the symbol of a corporate 'war profiteer.' Actually, that was *unfair.* Dow . . . napalm contracts . . . represented only one-fourth of 1 percent of . . . sales.

Facts, however, were *unimportant to antiwar activists;* napalm had become a symbol of the war, and by autumn 1966 the campaign against Dow had reached the university campus. Student activists held . . . demonstrations [and obstructed] interviews [emphasis mine].[65]

To claim that facts "were unimportant to antiwar activists" demeans these protestors and their protests. To argue that these protests were unfair to Dow Chemical ignores the effect that one-quarter of 1 percent had on the population of Vietnam and sheds no light on the root causes of these protests—namely the use of university facilities and faculty for defense-related research. This not only covers up the university's complicity in the prosecution of the Vietnam War, but also the tragic consequences of weapons research.[66]

In *Eichmann in Jerusalem,* Hannah Arendt notes that Eichmann's claim of innocence rested on the amoral claim that he had not broken the law "because Hitler's orders . . . had possessed the 'force of law' in the Third Reich."[67] Likewise, the claim made by American university presidents and senior faculty—during the Vietnam War—that defense-related research "was principally an act of public service"[68] was equally amoral. As was noted by Howard Zinn, attempts by universities to distance themselves from the consequences of such defense-related research can "not vitiate the moral issues. It is precisely the nature of modern mass murder that it . . . takes on a corporate character, where every participant has limited liability. The total effect, however, is a thousand times more pernicious."[69]

Similarly, and in spite of the fact that this research was often classified, university presidents and boards of regents/trustees argued it was not "incompatible with the spirit of the university. Surely the university and its members should not shun controversial areas of research; often it is there that *new knowledge* and . . . *insights* are sorely needed."[70]

This was grist for SDS's mill. And when the President of Harvard wrote that American universities should not withdraw their support for defense-related programs "because of repugnance to an unpopular war,"[71] Harvard SDS responded that "American universities [were now] absolutely central components of the social system of technological warfare-welfare capitalism. The functions, goals, structure, and organization of the universities are . . . determined by the needs and perspectives of that system."[72]

To ignore these responses and solely concentrate on their spectacular activities precludes their influence on the evolution of the civilian antiwar movement. For example, one cannot understand why certain activists came to join the Weathermen or endorse its stance without paying serious attention to the issue of Columbia University's affiliation with the military industrial complex through the Institute for Defense Analysis (IDA).

The IDA—supposedly founded "to promote the national security, the public welfare, and the advancement of scientific learning by making evaluations and reports on matters . . . of national security"[73]—was "given considerable responsibility for the development of techniques and weapons for use in counterinsurgency"[74] in South Vietnam. In devising how best to deal with such insurgency, an anonymous Columbia University professor developed

A model . . . for predicting the expected number of attacks to be made as a function of the target kill assessment (TKA) probabilities, the single attack kill probability, the confidence on the level of the kill desired, and the maximum number of attacks required if no TKA data are available. Finally, the maximum number of attacks that might be required to achieve the desired kill confidence is computed.[75]

While—as has been described by Philip Caputo, Bill Ehrhart, and other Vietnam veterans—these tactics did nothing to diminish but instead deepened support for the Viet Cong, their effect on the U.S. military was devastating.[76]

These GIs had arrived in Vietnam believing they would be welcomed as liberators who would ride atop a tank from Saigon to Hanoi mobbed by the kind of crowds they had seen in a thousand war movies. Instead, they were confronted by a hostile population, whose villages had been designated free-fire zones and destroyed. These Vietnamese civilians had become the unwitting victims of an American military behemoth expected to maximize the "number of attacks that might be required to achieve the desired kill confidence."[77] Consequently, they were more than willing to harbor, aid, and join with the North Vietnamese Army and Viet Cong in driving the Americans out of Vietnam.

Denied the support of civilians, GI dreams of liberation disintegrated when they or their fellow GIs were ripped apart by mines and booby traps set by these same civilians. As Bill Ehrhart writes in his memoir *Passing Time:*

You're out on patrol just strolling along and—*kerbloom!* And there's your buddy lyin' on the ground without any legs . . . and there's nobody . . . except Farmer Jones over in the ricefield behind his water buffalo. . . . Does he try to warn us? Hell no. Hell, he probably planted the damned thing—him or his wife or his daughter. . . . And every day you wake up wondering if today's the day *you* pack it in. You can't even begin to imagine what that does to your head after a while. It makes you crazy. And then one day you realize that you can blow away civilians and you don't get into trouble for it. Christ, you get promotions and medals for it. And when you realize that, there's nothing left to stop you. Next time some Marine steps on a mine, Farmer Jones gets turned into a piece of Swiss cheese: one

Vietcong guerilla killed in action. Maybe he was and maybe he wasn't, but once he's dead, he sure as hell is—and no questions asked.[78]

Stripped of these illusions and in some cases their humanity, GIs could not obscure the pointlessness of their sacrifice and brutality. Consequently, the military paradigm in Vietnam, which held that U.S. troops were in Vietnam to defend freedom and democracy, fell apart. Instead, it reinforced the claims and demands of GIs opposed to the war. As was pointed out by the editor of *Up Front*, GIs were radicalized by the military brass and their spurious justifications:

It is this very type of thought to which we oppose ourselves. It is the very fact that men die needlessly and are dying unjustly everyday in a war which we have concluded is altogether wrong, which causes our disapproval. Not because we are "misguided kids" without a purpose in life but because the purposes which you have forced on our lives are those of the Great American Dream which has undoubtedly become a nightmare of hunger, poverty, death, war, racism, and total human misunderstanding.[79]

For the editors of *The Ally*, it was "the war [that] created the antiwar GI. Men do not need the kind of stupid discipline the military hands out if they believe in what they are doing. When men are asked to fight an unjust war and . . . then harassed and abused while doing it, they begin to ask questions."[80] In testimony before the Senate Foreign Relations Committee, Lieutenant John Kerry argued he and his fellow Vietnam veterans were turned against the war by the strategies, tactics, and hollow justifications of the military elite:

We watched while men charged up hills because a general said that hill has to be taken, and after losing one platoon or two platoons, they marched away to leave the hill for reoccupation by the North Vietnamese. We watched pride allow the most unimportant battles to be blown into extravaganzas, because we couldn't lose, and we couldn't retreat, and because it didn't matter how many American bodies were lost to prove that point, and so there were Hamburger Hills and Khe Sahns and Hill 81s and Fire Base 6s and so many others.[81]

These speeches and editorials need to be read in the context of Articles 88[82] and 91[83] of the UCMJ, which collectively prohibit any criticism of superior officers, the President, the Vice President, the Cabinet, and Congress. When looked at in this way, the fact that GIs were willing to not only violate the UCMJ but to also do so openly, and in spite of threatened court-martials, suggests that the legitimacy of command and control in the minds of GIs had begun to crumble as a result of the Vietnam War. For example, the editor of *About Face!* declared the following:

You . . . the ruling class, have closed the doors of protest and frank discussion of your policies. We believe in democracy and we demand our rights under it. If the door remains closed too long, more than subtle protest is in store. Our numbers are growing . . . for after all, the future is in the hands of youth.[84]

The editor of *Top Secret* wrote the following:

Americans, have witnessed an unprecedented development in the history of this country . . . the active participation of servicemen in the demonstrations . . . against the war. . . . Because . . . the brass . . . [understands] the implications of antiwar activity in the armed forces [GIs] are subject to arbitrary harassment and repression that civilians are not. Even though there is nothing in the Constitution or . . . the law which gives [them] the right to . . . restrict [our] political activities . . . we have seen a conscious effort by the military to harass and discipline GI's who speak out against the war. It is absolutely essential that [our] right of free speech . . . be firmly established. It is imperative that all attempts by the authorities to deny GI's their civil liberties be exposed and defeated in order to ensure the growth of the anti-war movement among the troops who are in a key position to end this war.[85]

CONCLUSION

In this chapter, I first focus on the GI movement as a spectacular subculture that emerged among young working-class GIs. In looking at this, I interpret them through the prism of the Birmingham School's discussions of the between spectacular subcultures, their parent culture and the dominant culture, which had channeled them into the armed forces. I pay special attention to the influence and effect of a parent culture and mass media that encouraged young men to prepare for military service by watching war movies and playing war games. As Lloyd Lewis notes, these prepared a generation of Americans to wage a war "that in the 1960s only existed on celluloid, videotape and print. . . . The movies fed a generation a consistent diet of war images from which Americans might learn to interpret the nature of armed conflict."[86]

I then revisit the assertion that the GI movement was an extension of, and directed by, the civilian antiwar movement. To illustrate why this claim is false, I contrast the bases and army towns where the GI movement emerged with campuses and college towns where the primary sites of a civilian struggle against the war were located.

To date, scholars of the Vietnam War and the Vietnam-era antiwar movements have ignored these sites, preferring to focus on spectacular activities and individual actors.[87] This is a mistake that inevitably skews our interpretation of the period. To avoid this, scholars must view all the movements of the 1960s through the prism of the environments within which they emerged.

NOTES

1. Stuart Hall, "Cultural Studies and the Centre: Some Problematics and Problems," in *Culture, Media, Language: Working Papers in Cultural Studies* (London: Hutchinson, 1980), 20.

2. John Clarke, Stuart Hall, Tony Jefferson, and Brian Roberts "Subcultures, Cultures and Class," in *Resistance through Rituals: Youth Subcultures in Post-War Britain,* eds. Tony Jefferson and Stuart Hall (London: Hutchinson, 1976), 14.

3. Paul Johnson cited in Clarke et al., "Subcultures, Cultures and Class," 19.

4. See Clarke et al., "Subcultures, Cultures and Class," and Dick Hebdige, *Subculture: The Meaning of Style* (London: Methuen, 1979), chapter 1.

5. Phil Cohen, "Sub-Cultural Conflict & Working-Class Community," in *Working Papers in Cultural Studies* 2 (spring 1972): 23.

6. Clarke et al., "Subcultures, Cultures and Class," 19.

7. See Louis Althusser, "Ideology and Ideological State Apparatuses (Notes towards an Investigation)," in *Lenin and Philosophy,* trans. Ben Brewster (New York: Monthly Review Press, 1971), 127–86; Hebdige, *Subculture: The Meaning of Style*; Henri Lefebvre, *The Critique of Everyday Life,* vol. 1 (London: Verso, 1991); and V. N. Volosinov, *Marxism and the Philosophy of Language* (Cambridge, Mass.: Harvard University Press, 1971).

8. Clarke et al., "Subcultures, Cultures and Class," 12.

9. Althusser cited in Hebdige, *Subculture: The Meaning of Style,* 12.

10. Althusser, "Ideology and Ideological State Apparatuses," 145.

11. Lloyd Lewis, *The Tainted War: Culture and Identity in Vietnam War Narratives* (Westport, Conn.: Greenwood Press, 1985), 52.

12. Ibid., 52.

13. This use of literal signs was common throughout the Vietnam-era military. For example, the Marine Corps Recruitment Center at Parris Island was criss-crossed by yellow footsteps painted on the ground to give recruits direction.

14. "Growth of GI Power," in *The Ally* 1, no. 17 (June 1969): 3.

15. Department of Defense cited in House Committee on Internal Security, *Investigation of Attempts to Subvert the United States Armed Services,* 92nd Cong., 2nd sess., 1972, Committee Print 7310.

16. Clarke et al., "Subcultures, Cultures and Class," 14.

17. "Editorial," in *Top Secret* 1, no. 2 (21 March 1969): 2.

18. "Do you think we would risk jail, and that's what will happen when Uncle finds out who we are, if this was not important? . . . Many of us have . . . plans for when we get out of the military such as college, getting married, etc. and being jailed solely for publishing this newspaper would greatly upset these plans, but we're still doing it." ("Editorial," in *The Whig* 1 [4 July 1970]: 1).

19. Clarke et al., "Subcultures, Cultures and Class," 57–71.

20. Christian Appy, *Working-Class War: American Combat Soldiers and Vietnam* (Chapel Hill, N.C.: The University of North Carolina Press, 1993), 37.

21. Ibid., 27.

22. Clarke et al., "Subcultures, Cultures and Class," 45.

23. Appy, *Working-Class War*, 6–7.

24. Lewis, *The Tainted War*, 43–44.

25. While no one has applied Paul Willis' *Learning to Labor*, to this generation of servicemen, they appear to have internalized the modes, mores and morals of the military in much the same way, British working-class youths learnt to be working-class.

26. Appy, *Working-Class War*, 57.

27. "Peace is the GIs Cause," in *The Ally* 9 (September 1968): 3.

28. "When a GI goes AWOL, a notice goes to the MPs at his base, to local police, to his hometown police, to anywhere he might be likely to go (for instance, where his wife or girlfriend live) and to his parents. After 30 days, the FBI is notified. They distribute information on him to police all over the country." ("Desertion and Other Trips," in *The Ally* 5 [June 1968]: 4).

29. Gloria Emerson, *Winners and Losers* (New York: Random House, 1977), 125–27.

30. James W. Tollefson, *The Strength Not to Fight: An Oral History of Conscientious Objectors of the Vietnam War* (Boston: Little Brown and Company, 1993), 185.

31. Paul Willis, *Learning to Labor: How Working-Class Kids Get Working-Class Jobs* (Farnborough, U.K.: Saxon House, 1977), 2.

32. Fred Turner, *Echoes of Combat* (New York: Anchor Books, 1996), 21.

33. See Appy, *Working-Class War*.

34. Michael Herr cited in Lewis, *The Tainted War*, 24.

35. Hebdige, *Subculture: The Meaning of Style*, 2–3.

36. "Black Unity Band," in *Black Unity* 1 (August 1970): 3.

37. See Hebdige, *Subculture: The Meaning of Style*.

38. "Black Unity Band," in *Black Unity* 1 (August 1970): 3.

39. Jean Genet cited in Hebdige, *Subculture: The Meaning of Style*, 2.

40. "Black Unity Band," in *Black Unity* 1 (August 1970): 3.

41. Ibid., 3.

42. Appy, *Working-Class War*, 15.

43. Ibid., 301.

44. Herbert Marcuse cited in James Lewes, "The Visualization of the Columbia Crisis" (unpublished master's thesis, Annenberg School of Communication, University of Pennsylvania, 1990), 75.

45. Hebdige, *Subculture: The Meaning of Style*, 12.

46. For example, most of the officers quarters at the Presidio in San Francisco were at least 100 years old and now represent some of the most lucrative real estate in the Bay Area.

47. David Cortright, *Soldiers in Revolt: The American Military Today* (New York: Anchor Press, 1975), 50.

48. W. D. Ehrhart, *Vietnam-Perkasie: A Combat Marine Memoir* (Amherst, Mass.: University of Massachusetts Press, 1995), 14.

49. One of the more absurd regulations of the Vietnam-era military was the requirement that servicemen had to salute the most mundane objects bearing the commander's signature, including his car even if the commander is not present.

50. Curtis Stocker and Tom Roberts, "Know Your Rights," in *Aboveground* 1, no. 5 (December 1969): 4.

51. Ibid., 4.

52. Ibid., 4.

53. Ibid., 4. Given the media coverage of antiwar demonstrations, such as the October 1967 March on the Pentagon and the protests at the August 1968 Democratic Convention, any base commander could justifiably claim that he believed each and every public demonstration was likely to include breaches of law and order and result in violence.

54. Unclassified message received 28 August 1968, USAF Communications Center, cited in *Task Force* 2 (October 1968): 3.

55. Fred Halstead, *GIs Speak Out Against the War: the Case of the Fort Jackson 8* (New York: Pathfinder Press, 1970), 15.

56. Ibid., 15.

57. Ibid., 15.

58. *An Exciting Career Awaits You in the GI Movement* (Oakland, Calif.: SOS, 1970), 7.

59. Ibid., 7.

60. Ibid., 8.

61. Ibid., 8.

62. Ibid., 8.

63. See Terry Anderson, *The Movement and the Sixties: Protest in America from Greensboro to Wounded Knee* (New York: Oxford University Press, 1995); Lewes, "The Visualization of the Columbia Crisis" ; Straughton Lynd and Michael Ferber, *The Resistance* (Boston: Beacon Press, 1971); W. J. Rorabaugh, *Berkeley at War: The 1960s* (New York: Oxford University Press, 1989); Kirkpatrick Sale, *SDS* (New York: Random House, 1973); Peter Stansill and David Marovitz, eds., *BAMN: Outlaw Manifestos and Ephemera 1965–1970* (Harmondsworth, U.K.: Penguin Books, 1971); Massimo Teodori, ed., *The New Left: A Documentary History* (New York: The Bobbs-Merrill Company, 1969); Emanuel Wallerstein and Paul Starr, ed., *The University Crisis Reader*, vols. 1 and 2 (New York: Random House, 1970); Tom Wells, *The War Within: America's Battle over Vietnam* (Berkeley: University of California Press, 1994); Alfred Willener, *The Action Image of Society: On Cultural Politicization* (New York: Pantheon Books, 1968); Nancy Zaroulis and Gerald Sullivan, *Who Spoke Up?* (New York: Holt, Rinehart and Winston, 1984).

64. Anderson, *The Movement and the Sixties*, 1.

65. Terry Anderson, "The New American Revolution: the Movement and Business," in *The Sixties: From Memory to History*, ed. David Farber (Chapel Hill, N.C.: The University of North Carolina Press, 1994), 180–81.

66. Among other problems with such research is that it was, and is, classified. Consequently, the scholars pursuing it were unable to share it with their colleagues.

67. Hannah Arendt, *Eichmann in Jerusalem: A Report on the Banality of Evil* (Harmondsworth, U.K.: Penguin Books, 1979), 24.

68. Alan Barton, unpublished report on the attitudes of Columbia students and faculty (New York: Columbia University, 1968), 29.

69. Howard Zinn, *Dow Shalt Not Kill* (Washington, D.C.: Liberation News Service, 13 November 1967), 4.

70. Ibid., 20–21.

71. President Pusey cited in Lawrence Eichel et al., *The Harvard Strike* (Boston: Houghton Mifflin, 1970), 352.

72. Harvard SDS, in Lawrence Eichel et al., *The Harvard Strike*, 39.

73. See Lewes, "The Visualization of the Columbia Crisis," 33.

74. Michael Klare, "IDA, Cold War Think-Tank," in *The Rat* (8 May 1968): 8.

75. See Lewes, "The Visualization of the Columbia Crisis," 33.

76. I am not here suggesting these tactics had no effect on the populations of Southeast Asia; one only need consider the casualties and dislocations inflicted on the populations of Laos, Cambodia, and Vietnam to understand its effect.

77. Barton, unpublished report, 29.

78. W. D. Ehrhart, *Passing Time: Memoir of a Vietnam Veteran Against the War* (Amherst, Mass.: University of Massachusetts Press, 1995), 51–52.

79. "Letter to Lt. General Lewis W. Walt," in *Up Front* 1, no. 2 (June 1969):, 1, 3.

80. "Growth of GI Power," in *The Ally* 17 (June 1969): 3.

81. John Kerry, "How Do You Ask a Man to Be the Last Man to Die for a Mistake," in *The New Soldier*, eds. John Kerry with the Vietnam Veterans against the War (New York: The Macmillan Company, 1971), 16–18. John Kerry is currently the junior Senator from Massachussetts.

82. Article 88 prohibits the use of "contemptuous words against the President, the Vice President, Congress, the Secretary of Defense, the Secretary of a military department, the Secretary of Transportation, or the Governor or legislature of any State, Territory, Commonwealth, or possession in which he is on duty or present shall be punished as a court-martial may direct." (Found at [http://www4.law.cornell.edu/uscode/10/888.html].)

83. Article 91 prohibits any GI from treating "with contempt" or being "disrespectful in language or deportment toward a warrant officer, noncommissioned officer, or petty officer, while that officer is in the execution of his office; shall be punished as a court-martial may direct." (Found at [http://www4.law.cornell.edu/ uscode/10/891.html].)

84. "One Reason for *About Face!*" in *About Face!* 2 (April 1969): 1.

85. "Editorial," in *Top Secret* 1 (14 February 1969): 3–5.

86. Lewis, *The Tainted War*, 22.

87. Barbara Tischler notes: "Popular works about the United States in the 1960s often analyse the Vietnam war in terms of the actions of Lyndon Johnson, Melvyn Laird, and William Westmoreland juxtaposed to the protests of Abbie Hoffman, Mark Rudd and Bernadine Dohrn. But such a 'top down' approach is unsatisfactory in analyzing the decentralized and loosely structured opposition to United States military involvement in Southeast Asia." (Barbara Tischler, "Breaking Ranks: GI Antiwar Newspapers and the Culture of Protest," in *Vietnam Generation* 2, no. 1 [1990]: 20.)

Chapter 8

Conclusion

THE GI PRESS: UNDERGROUND OR ABOVEGROUND

Following the public outcry about the treatment of the Presidio 27 and the Fort Jackson 8, the Pentagon adopted a two-prong strategy of damage control. On the one hand, members of the Joint Chiefs of Staff—including General William Westmoreland and General Lewis Walt—blamed civilian activists for the military's problems. Simultaneously, however—with the "Guidance on Dissent"—the Pentagon liberalized the rules and regulations concerning the rights of GIs to publish and petition.

Despite the fact that no member of the Joint Chiefs of Staff was actively involved in its preparation, it is hard to believe their claims about civilians were not known to the authors of the *Guidance on Dissent* and may have been intended to influence its content. This is suggested both by the timing of Westmoreland's claim that there was strong evidence that civilians were actively "introducing the divisiveness found in our society" into the armed services and by the language the authors used to describe the GI press.

Regarding Westmoreland's timing, he made this claim in public testimony before the Senate Armed Services Committee less than a month before the *Guidance* was distributed. Consequently, I find it difficult to believe that its authors were not aware of his position, and given their subordinate status, may have interpreted his comments as directed at them.

The fact they did interpret his comments this way is suggested by their use of the label "underground" to describe these GI newspapers. While most GI newsworkers would come to refer to their papers as such, in May 1969, they did not. Consequently, it strikes me that the authors of the *Guidance on Dissent* branded these papers as underground so as to support the claims of the Joint Chiefs of Staff.

Given this observation, does it make any sense for me to label these GI papers as underground? To answer this, I revisit my preliminary definition of the underground press and attempt to apply it to the GI press.

A Preliminary Definition of the GI Press

The label "GI press," as I have used it in this book, stands in for a range of newspapers published by and serving the interests of active duty servicemen. While I have concentrated on those papers printed between 1968 and 1970, the first GI paper was published in June 1967 and the last after U.S. troops were finally withdrawn from South Vietnam in March 1973.

My preliminary definition of the civilian press can be broken down into three subsets. First, these papers were either members of the Underground Press Syndicate (UPS), Liberation News Service (LNS) subscribers, or both. Second, they were countercultural community newspapers whose staffs not only lived in—and saw themselves as part of—the same countercultural communities that they reported on, they were active participants in the events they covered. Third, these papers were not actively interested in the myriad of political struggles of the period, but their reporting favored the claims of demonstrators and activists over those of the authorities.

Regarding the first of these subsets, while I found no GI paper that belonged to UPS, slightly less than one-third—fifteen out of forty-eight—of stateside-published GI underground papers were listed by LNS as active subscribers in January 1970.

Furthermore, the fact that only fifteen out of these forty-eight papers subscribed to LNS does not mean that these other papers were unable to use materials from the civilian press (Figure 8.1). All forty-eight, plus nine published in Europe and Asia, subscribed to the GI Press Service (GIPS), which mailed out news packets every two weeks on the understanding that their materials "may be used by GI papers, with or without acknowledgment of the GI press service."[1] Because GIPS subscribed to LNS, any materials printed in the thrice-weekly newspackets distributed by LNS could have been reprinted in a GI newspaper. Furthermore, GIPS—like UPS and LNS—provided GI papers with a wealth of national and international news to supplement local material.

With regard to the second of my subsets, namely, that the underground newspapers were countercultural community newspapers, I offer the following observations. The visions and representations published in the GI underground press not only served to center and focus the movement, but they also enabled movement activists to define and fill in the movement's maps of meaning.

Furthermore, like their civilian counterparts, GI newsworkers not only saw themselves as part of the GI community their papers served, they

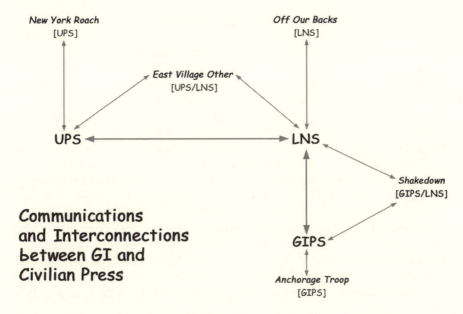

Figure 8.1. Networking the Underground Press. Artist: James Lewes.

were actively involved in organizing and participating in the marches, teach-ins and demonstrations that they covered. However, unlike most civilians, these GIs had no choice as to where they lived. Lastly, GI news-workers were actively interested in reporting on the myriad of national and international political struggles of the period. Like civilian news-workers, they favored the claims of demonstrators, revolutionaries, and activists over those of authorities whom they distrusted and dismissed as pigs.

A FEW FINAL OBSERVATIONS AND A CONCLUSION OR TWO

In chapter 3 I briefly sketch out what I claimed was the institutional locus of the GI press. I close with an all-too-brief excursus on the relative roles of the GI movement, the GI press, and the antiwar coffeehouses and their effects on the brass. It is important to remember that each institution afforded GIs an opportunity to question the legitimacy not only of U.S. involvement in Southeast Asia but also of the military as an institution. Once given this opportunity, it is only a matter of time before "the system of military indoctrination breaks down and military discipline is threat-ened."[2]

As I discuss in chapter 7, each of these counterinstitutions afforded GIs different degrees of protection from harassment. Most GI organizations—

while offering GI activists security through numbers—were least able to protect these same activists because they tended to be riddled with informants and agent provocateurs. While it is impossible to quantify how many supposed activists were, in fact, working for military intelligence, the editors of *Counterpoint* estimated that any group of ten or more members was more than likely infiltrated by military intelligence.

Likewise, and because of the fact that they offered a supportive civilian space where GIs could rest outside the military reservation, coffeehouses could be, and often were, placed off limits by the local brass. Those that were not off limits were kept under constant surveillance by the local police department, who then provided the brass with detailed photographic records of all GIs coming and going from the premises.

Unfortunately, few coffeehouses lasted more than a few months before they were sabotaged, shot up, or firebombed by unknown persons. Those that were not vandalized fared little better. They either closed because there was no one to staff them after local townspeople had driven their original staff out of town. Or they were shut down by force of law because they were found in violation of ordinances that did not exist before they opened.

GI newspapers, on the other hand, not only provide "a means of communication among anti-war GIs,"[3] they break "down the isolation many GIs feel. They also help morale, because they are a way of expressing criticism and anger, as well as poking fun at the military—which is pretty hard for a GI to do in the normal course of military life."[4] They did so by offering GI activists and their sympathizers anonymity.

To return to the question of whether it makes any sense for me to label these GI-produced papers as underground, I would say yes. In fact, I would go further and note that by 1970, about the only thing GI movement activists, the brass, and their respective civilian supporters agreed on was the fact that these GI-produced papers were underground.

While we may never be privy to the effect these GI activists had on the Joint Chiefs of Staff or Nixon and his advisors, the fact a plurality of GIs opposed any further U.S. involvement in Vietnam's civil war had to have added to the administration's predicament. When all else is said and done, the fact that the GI press provided these GIs concrete evidence that they were not alone in their opposition means that these papers—and their newsworkers—helped end U.S. intervention in South Vietnam.

NOTES

1. Frontispiece, in *GI Press Service* 1, no. 1 (26 June 1969): 1.
2. Ibid., 3.
3. Ibid., 3.
4. Ibid., 3.

Appendix 1

Partial Chronology of Dissent, 1965–1970

6 November 1965	Lt. Henry Howe (El Paso) participates in anti-war rally.
February 1966	M.Sgt. Donald Duncan retired publishes "The Whole Thing Was a Lie" in *Ramparts*.
30 June 1966	James Johnson, Paul Mora, and David Samas (Fort Hood) announce intention to refuse orders to Vietnam at a press conference.
October 1966	Dr. Howard Levy refuses to train Green Beret medics on the grounds that the Green Berets were responsible for war crimes in Vietnam.
May 1967	United States found guilty of war crimes in Vietnam by an International War Crimes Tribunal in Stockholm, which heard testimony from vets and deserters.
1 May 1967	Pvt. Philip Wagner deserts in opposition to the Vietnam War.
June 1967	Pvt. Andy Stapp and five other GIs (Fort Sill) send telegram expressing their support for Howard Levy.
16 June 1967	Senator Fulbright reads a letter from a marine second lieutenant into the Congressional Record, in which he says "I wanted to tell you

that there are many, many of us in the military who oppose this war."

23 June 1967   First GI underground paper, *The Bond*, begins publication.

July 1967   Committee for GI Rights founded.

July 1967   Pfc. George Daniels and Cpl. William Harvey call an on-base meeting to discuss whether Blacks should have to serve in the U.S. military.

4 July 1967   300 vets (Philadelphia) hold an antiwar rally opposite Independence Hall.

27 July 1967   Pvt. Richard Perrin publishes antiwar statement in issue 3 of *The Bond*.

31 July 1967   Pvt. Andy Stapp (Fort Sill) charges dismissed in second court-martial.

3 October 1967   Riot (Fort Hood).

23 October 1967   Craig Anderson, John Barella, Richard Bailey, and Michael Lindner (Yokusaka) hold press conference to announce their desertion from USS Intrepid and then travel overland, via USSR to Sweden.

15 November 1967   Pfc 3 Dennis Cisielski (Norfolk Navy Base) refuses to obey orders to Vietnam.

November 1967   Pvt. Ronald Lockman refuses to obey orders to Vietnam.

November 1967   Fred Chard refuses to obey orders to Vietnam.

November 1967   Steve Masono (Fort Benning) is AWOL to avoid shipment to Vietnam.

December 1967   Fred Gardner opens first GI coffeehouse, the UFO, in Columbia, South Carolina.

November 1967   American Servicemen's Union founded.

19 January 1968   Antiwar pamphlet distributed (Fort Sam Houston).

24 January 1968   Pfc. Terry Wilsono deserts in opposition to Vietnam War.

13 February 1968	Twenty-five GIs (Fort Jackson), hold "pray-in" against the war.
20 February 1968	U.S. Ninth Infantry Division (Me Tho Province) reported Combat Refusal.
21 February 1968	Pvt. Ken Stolte and Pfc. Dick Amick (Fort Ord) distribute antiwar leaflet.
4 March 1968	Pfc. Mike Nelson visits congressman in Washington to complain about the treatment of troops at Fort Story.
8 March 1968	Capt. Dale Noyd (Cannon Air Force Base [AFB]) refuses to obey orders to train pilots for service in Vietnam.
10 March 1968	Lt. Dennis Mottiseau pickets White House with sign reading "120,000 U.S. Casualties. Why?"
April 1968	David Crane (Santa Cruz) is military ordered by Judge Weigel to let him resign from military as conscientious objector.
April 1968	Pfc. Walter Kos (Germany) attempts to organize Day of Mourning in remembrance of Martin Luther King.
April 1968	E. Arnet, P. Callicote, C. Kennette, J. Knetz, M. Shapiro, and T. Whitmore desert from Marine Corps in opposition to Vietnam War.
11–12 April 1968	Riot (Fort Campbell).
27 April 1968	GIs from Hamilton AFB, Fort Ord, and Travis AFB lead civilian antiwar demonstration in San Francisco.
May 1968	Pvt. John Perry (Oakland Army Base) refuses to obey orders to Vietnam.
May 1968	Ten GIs granted asylum in Sweden.
10 May 1968	Pfc. Richard Decker is AWOL to avoid further inoculations.
20 May 1968	Sp4c. William Chase (Boston) is granted sanctuary at Arlington Unitarian Church.

June 1968	Navyman Fred Patrick (Naval Air Facility, El Centro) returns from AWOL but refuses all duty.
June 1968	Court-martial rules conscientious objection is a valid defense against charge of being AWOL for Navyman Fred Patrick.
12 June 1968	Seventy GIs (Lai Khe, Vietnam) reported Combat Refusal.
23 June 1968	Sailor Allen Loehmer (Providence, RI), granted sanctuary.
4 July 1968	Riot (Presidio stockade).
15 July 1968	Five army, one marine, two navy, and one air force GIs (San Francisco) are granted sanctuary at Howard Presbyterian Church.
23 July 1968	238 inmates riot (Fort Bragg stockade).
26 July 1968	L.Cpl. Barry Laing (Camp Pendelton) sends letter of resignation from the Marine Corps citing moral and religious opposition to the war.
29 July 1968	Ken Shilman (Oakland Navy base) petitions to hold antiwar meeting on base.
August 1968	200 inmates riot (Marine Brig, DaNang).
August 1968	150 GIs (Fort Carson, Colorado), refuse Chicago Convention duty.
August 1968	113 army reservists (Cleveland) file suit to block recall.
August 1968	1,113 army reservists (Baltimore) file suit to block recall.
August 1968	Pvt. Griswold Wilson (Berkeley) offered sanctuary at Quaker Meeting House.
August 1968	Pvt. Michael Locianto (New York) offered Sanctuary in Greenwich Village Church.
August 1968	Allan Wakoski (Seattle) offered sanctuary.
10 August 1968	GI teach-in (Provo Park, Berkeley).
16–18 August 1968	Riot (Long Binh Jail).
23 August 1968	Sixty-four GIs (Fort Hood) demonstrate

against riot control duty at Democratic National Convention.

25 August 1968 — Forty-three GIs (Fort Hood) refuse Chicago Convention duty.

29 August 1968 — Riot (Long Binh Jail).

September 1968 — Supreme Court considers suit of 700 reservists to block recall.

September 1968 — Pvt. Gerald Condon (Fort Bragg) resigns from Green Berets in opposition to the war.

2 September 1968 — 206 reservists file suit to declare recall illegal.

October 1968 — Maj. Lewis Olive resigned commission because of limitations on right to speak out on civil rights.

October 1968 — GI Civilian Alliance for Peace formed.

October 1968 — GI teach-in (Fort Knox).

1 October 1968 — Sp4c. Allen Myers (Fort Dix), charged of "distribution of leaflets and other printed matter in bad taste," is dismissed ("Myer Wins," in *Flag in Action* 3 [December 1968]: 4).

10 October 1968 — Lt. Susan Schnall bombs naval vessels with leaflets announcing antiwar March in San Francisco on 12 October.

12 October 1968 — 450–500 GIs and 15,000 civilians (San Francisco), GI- and Vietnam veteran–sponsored march for peace.

12 October 1968 — 150 GIs and 150 civilians (Austin) attend GI Solidarity Day picnic.

14 October 1968 — Twenty-three inmates (Presidio stockade) sit-down strike in protest of the killing of Pvt. Richard Bunch by a guard.

26 October 1968 — Thirty to forty GIs and 1,200 civilians (Chicago) attend antiwar rally.

27 October 1968 — Fifty GIs and 600 civilians (Atlanta) attend antiwar rally.

27 October 1968 — Fifty GIs and 1,500 civilians (Austin) attend antiwar rally.

27 October 1968	200 GIs and 100 civilians (Seattle) attend anti-war rally.
27 October 1968	Three GIs killed and ten wounded as a result of bungled suicide attempt.
29 October 1968	Pvt. John Michael O'Connor offered sanctuary at Massachusetts Institute of Technology.
November 1968	Glen Davis (Portland), AWOL marine, announces resignation from corps at news conference.
November 1968	Four GIs given political asylum in France.
November 1968	116 GIs (San Francisco) file suit on behalf of Presidio soldier.
7 November 1968	Riot (Camp Pendelton Brig).
7 November 1968	Fort Dix Free Speech Movement organizes GI teach-in (University of Pennsylvania).
8 November 1968	Pvt. W. Brakefield, Airman D. Copp (New York) offered sanctuary at New York University.
29 November 1968	Sixty-seven men of Company B, Sixth Battalion, Second Basic Combat Training Brigade (Fort Jackson) sign antiwar letter addressed to President Nixon.
20 November 1968	Sp4. Wayne Morse and Pfc. Gary Wisby (editors of *The Logistic*) file suit to block their transfer to Korea.
27 November 1968	3,000 GIs from Twenty-fifth Division (Dong Du Base, Cu Chi, South Vietnam) participate in antiwar demonstration.
27–29 November 1968	GI-Civilian Conference (Chicago).
January 1969	Ninth Infantry Division (South Vietnam) reported "Combat Refusal."
6 January 1969	Riot (Camp Pendelton Brig).
19 January 1969	GIs participate in anti-(Nixon)-inauguration (Washington, D.C.).
21 January 1969	GIs United formed (Fort Jackson).

2 February 1969	Riot (Fort Hood Stockade).
16 February 1969	200 GIs and 4,500 civilians attend antiwar march (Seattle).
23 February 1969	Riot (Duc Hoa, South Vietnam).
26 February 1969	GIs United petition to hold meeting (Fort Jackson).
March 1969	100 GIs riot (Fort Bliss).
March 1969	Tom Sincavich quits Reserves after he was offered sanctuary in a Detroit church.
March 1969	GI Day (University of Pennsylvania).
March 1969	Henry Mills refuses orders to South Vietnam (Fort Dix).
2 March 1969	GI-Civilian Conference (Wright State University).
18 March 1969	Combat Refusal (Son Phu, South Vietnam).
20 March 1969	100 GIs attend antiwar meeting (Fort Jackson).
April 1969	Fifteen GIs refuse orders to South Vietnam (Fort Sill).
April 1969	Riot (Binh Duc, South Vietnam).
April 1969	*About Face!* issue no. 2 lists 150 GIs as jailed for their opposition to the war in Vietnam and racism at home and claims the list is partial.
1 April 1969	Suit filed for GIs United against the War in Vietnam, asking for GIs to be covered by same Constitutional laws as all other U.S. citizens (Spartanburg, North Carolina).
5 April 1969	200 GIs and 75,000–100,000 civilians attend GI-Civilian March (New York).
5 April 1969	Thirty GIs and 30,000 civilians attend GI-Civilian March (Chicago).
6 April 1969	Fifty GIs and 6,000 civilians attend "Free the Presidio 27" march (Los Angeles).
6 April 1969	Fifty GIs and 4,000 civilians attend GI-Civilian March (Atlanta).

6 April 1969   Riot (Fort Riley Stockade).

10 April 1969   Army admits that one of the Fort Jackson 8—Pvt. John Huffman—is an agent provocateur (Fort Jackson).

12 April 1969   100 GIs and 1,200 civilians attend GI-Civilian March (Austin).

19 April 1969   Riot (Camp Pendelton Brig).

21 April 1969   Permission sought for the right to distribute *Rough Draft* on base (Fort Eustis).

24 April 1969   Sp4. Allan Myers (Editor of *The Ultimate Weapon*) applies for permission to distribute *The Ultimate Weapon* at Fort Dix.

28 April 1969   Steve Gilbert (Editor of *FTA*) deserts to avoid shipment to Korea.

May 1969   Charges dropped against Fort Jackson 8 (Fort Jackson).

May 1969   Eighteen GIs in 101st Airborne issue "Statement in Support of Presidio 27" (Phu Bai, South Vietnam).

May 1969   Sp4. Allan Myers (editor of GI Press Service) found not guilty in two court-martials (Fort Dix).

7 May 1969   Protest/riot in support of Presidio 27 (Fort Ord Stockade).

13 May 1969   Riot (Fort Carson).

17 May 1969   Pvt. Joe Miles and nineteen others file suit against the secretary of the army and Fort Bragg commander, seeking an injunction that would prohibit the defense from interfering with the constitutional rights of GIs at Fort Bragg.

18 May 1969   Dennis Ciesielski (Editor of *Rough Draft*) requests permission to distribute paper on base (Fort Eustis).

20 May 1969   500 inmates boycott mess hall (Fort Ord Stockade).

20 May 1969   Demonstration in support of Presidio 27 (Fort Ord Stockade)

21 May 1969	Fort Jackson 8 released from the stockade (Fort Jackson).
24 May 1969	GIs and Vietnam Veterans against the War organize GI-Student Antiwar picnic (Riverside).
June 1969	GIs in 101st Airborne who survived Hamburger Hill offer $10,000 reward to anybody who succeeded in fragging their commanding officer (South Vietnam).
June 1969	One GI Combat Refusal (South Vietnam).
June 1969	Riot (Fort Leonard Wood stockade).
3 June 1969	Charges of "unauthorized distribution" of antiwar literature dropped for Pfc. Robert Bower (Fort Hood).
5 June 1969	200 inmates riot (Fort Dix stockade).
11 June 1969	11 GIs request permission to distribute *The Ultimate Weapon* on post (Fort Dix).
14 June 1969	150 inmates sit in (Fort Jackson Stockade).
14 June 1969	100 or more GIs sign petition calling for GIs to have the right to speak out against the war and racism (Fort Jackson).
14 June 1969	GI-Civilian Victory Picnic.
16 June 1969	Jeff Sharlett (Editor of *Vietnam GI*) dies of cancer.
19 June 1969	Cpl. Bob Kukiel (Editor of *Head On!*) petitions to distribute the Bill of Rights and *Head On!* on base (Camp Lejeune).
20 June 1969	Antiwar leaflets distributed on base (Fort Meade).
22 June 1969	Riot (Camp Pendelton Brig).
22 June 1969	Riot (Fort Riley Stockade).
25 June 1969	Sgt. Rossaire Bisson (Editor of USAF) acquitted of charges that he violated order not to distribute paper on base (Wright-Patterson AFB).

30 June 1969	Committee of Fort Jackson Conscientious Objectors formed (Fort Jackson).
July 1969	Pvt. Benny Amos immolates self in protest of the war but is not seriously hurt (Fort Ord).
July 1969	GI reported to have invented a portable duplicator, which could produce 3–400 copies an hour with three people working on it. It was designed to fit in foot locker.
July 1969	Pfc. Michael Madler has antiwar letter published in *Playboy*, claiming 75% of GIs opposed the war.
1 July 1969	David Egan (Editor of *Huachuca Hard Times*) requests permission to distribute the *Huachuca Hard Times* on post. Base commander agrees to it being distributed on 12 July 1969 (Fort Huachuca).
1 July 1969	Bob Kukiel (Editor of *Head On!*) given honorable discharge three months early because of his paper (Camp Lejeune).
4 July 1969	Request to distribute *Bragg Briefs* on base filed (Fort Bragg).
4–5 July 1969	First national antiwar conference, involoving GIs (Cleveland).
11 July 1969	Riot (Camp Lejeune Stockade).
16 July 1969	Airman Ralph Dady petitions to distribute Bill of Rights and Oath of Enlistment on base filed (Chanute AFB).
20 July 1969	Riot (Camp Lejeune).
21 July 1969	Riot (naval airstation north of Memphis).
21 July 1969	200 inmates riot (Fort Riley stockade).
26 July 1969	Riot (Fort Hood).
30 July 1969	100 GIs demonstrate, demanding peace, end to U.S. aggression in Vietnam, and immediate withdrawal (Qui Nhon, South Vietnam).
30 July 1969	Riot (Fort Carson).
30 July 1969	Request to distribute *Bragg Briefs* filed a second time (Fort Bragg).

August 1969	At least thirty-five GIs get sanctuary for a month (Hawaii).
August 1969	GIs for Peace founded (Fort Bliss).
2 August 1969	600 GIs and civilians demonstrate in support of the Fort Dix 38 (Penn Station, New York).
4 August 1969	Unidentified GI in Vietnam told *New York Times* reporter "I fight because that's the only way to stay alive out here in the boonies. I don't believe this war is necessary. I just work hard at surviving so I can go home and protest all this killing." (*New York Times* [4 August 1969], quoted in *GI Press Service* 1, no. 5 [21 August 1969], 66.)
11 August 1969	Riot (Fort Bragg).
16 August 1969	GIs for Peace granted permission to distribute antiwar leaflet (Fort Bliss).
17 August 1969	Riot (Camp Pendelton Brig).
17 August 1969	Demonstration at Nixon's Summer Whitehouse (San Clemente).
24 August 1969	A Company, 101st Airborne Combat Refusal (Vietnam).
30 August 1969	Riot (Koza, Okinawa).
7 September 1969	GIs from four posts in Washington, D.C., form GI mobilization committee.
28 September 1969	*Rough Draft* legally distributed on base (Fort Eustis).
11 October 1969	Fort Bragg GIs United against the War organize antiwar demonstration (Fayetteville, North Carolina).
15 October 1969	National Moratorium against the War.
November 1969	200 or more GIs send letter to Richard Nixon announcing a protest fast for Thanksgiving (Pleiku, South Vietnam).
November 1969	200 or more GIs participate in Thanksgiving fast in protest of the war (Pleiku, South Vietnam).
9 November 1969	1,365 GIs attach signatures to full-page antiwar statement published in the *New York Times*.

11 November 1969	100 GIs hold Veteran's Day demonstration (El Paso, Texas).
13 November 1969	GIs in West Germany wear black armbands in support of the Moratorium.
13 November 1969	125 GIs sign petition expressing support of the Moratorium (Long Binh, South Vietnam).
13 November 1969	GI-civilian march from Mannheim University to Turley Barracks (Mannheim, West Germany).
13 November 1969	GI teach-in and forum (Mannheim, West Germany).
13 November 1969	Moratorium Sick Call (Fort Knox).
13–14 November 1969	National Conference on GI Rights organized by the GI Defense Organization (Washington, D.C.).
15 November 1969	National Moratorium against the War (Washington, D.C.).
15 November 1969	GIs wear black armbands in solidarity with moratorium (Vietnam).
15 November 1969	160 GIs and 440 civilians attend antiwar demonstration (El Paso, Texas).
16 November 1969	Soldiers Liberation Front formed (Fort Dix).
16 November 1969	GI demonstration (Washington, D.C.).
23 November 1969	Louis Anthony Franchina given sanctuary (First Unitarian Church, Los Angeles).
January 1970	Roger Priest's GI Refendum on Vietnam distributed.
5 January 1970	Eighty GIs join GIs for Peace picket of General Westmoreland (Fort Bliss).
February 1970	Baltimore GIs United founded.
27 February 1970	1st Lt. Louis P. Font, a West Point graduate, asks to be released from military because its actions in Vietnam counter his religious beliefs.
13 March 1970	Riot (Mannheim Brig).

15 March 1970	GI Peace Rally (El Paso).
20 March 1970	Pvt. David H. O'Brien, released from the army after having been in basic training for twenty months and seventeen days, struggling to gain conscientious objector status (Fort Bragg).
4 April 1970	Al Rita (editor of *Potemkin*) given early discharge, four years and three months ahead of schedule.
23 April 1970	Roger Priest (Editor of *OM*), cleared of all but two counts of promoting disloyalty and disaffection.
May 1970	GI movement calls for national demonstrations to celebrate Armed Farces Day.
2 May 1970	470 reservists sign antiwar petition published in the *New Republic*.
11 May 1970	Reservists file suit against 122 members of Congress demanding they resign their National Guard commissions.
16 May 1970	200 GIs participate in Armed Farces Day demonstration (Camp Pendelton).
16 May 1970	100 GIs participate in Armed Farces Day demonstration (Fort Benning).
16 May 1970	750–1,000 GIs participate in Armed Farces Day demonstration (Fort Bragg).
16 May 1970	Twenty GIs participate in Armed Farces Day demonstration (Fort Devens).
16 May 1970	Thirty GIs participate in Armed Farces Day demonstration (Fort Carson).
16 May 1970	700–800 GIs participate in Armed Farces Day demonstration (Fort Hood).
16 May 1970	Sixty GIs participate in Armed Farces Day demonstration (Fort Lewis).
16 May 1970	Fifty GIs participate in Armed Farces Day demonstration (Fort McClellan).
16 May 1970	Seventy-five GIs participate in Armed Farces Day demonstration (Fort Meade).

16 May 1970	100 GIs participate in Armed Farces Day demonstration (Fort Ord).
16 May 1970	400 GIs participate in Armed Farces Day demonstration (Fort Riley).
29 May 1970	National GI Alliance formed.
June 1970	Antiwar reservists picket the annual convention of the Reserve Officers Association (Philadelphia).
30 June 1970	Call for national GI strike.
July 1970	Fort Hamilton GI's United formed.
4 July 1970	1000 GIs attend antiwar rally (Heidelberg).
4 July 1970	United Black Servicemen founded (Heidelberg).
15 August 1970	1,000 or more national guardsmen and reservists sign petition calling for immediate total withdrawal from Vietnam.
October 1970	Eight GIs file federal suit against their commanding officers charging the GIs' military and constitutional rights are being violated by the continued use of the "correctional custody facility."
21 October 1970	Pfc. James Williams (editor of *Freedom Rings*) calls press conference to discuss his opposition to the War (Yuraku-Cho, Japan).
November 1970	GI band members hold a series of peace concerts given in New York area.
8 November 1970	Terry Klug, Russ Malone, and Susan Schnall, former military resisters, are honored by the War Resisters League.

Appendix 2

GI Publications, 1967–1970

A'BOUT FACE (HEIDELBERG)[1]

vol. 1, no. 1 (4 July 1970)

vol. 1, no. 6 (12 September 1970)

ABOUT FACE! (LOS ANGELES)[2]

no. 1 (March 1969)

no. 2 (April 1969)

no. 3 (May 1969)

no. 4 (June 1969)

no. 5 (July 1969)

ABOVEGROUND (FORT CARSON, COLORADO)

vol. 1, no. 1 (August 1969)

vol. 1, no. 2 (September 1969)

vol. 1, no. 3 (October 1969)

vol. 1, no. 4 (November 1969)

vol. 1, no. 5 (December 1969)

vol. 1, no. 6 (February 1970)

vol. 1, no. 7 (March 1970)

vol. 1, no. 8 (April 1970)

Final issue (May 1970)

ACT (PARIS)[3]

vol. 1, no. 1 (undated)[4]
vol. 1, no. 2 (ca. 1970)
vol. 1, no. 3 (undated)[5]
vol. 1, no. 4 (undated)
vol. 2, no. 1 (undated)
vol. 2, no. 2 (undated)
vol. 2, no. 2 (undated)[6]

AEROSPACED (GRISSOM AIR FORCE BASE, INDIANA)[7]

vol. 1, no. 1 (undated)[8]
vol. 1, no. 2 (undated)[9]
vol. 1, no. 3 (undated)[10]
vol. 2, no. 1 (undated)[11]
vol. 2, no. 2 (undated)[12]
vol. 2, no. 3 (undated)[13]
vol. 2, no. 4 (undated)[14]

ALL HANDS ABANDON SHIP (NEWPORT, RHODE ISLAND)[15]

no. 1. (August 1970)
no. 2. (October 1970)

ALL READY ON THE LEFT (CAMP PENDELTON, CALIFORNIA)[16]

vol. 1, no. 1 (August 1970)
vol. 1, no. 2 (September 1970)
vol. 1, no. 3 (December 1970)
vol. 2, no. 1 (April 1971)

THE ALLY (BERKELEY)

no. 1 (February 1968)
no. 2 (March 1968)
no. 3 (April 1968)
no. 4 (May 1968)
no. 5 (June 1968)

no. 6 (July 1968)

no. 7 (July/August 1968)

no. 8 (August 1968)

no. 9 (September 1968)

no. 10 (October 1968)

no. 11 (November 1968)

no. 12 (December 1968)

no. 13 (January 1969)

no. 14 (February 1969)

no. 15 (March/April 1969)

no. 16 (May 1969)

no. 17 (June 1969)

no. 18 (July/August 1969)

no. 19 (September 1969)

no. 20 (October 1969)

no. 21 (November 1969)

no. 22 (December 1969)

no. 23 (January/February 1970)

no. 24 (March 1970)

no. 25 (April 1970)

no. 26 (May 1970)

no. 27 (June 1970)

no. 28 (July 1970)

no. 29 (August 1970)

no. 30 (September 1970)

no. 31 (October 1970)

no. 32 (November 1970)

no. 33 (December 1970)

THE AMERICAN EXILE IN BRITAIN (OXFORD, U.K.)[17]

no. 1 (5 March 1969)

no. 2 (16 April 1969)

THE AMERICAN EXILE IN CANADA (TORONTO)[18]

no. 8 (29 December 1968)

no. 9 (12 January 1969)

no. 10 (26 January 1969)

no. 11 (09 February 1969)

no. 12 (ca. March 1969)

no. 13 (30 March 1969)

no. 14 (24 April 1969)

no. 15 (May 1969)

no. 16 (July 1969)

vol. 2, no. 1 (October 1969)

ANCHORAGE TROOP (FORT RICHARDSON, ALASKA)

vol. 1, no. 1 (January 1970)

vol. 1, no. 2 (February 1970)

vol. 1, no. 3 (March 1970)

vol. 1, no. 4 (March 1970)

ANTIBRASS (LOS ANGELES)

no. 1 (ca. 1970)

ASH (KAISERSLAUTERN, W. GERMANY)

2 issues 1969 (date unknown)

AS YOU WERE (FORT ORD, CALIFORNIA)

no. 1 (April 1969)

no. 2 (May 1969)

no. 3 (May 1969)

no. 4 (June 1969)

no. 5 (July 1969)

no. 6 (August 1969)

no. 7 (August 1969)

no. 9 (November 1969)

no. 10 (November 1969)

no. 13 (April 1970)

ATTITUDE CHECK (CAMP PENDELTON, CALIFORNIA)

vol. 1, no. 1 (1 November 1969)

vol. 1, no. 2 (1 December 1969)

vol. 2, no. 1 (1 February 1970)

vol. 2, no. 1 (1 March 1970)[19]

vol. 2, no. 3 (1 April 1970)
special issue (May 1970)

THE AWOL PRESS (FORT RILEY, KANSAS)

vol. 1, no. 1 (undated)[20]
vol. 1, no. 2 (undated)[21]
vol. 1, no. 3 (undated)[22]
vol. 1, no. 4 (undated)[23]
vol. 1, no. 5 (undated)[24]
vol. 1, no. 6 (undated)[25]
vol. 1, no. 7 (undated)[26]
vol. 1, no. 8 (undated)[27]
vol. 1, no. 9 (undated)[28]
vol. 1, no. 10 (undated)[29]
vol. 1, no. 11 (undated)[30]

B TROOP NEWS (FORT LEWIS, WASHINGTON)

vol. 1, no. 3 (May 1970)
vol. 1, no. 4 (June 1970)

BLACK UNITY (CAMP PENDELTON, CALIFORNIA)[31]

vol. 1, no. 1 (August 1970)
vol. 1, no. 2 (September 1970)

THE BOND (BERKELEY AND NEW YORK)[32]

vol. 1, no. 1 (23 June 1967)
vol. 1, no. 2 (7 July 1967)
vol. 1, no. 3 (7 July 1967)
vol. 1, no. 4 (4 August 1967)
vol. 1. no. 10 (3 November 1967)
vol. 1, no. 11 (17 November 1967)
vol. 2, no. 1 (28 January 1968)
vol. 2, no. 2 (18 February 1968)
vol. 2, no. 3 (18 March 1968)
vol. 2, no. 4 (14 April 1968)
vol. 2, no. 5 (13 May 1968)

vol. 2, no. 6 (11 June 1968)

vol. 2, no. 7 (17 June 1968)

vol. 2, no. 8 (15 August–15 September 1968)

vol. 2, no. 9 (18 September 1968)

vol. 2, no. 10 (16 October 1968)

vol. 2, no. 11 (18 November 1968)

vol. 2, no. 12 (16 December 1968)

vol. 3, no. 1 (21 January 1969)

vol. 3, no. 2 (17 February 1969)

vol. 3, no. 3 (17 March 1969)

vol. 3, no. 4 (15 April 1969)

vol. 3, no. 5 (20 May 1969)

vol. 3, no. 6 (17 June 1969)

vol. 3, no. 7 (22 July 1969)

vol. 3, no. 8 (25 August 1969)

vol. 3, no. 9 (22 September 1969)

vol. 3, no. 10 (20 October 1969)

vol. 3, no. 11 (18 November 1969)

vol. 3, no. 12 (16 December 1969)

vol. 4, no. 1 (15 January 1970)

vol. 4, no. 2 (18 February 1970)

vol. 4, no. 3 (18 March 1970)

vol. 4, no. 4 (22 April 1970)

vol. 4, no. 5 (13 May 1970)

vol. 4, no. 6 (17 June 1970)

vol. 4, no. 7 (22 July 1970)

vol. 4, no. 8 (26 August 1970)

vol. 4, no. 10 (21 October 1970)

vol. 4, no. 11 (18 November 1970)

vol. 4, no. 12 (16 December 1970)

BRAGG BRIEFS (FORT BRAGG, NORTH CAROLINA)[33]

vol. 1, no. 1 (4 July 1969)[34]

vol. 2, no. 1 (August 1969)

vol. 2, no. 2 (September 1969)

vol. 2, no. 3 (November 1969)

vol. 2, no. 4 (December 1969)

vol. 2, no. 5 (Christmas 1969)

vol. 2, no. 6 (February 1970)

vol. 3, no. 1 (April 1970)

vol. 3, no. 3 (May 1970)[35]

special May 16th issue (16 May 1970)[36]

vol. 3. no. 3 (June 1970)

BROKEN ARROW (SELFRIDGE AFB, MICHIGAN)[37]

vol. 1, no. 1 (undated)[38]

vol. 1, no. 2 (22 July 1969)

vol. 1, no. 4 (20 August 1969)

vol. 1, no. 5 (17 September 1969)

vol. 1, no. 6 (2 October 1969)

vol. 1, no. 7 (23 September 1969)[39]

vol. 1, no. 7 (1 December 1969)

vol. 1, no. 9 (10 February 1970)[40]

vol. 1, no. 10 (30 May 1970)

vol. 2, no. 1 (12 July 1970)

vol. 2, no. 2 (15 October 1970)

vol. 2, no. 3 (17 November 1970)

Christmas issue (December 1970)

CALL UP (PATTON BARRACKS, HEIDELBERG)[41]

vol. 1, no. 1 (26 September 1970)

CATHARSIS (QUONSET-DAVISVILLE NAVAL AIR STATION, RHODE ISLAND)[42]

no. 1 (August 1970)

unnumbered issue (October 1970)

CHESSMAN (MARINE CORPS AIR STATION, BEAUFORT, SOUTH CAROLINA)[43]

vol. 1, no. 1 (July 1969)

COFFEEHOUSE NEWS (SAN FRANCISCO)

vol. 1, no. 1 (12 February 1969)

COM MON SENSE (WASHINGTON, DC)

vol. 2 no. 1 (December 1970)

vol. 2, no. 2 (March 1971)

COM NEWSLETTER (WASHINGTON, D.C.)[44]

no. 3 (July 1970)

CONFINEE SAYS (CAMP PENDELTON BRIG, CALIFORNIA)[45]

1 issue undated

COUNTER-ATTACK (FORT CARSON, COLORADO)[46]

vol. 1, no. 1 (undated)

vol. 1, no. 2 (undated)

vol. 1, no. 3 (undated)

COUNTERPOINT (FORT LEWIS, WASHINGTON)[47]

vol. 1, no. 1 (29 October 1968)

vol. 1, no. 4 (14 December 1968)

vol. 1, no. 5 (6 January 1969)

vol. 2, no. 1 (24 February 1969)

vol. 2, no. 2 (3 March 1969)

vol. 2, no. 3 (10 March 1969)

vol. 2, no. 4 (17 March 1969)

vol. 2, no. 5 (24 March 1969)

vol. 2, no. 6 (31 March 1969)

vol. 2, no. 7 (7 April 1969)

vol. 2, no. 8 (14 April 1969)

vol. 2, no. 10 (28 April 1969)

vol. 2, no. 11 (12 May 1969)

vol. 2, no. 12 (2 June 1969)

vol. 2, no. 13 (23 June 1969)

vol. 2, no. 14 (7 August 1969)

vol. 2, no. 15 (20 September 1969)

DARE TO STRUGGLE (SAN DIEGO)[48]

vol. 1, no. 1 (undated)[49]

vol. 1, no. 2 (25 September 1970)

vol. 1, no. 3 (9 October 1970)

DEMAND FOR FREEDOM (KADENA AIR FORCE BASE, OKINAWA)

no. 1 (7 October 1970)

no. 2 (16 November 1970)

no. 3 (25 December 1970)

THE DESTROYER (PHILADELPHIA)

vol. 1, no. 2 (18 September 1970)

vol. 1, no. 3 (05 April 1971)

DUCK POWER (SAN DIEGO)[50]

vol. 1, no. 3 (24 September 1969)[51]

vol. 1, no. 4 (4 October 1969)

vol. 1, no. 5 (22 October 1969)

vol. 1, no. 6 (6 November 1969)[52]

vol. 1, no. 7 (1 December 1969)

vol. 1, no. 7 (22 December 1969)[53]

vol. 2, no. 1 (22 January 1970)

vol. 2, no. 3 (undated)[54]

vol. 2, no. 7 (20 June 1970)

vol. 2, no. 8 (10 July 1970)

DULL BRASS (FORT SHERIDAN, ILLINOIS)

vol. 1, no. 1 (14 April 1969)

vol. 1, no. 2 (15 May 1969)

vol. 1, no. 3 (undated)[55]

vol. 1, no. 4 (undated)[56]

special edition (undated)[57]

EAT THE APPLE (DETROIT)

no. 2 (August 1969)

no. 3 (September 1969)

no. 4 (October 1969)

no. 5 (November 1969)

no. 6 (March 1970)

EM-16 (FORT KNOX, KENTUCKY)

no. 1 (25 March 1970)

EYES LEFT (TRAVIS AFB, CALIFORNIA)

no. 1 (May 1969)

no. 2 (June 1969)

no. 3 (July 1969)

no. 4 (September 1969)

no. 5 (October 1969)

no. 6 (November 1969)

no. 7 (December 1969)

FALL IN AT EASE (TOKYO)[58]

no. 1 (Autumn 1970)

no. 2 (Winter 1970)

FATIGUE PRESS (FORT HOOD, TEXAS)

no. 8 (September 1968)

no. 10 (October 1968)

no. 11 (December 1968)

no. 13 (undated)

no. 20 (May 1970)

no. 21 (June 1970)

no. 22 (July 1970)

no. 23 (August 1970)

no. 24 (September 1970)

no. 25 (October 1970)

no. 26 (November 1970)

no. 27 (December 1970)

no. 28 (January 1971P)

FED UP! (FORT LEWIS, WASHINGTON)

vol. 1, no. 1 (13 October 1969)

vol. 1, no. 3 (16 January 1970)

vol. 1, no. 4 (26 February 1970)

FIGHT BACK (LOS ANGELES)

4 issues undated and unnumbered (ca. 1970)

FIRST AMENDMENT (FORT WAYNE, INDIANA)

no. 1 (May 1970)

no. 2 (undated)

FLAG IN ACTION (FORT CAMPBELL, KENTUCKY)

no. 1 (November 1968)

no. 2 (December 1968)

no. 3 (ca. 1969)

A FOUR YEAR BUMMER (CHANUTE AFB, ILLINOIS)[59]

vol. 1, no. 1 (May 1969)

vol. 1, no. 2 (undated)

vol. 1, no. 3 (August 1969)

vol. 1, no. 4 (September 1969)

vol. 1, no. 5 (October/November 1969)

vol. 1, no. 6 (December 1969)

vol. 2, no. 1 (February 1970)

vol. 2, no. 2 (4 March 1970)

vol. 2, no. 3 (May 1970)

vol. 2, no. 4 (June 1970)

vol. 2, no. 5 (July 1970)

vol. 2, no. 6 (August 1970)

vol. 2, no. 7 (September 1970)

vol. 2, no. 8 (October 1970)

vol. 2, no. 9 (November 1970)[60]

vol. 2, no. 10 (December 1970/January 1971)

FREEDOM RINGS (TOKYO)

no. 1 (14 August 1970)

no. 3 (21 November 1970)

FT POLK GI VOICE (FORT POLK, TEXAS)

no. 1 (March 1969)

FUN TRAVEL ADVENTURE (FORT KNOX, KENTUCKY)

no. 1 (23 June 1968)

no. 2 (ca. August 1968)

no. 3 (ca. September 1968)

no. 4 (ca. October 1968)

no. 5 (November 1968)

no. 6 (December 1968)

no. 7 (March 1969)

no. 8 (May 1969)

no. 9 (June 1969)[61]

no. 10 (August 1969)[62]

no. 11 (September 1969)[63]

no. 12 (October 1969)[64]

no. 13 (November 1969)[65]

no. 14 (December 1969)[66]

no. 16 (March 1970)[67]

no. 17 (May 1970)[68]

no. 18 (June 1970)

no. 19 (July 1970)

no. 20 (August 1970)

no. 21 (September 1970)

no. 22 (November 1970)

no. 23 (December 1970)

GAF (BARKSDALE AFB, LOUISIANA)

vol. 1, no. 1 (4 July 1969)

vol. 1, 2 (13 December 1969)

GI ALLIANCE (WASHINGTON, D.C.)

newsletter 1 (3 June 1970)

newsletter 2 (24 June 1970)

THE GI ORGANIZER (FORT HOOD, TEXAS)

no. 1 (2 April 1969)

no. 2 (28 April 1969)

no. 3 (26 May 1969)

no. 4 (1 July 1969)

no. 5 (5 August 1969)

GI PRESS SERVICE (NEW YORK CITY)

vol. 1, no. 1 (26 June 1969)

vol. 1, no. 2 (10 July 1969)

vol. 1, no. 3 (24 July 1969)

vol. 1, no. 4 (7 August 1969)

vol. 1, no. 5 (21 August 1969)

vol. 1, no. 6 (4 September 1969)

vol. 1, no. 7 (18 September 1969)

vol. 1, no. 8 (2 October 1969)

vol. 1, no. 9 (16 October 1969)

vol. 1, no. 10 (30 October 1969)

vol. 1, no. 11 (13 November 1969)

vol. 1, no. 12 (27 November 1969)

vol. 1, no. 13 (11 December 1969)

vol. 2, no. 1 (21 January 1970)

vol. 2, no. 2 (4 February 1970)

vol. 2, no. 3 (26 February 1970)

GI SAYS (VIETNAM)

1 issue (ca. 1970)

GI VOICE (NEW YORK)[69]

no. 1 (February 1969)

no. 2, special edition (April 1969)

no. 2–3 (May 1969)

no. 4 (July 1969)

Special Edition for Cleveland Antiwar Conference (5 July 1969)

no. 5 (November 1969)

GIGLINE (FORT BLISS, TEXAS)[70]

vol. 1, no. 2 (August 1969)

vol. 1, no. 3 (October 1969)

vol. 1, no. 4 (November 1969)

vol. 1, no. 5 (Christmas 1969)

vol. 2, no. 1 (January 1970)

vol. 2, no. 2 (February 1970)

vol. 2, no. 3 (March 1970)

vol. 2, no. 4 (April 1970)

vol. 2, no. 5 (May 1970)

THE GRAFFITTI (HEIDELBERG)[71]

no. 1 (June 1969)

no. 2 (undated)[72]

no. 3 (undated)[73]

no. 4 (undated)[74]

no. 5 (July 1970)

THE GREEN MACHINE (FORT WAINWRIGHT, ALASKA)[75]

no. 1 (undated)

no. 2 (March 1970)

no. 3 (April 1970)

no. 5 (July 1970)

no. 6 (August 1970)

no. 7 (October 1970)

HAIR (AOMORI-KEN, JAPAN)

no. 1 (ca. July 1969)

no. 2 (ca. July 1969)

no. 3 (ca. July 1969)

HAIR REVIVED (AOMORI-KEN, JAPAN)

no. 3 + 1 (December 1970)

no. 3 + 2 (15 December 1970)

HEAD-ON! (CHERRY POINT NAS, NORTH CAROLINA)[76]

vol. 1, no. 1 (25 December 1968)

vol. 1, no. 2 (14 February 1969)

vol. 1, no. 3 (24 March 1969)

vol. 1, no. 4 (15 April 1969)

vol. 1, no. 7 (4 July 1969)[77]

HEAD-ON WISH (CHERRY POINT NAS, NORTH CAROLINA)[78]

vol. 1, no. 8 (21 July 1969)

vol. 1, no. 9 (18 August 1969)

HERESY II (NO PLACE OF PUBLICATION)

vol. 1, no. 1 (November 1969)

HUACHUCA HARD TIMES (FORT HUACHUCA, ARIZONA)

no. 1 (April 1969)

no. 2 (June 1969)

KILL FOR PEACE (TOKYO)

no. 1 (November 1969)

no. 2 (December 1969)

LAST HARASS (FORT GORDON, GEORGIA)

no. 1 (October 1968)

no. 2 (December 1968)

no. 3 (March 1969)

no. 4 (May 1969)

no. 6 (May 1970)

no. 7 (June 1970)

LEFT FACE (FORT McCLELLAN, ALASKA)[79]

vol. 1, no. 1 (October 1969)

vol. 1, no. 2 (November 1969)

vol. 1, no. 4 (December 1969)

vol. 1, no. 5 (January 1970)

vol. 2, no. 1 (April 1970)

vol. 2, no. 2 (May 1970)

LEWIS-McCHORD FREE PRESS (FORT LEWIS, WASHINGTON)

vol. 1, no. 1 (August 1970)[80]

vol. 1, no. 2 (September 1970)

vol. 1, no. 3 (October 1970)
vol. 1, no. 4 (November 1970)
vol. 1, no. 5 (December 1970)

LINK NEWS (WASHINGTON, D.C.)[81]

no. 1 (November 1969)

THE LOGISTIC (FORT SHERIDAN, ILLINOIS)

2 undated and unnumbered issues.[82]

THE LOOPER (SAN FRANCISCO)[83]

1 unnumbered issue published in April 1969

MARINE BLUES (SAN FRANCISCO)[84]

vol. 1, no. 1 (April/May 1969)
vol. 1, no. 7 (December 1969)
vol. 1, no. 12 (April 1970)[85]

MILITARY INTELLIGENCE (LOS ANGELES)

vol. 1, no. 3 (September 1970)

MORNING REPORT (FORT DEVEN, MASSACHUSETTS)

vol. 1, no. 1 (May 1970)
vol. 1, no. 2 (June 1970)
vol. 1, no. 3 (undated)[86]
vol. 1, no. 4 (ca. 1970)
vol. 1, no. 5 (undated)[87]

MY KNOT (MINOT AFB, NORTH DAKOTA)

no. 1 (undated)[88]

NAPALM (FORT CAMPBELL, KENTUCKY)

vol. 1, no. 1 (June 1970)
vol. 1, no. 2 (undated)[89]
vol. 1, no. 3 (undated)[90]
vol. 1, no. 4 (September 1970)
vol. 1, no. 5 (undated 1970)

NAVY TIMES ARE CHANGIN' (CHICAGO)[91]

vol. 1, no. 1 (February 1970)

NEW SALUTE (BALTIMORE)[92]

vol. 1, no. 1 (October 1969)[93]

NEW SOS NEWS (SAN FRANCISCO)

vol. 1, no. 4 (27 July 1969)

THE NEXT STEP (HEIDELBERG)[94]

vol. 1, no. 1 (4 July 1970)
vol. 1, no. 2 (19 July 1970)
vol. 1, no. 3 (3 August 1970)
vol. 1, no. 4 (20 August 1970)
vol. 1, no. 9 (16 November 1970)

THE OBLIGORE (NEW YORK)

no. 1 (September 1969)
no. 2 (November 1969)
no. 3 (December 1969)
no. 4 (January 1970)
no. 5 (March 1970)
no. 6 (April 1970)

OM (WASHINGTON, D.C.)[95]

vol. 1, no. 1 (April 1969)
vol. 1, no. 2 (May 1969)
vol. 1, no. 3 (June 1969)
vol. 1, no. 4 (October 1969)
vol. 1, no. 5 (January 1970)
vol. 1, no. 6 (undated 1970)
"Stop The Trial" (undated 1970)

ON THE BEACH (DAM NECK, VIRGINIA BEACH, VIRGINIA)

vol. 1, no. 1 (September 1970)
vol. 1, no. 2 (October 1970)[96]

vol. 1, no. 3 (23 October 1970)

vol. 1, no. 4 (December 1970)

OPEN RANKS (FORT HOLABIRD, MARYLAND)[97]

vol. 1, no. 4 (January 1970)

vol. 1, no. 5 (February 1970)

vol. 1, no. 8 (May 1970)

vol. 1, no. 9 (June 1970)

vol. 1, no. 10 (July 1970)

OPEN SIGHTS (WASHINGTON, D.C.)

vol. 1, no. 1 (February 1969)

vol. 1, no. 2 (March 1969)

vol. 1, no. 3 (April 1969)

Special issue — Fall 1969

vol. 2, no. 1 (February 1970)

vol. 2, no. 2 (March 1970)

vol. 2, no. 3 (April 1970)

vol. 2, no. 4 (May 1970)

vol. 2, no. 5 (June/July 1970)

vol. 2, no. 6 (August 1970)

OUR THING (REDSTONE ARSENAL, ALABAMA)[98]

vol. 1, no. 1 (June 1970)

OUT NOW (LONG BEACH, CALIFORNIA)[99]

vol. 1, no. 1 (May 1970)[100]

vol. 1, no. 2 (June 1970)

vol. 1, no. 3 (July 1970)

vol. 1, no. 4 (August 1970)

vol. 1, no. 5 (October 1970)

vol. 2, no. 1 (ca. 1970)[101]

THE PAPER BAG (PETERSBURG, VIRGINIA)

vol. 3, no. 3 (November 1970)

THE PAWN (FORT DETRICK, MARYLAND)[102]

vol. 1, no. 1 (November 1969)
vol. 1, no. 2 (December 1969)
vol. 1, no. 3 (February 1970)[103]
vol. 1, no. 4 (April 1970)

PAY BACK (SANTA ANNA, CALIFORNIA)

vol. 1, no. 1 (July 1970)

PEACE (ROYAL AIR FORCE, MILDENHALL, U.K.)[104]

vol. 1, no. 1 (1 August 1970)
vol. 1, no. 2 (1 September 1970)
vol. 1, no. 3 (1 October 1970)
vol. 1, no. 4 (1 November 1970)
vol. 1, no. 5 (1 December 1970)

PEACE EXCHANGE (ST. CATHARINE, ONTARIO)[105]

vol. 1, no. 1 (undated)[106]

PENTAGON GI COFFEEHOUSE (OAKLAND, CALIFORNIA)[107]

no. 1 (24 November 1970)

POLYLOGUE (AUGUSTA, GEORGIA)[108]

vol. 1, no. 1 (12 November 1969)

POTEMKIN (USS FORRESTAL)[109]

vol. 1, no. 1 (January 1970)

P.O.W. (FORT ORD, CALIFORNIA)

vol. 1, no. 1 (March 1971)

RAP! (FORT BENNING, GEORGIA)

no. 1 (November 1969)
no. 2 (ca. 1969)
vol. 1, no. 3 (ca. 1970)

vol. 1, no. 4 (March 1970)

vol. 1, no. 5 (April 1970)

vol. 1, no. 6 (May 1970)

vol. 1, no. 7 (June 1970)

vol. 1, no. 8 (July 1970)

vol. 1, no. 9 (August 1970)[110]

vol. 1, no. 10 (November 1970)

vol. 1, no. 11 (February 1971)

RESERVISTS COMMITTEE TO STOP THE WAR NEWSLETTER (NEW YORK) [111]

Six issues published in 1970, each undated.

THE RETALIATION[112]

no. 1 (September 1969)

REVEILLE (CARMEL, CALIFORNIA)

vol. 1, no. 1 (April 1968)

RIGHT-ON POST (SEASIDE, CALIFORNIA)[113]

vol. 1, no. 1 (May 1970)

vol. 1, no. 2 (1 June 1970)

vol. 1, no. 4 (August 1970)

RITA BULLETINS (PARIS)[114]

no. 8, Resistance in the United States Armed Forces

no. 11, Note on resister who returned to U.S. Army

no. 13 (open bulletin), Article by Terry Klug

no. 14, Letter to the Editor of *Overseas Weekly* from Terry Klug

no. 18, Internal Letter Concerning Coverage of Sanctuary in Canada for Deserters

no. 19, Free Pvt Sood! Stop the Presidio Murderers!

no. 20, Prisoner of War (POW) Front

no. 21, Letter to the Editor of *Overseas Weekly*, Correcting Some Errors in Their Coverage of RITA

no. 23, Dear Danish Friends

no. 25, Report by Terry Klug from the Fort Dix stockade

no. 28, Going up the Country[115]

no. 39, Direct Work with GIs is Very Exhausting

no. 40, Useful Addresses for GIs and Vets

no. 45, Announcement of a Rally/Demonstration

no. 46, Announcement of Visit to Germany of Two Black Panther Spokesmen

no. 48, American Servicemen Have Rights. Do You Know Yours?[116]

no. 49, December Issue of *What's Happening*

no. 55, More Detailed Description of Black Panther's Visit to Germany

no. 61, Vietnam-Cambodia-Ohio

no. 62, Petition Calling for the Release of 15 Imprisoned GIs in Berlin

no. 63, Boycott *Overseas Weekly*, Support *GI Press*!

no. 77, The Situation in Sweden

no. 87, You May Be Irish

no. 88, First American Deserter Gets Political Asylum in West Germany

no. 92, To American GIs in Germany

ROUGH DRAFT (FORT EUSTIS, VIRGINIA)

no. 1 (March 1969)

no. 2 (March–April 1969)

no. 3 (May 1969)

no. 4 (June 1969)

special edition (June 1969)

no. 5 (August 1969)

no. 6 (September/October 1969)

SHAKEDOWN (FORT DIX, NEW JERSEY)

vol. 1, no. 7 (15 August 1969)

vol. 1, no. 10 (4 October 1969)

vol. 1, no. 11 (17 October 1969)

vol. 1, no. 13 (24 November 1969)

vol. 1, no. 16 (2 February 1970)

vol. 1, no. 17 (6 March 1970)

vol. 2, no. 1 (28 March 1970)

vol. 2, no. 2 (24 April 1970)

vol. 2, Special Issue (8 May 1970)

vol. 1, no. 1 (21 March 1969)

vol. 1, no. 2 (11 April 1969)

vol. 1, no. 7 (15 August 1969)

vol. 1, no. 9 (24 September 1969)

vol. 1, no. 10 (4 October 1969)

vol. 1, no. 13 (24 November 1969)

vol. 1, no. 16 (2 February 1970)

vol. 1, no. 17 (6 March 1970)

vol. 2, no. 1 (28 March 1970)

vol. 2, no. 2 (24 April 1970)

vol. 2, no. 3 (7 June 1970)

vol. 2, no. 6 (8 September 1970)

SHORT TIMES (FORT JACKSON, SOUTH CAROLINA)

no. 1 (January 1970)

no. 2 (6 December 1968)

no. 3 (March 1969)

no. 4 (April 1970)

no. 5 (July 1969)

SNORTON BIRD (NORTON AFB, CALIFORNIA)

vol. 1, no. 1 (16 June 1970)

vol. 1, no. 2 (4 July 1970)

SPARTACUS (FORT LEE, VIRGINIA)

vol. 1, no. 2 (4 August 1969)

SPD NEWS (FORT DIX, NEW JERSEY)

no. 10 (1 November 1969)

no. 11 (1 December 1969)

no. 12 (9 December 1969)

STAR SPANGLED BUMMER (WRIGHT-PATTERSON AFB, OHIO)[117]

vol. 1, no. 1 (July 16, 1970)

vol. 1, no. 2 (July 31, 1970)

vol. 1, no. 3 (October 1970)

THE STARS-N-BARS (IWAKUNI BRIG, JAPAN)

no. 1 (October 27, 1970)

no. 2 (ca. 1970)

STRIKE BACK (FAYETTEVILLE, NORTH CAROLINA)

Published during 1970. No information known, only vol. 1, no. 2 seen, has no date or relevant/useful bibliographic data.

STUFFED PUFFIN (KEFLAVIK, ICELAND)

vol. 1, no. 1 (4 September 1970)[118]

TASK FORCE (BERKELEY)

vol. 1, no. 1 (10 August 1968)
vol. 1, no. 2 (25 September 1968)
vol. 1, no. 3 (25 October 1968)
vol. 1, no. 4 (25 March 1969)

TOP SECRET (FORT DEVENS, MASSACHUSETTS)

vol. 1, no. 1 (14 February 1969)
vol. 1, no. 2 (21 March 1969)
vol. 1, no. 3 (May 1969)
no. 4 (April 1970)
vol. 1. no. 4 (undated)[119]
vol. 1, no. 5 (undated)[120]

TWIN CITIES PROTESTER (MINNEAPOLIS)

vol. 1, no. 1 (3. 1 1970)

THE ULTIMATE WEAPON (FORT DIX, NEW JERSEY)

no. 1 (18 December 1968)
no. 2 (15 January 1969)
no. 3 (5 February 1969)
no. 4 (24 February 1969)
no. 5 (15 March 1969)
special issue (5 April 1969)
no. 6 (19 April 1969)
no. 7 (17 May 1969)
no. 8 (14 June 1969)
no. 9 (24 July 1969)
no. 10 (15 November 1969)
no. 11 final issue (27 January 1970)

UNDERGROUND OAK (OAK KNOLL NAVAL HOSPITAL, OAKLAND, CALIFORNIA)

vol. 1, no. 1 (22 December 1968)

UNDERWOOD (ST. LOUIS)[121]

vol. 1, no. 3 (May 1970)

UNITY NOW (FORT ORD, CALIFORNIA)

vol. 1, no. 1 (6 October 1970)
vol. 1, no. 2 (16 October 1970)

UP AGAINST THE BULKHEAD (ALAMEDA, CALIFORNIA)[122]

no. 1 (undated)
vol. 1, no. 3 (15 June 1970)

UP AGAINST THE WALL (WEST BERLIN)

4 issues, each unnumbered and undated[123]

UP FRONT (LOS ANGELES)

vol. 1, no. 1 (May 1969)
vol. 1, no. 2 (June 1969)
vol. 1, no. 3 (July 1969)
vol. 1, no. 4 (August 1969)
vol. 1, no. 5 (September 1969)
vol. 1, no. 6 (November 1969)
vol. 1, no. 7 (December 1969)

UP TIGHT (EL PASO, TEXAS)

vol. 1, no. 1 (July 1969)

USAF (WRIGHT-PATTERSON AFB, OHIO)[124]

vol. 1, no. 1 (1 April 1969)
vol. 1, no. 2 (1 May 1969)
vol. 1, no. 3 (4 July 1969)
vol. 1, no. 3a (extra) (4 July 1969)

VENCEREMOS (FRANKFURT)[125]

no. 1 (undated)

VIETNAM GI (MIAMI)[126]

January 1968
February 1968
March 1968
April 1968
May 1968
June 1968
July 1968
August 1968
September 1968[127]
October 1968
November 1968
December 1968
January 1969
February 1969
March 1969
April 1969
May 1969
June 1969
July 1969
August 1969
October 1969
November 1969
December 1969
January 1970
February 1970
March 1970
April 1970
May 1970

WE GOT THE brASS (GERMAN ED., FRANKFURT)[128]

no. 1 (undated)
no. 2 (undated)[129]
no. 3 (undated)[130]

WE GOT THE brASS (ASIAN ED., TOKYO)

no. 1 (fall 1969)

WE GOT THE brASS (VIETNAM ED., TOKYO)

no. 1 (early 1970)

WHAT'S HAPPENING (PARIS)[131]

1 issue seen by me (December 1969)

WHERE IT'S AT (WEST BERLIN)[132]

vol. 1, no. 1 (April 1968)
vol. 1, no. 4 (April 1968)
vol. 1, no. 5 (undated)
vol. 2, no. 1 (undated)

THE WHIG (ANGELES CITY, PAMPANGA, PHILIPPINES)[133]

vol. 1, no. 1 (4 July 1970)
vol. 1, no. 2 (9 August 1970)
vol. 1, no. 3 (October 1970)
vol. 1, no. 4 (December 1970)

XPRESS (NEW YORK)[134]

vol. 1, no. 1 (September 1970)
vol. 1, no. 2 (October 1970)
vol. 1, no. 3 (November 1970)
vol. 1, no. 4 (December 1970)

YAND (FUKOKA, JAPAN)[135]

vol. 1, no. 1 (October 1970)

YOKOSUKA DAVID (TOKYO)[136]

no. 2 (31 October 1970)
no. 4 (14 November 1970)
no. 6 (19 December 1970)

YOUR MILITARY LEFT (SAN ANTONIO, TEXAS)[137]

vol. 1, no. 7 (ca. February 1970)

vol. 1, no. 8 (15 March 1970)

vol. 1, no. 10 (15 May 1970)

vol. 2, no. 1 (15 June 1970)

vol. 2, no. 2 (15 July 1970)

vol. 2, no. 3 (August 1970)

vol. 2, no. 4 (September 1970)

NOTES

1. Published by Unsatisfied Black Soldiers (USB).

2. Published by GIs and Vietnam Veterans against the War in Vietnam (GIVAWV).

3. Published by Resistors inside the Army in Paris—listed address c/o J. P. Satre.

4. *ACT* 1 was published between January and March 1968. This issue reprints an article from the 28 January 1968 issue of *The Bond,* and the 18 March 1968 issue of *The Bond* reprints an article from *Act* 1, no. 1.

5. Probably September or October 1968, given their referencing Johnson Administration peace talks.

6. 1970 is printed on page 1, but no month is given. Temple University Libraries date stamped their copy on 2 July 1970.

7. Published by GI's against the War.

8. Received at the Swarthmore College Peace Collection 29 January 1970.

9. Ibid.

10. Ibid.

11. Ibid.

12. Received at the Swarthmore College Peace Collection on 13 February 1970.

13. Has word "Feb" handwritten below the title.

14. Has a cartoon about Kent State on the cover.

15. Published by the Bureau of Revolutionary Personnel.

16. Published by ex-members of Movement for a Democratic Military (MDM) at Camp Pendelton.

17. Affiliated with the Union of American Exiles (U.K.).

18. Affiliated with the Union of American Exiles (Canada).

19. Misnumbered by publisher, most probably vol. 2, no. 2.

20. State Historical Society of Wisconsin lists "April 1969?" as the date of publication.

21. Has note saying General Westmoreland will be giving talk at K State University on 9 April about "creative uses of napalm on campus." (Author did not list anything but "K State University," but it most likely refers to Kansas State University, as *AWOL Press* was published by GIs at Fort Riley, Kansas.)

22. Published after 25 April 1969.

23. Published after 1 May 1969.

24. Printed in late June or July 1969; there is a report on the acquittal of the Fort Jackson 8 as having occurred two weeks previously.

25. Published after 28 May 1969 when "Airman 1/c Larry Fridburg and Sgt Rosarie Bisson were arrested for distributing leaflets." (*Awol News* no. 6: 2)

26. Published after 22 June 1969.

27. Published after 22 July 1969.

28. Published after 3 July 1969.

29. Published after 28 August 1969.

30. Published after 15 October 1969.

31. Produced by GIs who previously worked on *Attitude Check*. David Cortright (*Soldiers in Revolt* [New York: Anchor Press, 1975]) lists it as being published by black members of MDM; however, in the first issue it is noted that prior to publication MDM had split up because "we weren't getting the full support of the people. Third World people (black, brown, red, yellow) couldn't relate to it because they thought it was a white organization. White people couldn't relate to it because they thought it was a black struggle" ("Black Unity," in *Black Unity* 1 [1970]: 7).

32. Affiliated with American Servicemen's Union.

33. Published by GI's United against the War in Vietnam from 1969 to 1971.

34. Unseen by me.

35. Misnumbered by publisher.

36. As a response to the invasion of Cambodia, GI's United against the War in Vietnam renamed themselves GI's United against the War in Indo China.

37. Publishing address listed as Detroit.

38. Published sometime between 22 May and 22 July 1969.

39. Misdated by the publisher, most probable date is 23 October 1969, given the reporting of events on 15 October at the October Moratorium.

40. Announced that the paper was now affiliated with the American Servicemen's Union.

41. Published by "Soldiers for Democratic Action."

42. Published by members of "Quonset-Davisville GIs for Peace."

43. David Cortright lists it as being published from 1969 to 1970 (*Soldiers in Revolt*, 287).

44. Published by members of the Concerned Officers Movement. Dates of publication except no. 3 unknown. Title is not listed by David Cortright and not in the collection of the State Historical Society of Wisconsin.

45. The voice of the Camp Pendelton Brig Rat.

46. Published in 1970 by Colorado Springs MDM.

47. Published by the GI-Civilian Alliance for Peace.

48. Published by San Diego MDM.

49. State Historical Society of Wisconsin dates this issue as being published in August 1970.

50. Published by San Diego MDM.

51. Published by "GI's against Fascism."

52. Published by MDM.

53. Misnumbered; should be vol. 1, no. 8.

54. Published between 18 April 1970 and 10 May 1970.

55. Has announcement for a rally on 9 August 1969.

56. Published before 18 September 1969, it was received at Temple University on that date.

57. Received at Swarthmore College Peace Collection on 22 October 1969.

58. Originally the Asian edition *WE GOT THE brASS.*

59. Originally entitled *Harass the Brass,* changed to *A Four Year Bummer* after one issue.

60. With this issue, *A Four Year Bummer* affiliates itself with the ASU.

61. Also numbered vol. 2, no. 1.

62. Also numbered vol. 2, no. 2.

63. Also numbered vol. 2, no. 3.

64. Also numbered vol. 2, no. 4.

65. Also numbered vol. 2, no. 5.

66. Also numbered vol. 2, no. 6.

67. Also numbered vol. 2, no. 7.

68. Also numbered vol. 2, no. 8.

69. Published by Ex-Pfc. Gallatin Deitz.

70. Published by Fort Bliss GIs for Peace.

71. Afiliated with the ASU.

72. Published after 15 November 1969.

73. Published after 16 January 1970.

74. Published after 5 May 1970.

75. Published by United Servicemen of Fort Wainwright, Alaska.

76. Published by GIs affiliated with the ASU.

77. Merged with *Wish* and continued publication as *Head-On Wish.*

78. Continuation of *Head-On!.*

79. Published by Fort McClellan GIs-WACs United against the War in Vietnam.

80. Published as *Ft. Lewis Free Press,* changed to *Lewis-McChord Free Press* after one issue.

81. Published by The Serviceman's Link to Peace.

82. One of the issues is dated by State Historical Society of Wisconsin as being received on 28 December 1968.

83. Aligned with the GI Association.

84. Published c/o GI Association.

85. Published as a supplement to *Obligore* no. 6.

86. Has suggested activities for week of 30 June 1970 and a stamp from State Historical Society of Wisconsin dated 19 July 1970.

87. Has stamp dating its arrival at State Historical Society of Wisconsin as 14 October 1970.

88. David Cortright (*Soldiers in Revolt,* 300) lists its dates of publication as 1971–1972.

In the bibliography of the State Historical Society of Wisconsin, issue no. 1 publication date is listed as Jan 197?.

In a list of publications submitted to the Committee on Internal Security—House of Representatives—in September 1971, *My Knot* was listed as one of the GI publications currently published.

89. Published before 7 July 1970.

90. Published before 16 September 1970.

91. Published by the Great Lakes MDM.

92. Published by members of Baltimore GIs United.

93. Merges with *Open Ranks.*

94. Affiliated with Unsatisfied Black Soldiers (UBS).

95. Published by Roger Priest.

96. Issues 2–4 published by Dam Neck GIs affiliated with GI's Unite against the War in Indo China.

97. Published by members of Baltimore GIs United against the War in Vietnam.

98. Published by the Redstone Peace Force.

99. Affiliated with Long Beach MDM. In 1970 it briefly suspended publication and renamed itself *Now Hear This.*

100. Issues 1–5 titled *Out Now.*

101. Published as *Now Hear This.*

102. Published by GIs and Civilians in the Frederick, Maryland Area. David Cortright *(Soldiers in Revolt)* notes that they were members of Frederick GIs United.

103. Has two inserts: one is a pamphlet entitled "This Is the Army," the other is a high school underground entitled "Hard Ball."

104. Published by People Emerging against Corrupt Establishments.

105. Published by deserters and civilian supporters.

106. Has a stamp from Swarthmore dated 9 June 1970 on cover.

107. Published by GIs from Alameda NAS and the staff of the Pentagon GI Coffeehouse.

108. Published by GIs and civilians under the name Educational News Cooperative.

109. Published by members of ASU.

110. Affiliates with ASU.

111. Published by the Reserve Committee to Stop the War.

112. No address is given, and there is no reference to this paper in any of the literature.

113. Published by the Fort Ord Movement for a Democratic Military.

114. Origins of RITA lie in 1966, when opposition to the Vietnam War within the United States becomes public with the Fort Hood 3. None of these bulletins are dated.

115. Fact sheet on getting to Sweden, where deserters could find safe haven.

116. Pamphlet prepared by the GI Counseling Services.

117. Published by members of GI's United.

118. Published by naval officers of the Concerned Officers Movement.

119. Published in August or September 1969.

120. Fall 1969.

121. Bimonthly publication from Fort Leonard Wood; the successor to *HERESY II.*

122. Published by Alameda MDM.

123. Earliest from either February or March 1970, the next from April 1970, the next from May 1970, and the last from July 1970.

124. Published by United Servicemen's Actions for Freedom.

125. Published by soldiers of the Ninety-seventh Hospital in Frankfurt.

126. Founded by Jeff Sharlet in 1967, it closed with his death in 1969.

127. In late 1968, two editions of *Vietnam GI were* published: an Asian edition and a stateside edition with the subtitle *"Stateside Edition."*

128. The German and Asian editions of *WE GOT THE brASS* are essentially the same. The contents of both reflect an internationalist stance with heavy reliance on reproduction for contents. From the available evidence, it would seem that the German edition preceded the Japanese edition and the latter is a reproduction of the former with few changes.

129. Contains a call for a "puke-in" on 30 August 1969.

130. After 15 October 1969 and before 30 November 1969.

131. Published by RITA.

132. Published by GIs and civilian activists in the German SDS.

133. Published by "Airmen for a Democratic Airforce."

134. Published by members of Fort Hamilton GI's United.

135. Published by "Young Americans for a New Direction."

136. Founded in 1970 by sailors affiliated with the ASU. Published c/o the Pacific Counseling Service.

137. Published by the GI Co-ordinating Committee.

Bibliography

"20 GIs Celebrate 4th of July by Joining Union." *The Bond* 4 , no. 7 (22 July 1970): 4.

"1000 GIs March in Killeen." *Fatigue Press* 23 (August 1970): 1.

"'A' Company Returns to War." *GI Press Service* 1, no. 6 (4 September 1969): 91–93.

Advertisement for the *Voice of the 'Underground Press.'* Published in *Williamette Bridge* 1–20 (June 1968): n.p.

"AG Unclassified." *Aboveground* 1, no. 1 (August 1969): 2.

"Alaska GIs in Antiwar Action." *The Bond* 4, no. 5 (13 May 1970): 4.

Allen, Gary. "Underground for Adults Only." *American Opinion* (December 1967): 1–16.

"All Ready on the Left." *All Ready on the Left* 1, no. 1 (August 1970): 6.

Althusser, Louis. *Lenin and Philosophy.* Translated by Ben Brewster. New York: Monthly Review Press, 1971.

———. "Ideology and Ideological State Apparatuses (Notes towards an Investigation)." In *Lenin and Philosophy.* Translated by Ben Brewster. New York: Monthly Review Press, 1971, 121–73.

Anderson, Terry. "The GI Movement and the Response from the Brass." In *Give Peace a Chance: Exploring the Vietnam Antiwar Movement, Essays from the Charles DeBenedetti Conference.* Edited by Melvyn Small and William D. Hoover. Syracuse, N.Y.: Syracuse University Press, 1992, 93–115.

———. *The Movement and the Sixties: Protest in America from Greensboro to Wounded Knee.* New York: Oxford University Press, 1995.

———. "The New American Revolution: The Movement and Business." In *The Sixties: From Memory to History.* Edited by David Farber. Chapel Hill, N.C.: The University of North Carolina Press, 1994, 175–205.

Angleman, Jack. *The Underground Press.* Las Vegas: Ram Classics, M-T Publishers, 1969.

"Apple Pie, Motherhood and the American Flag." *The Blue Bus* 1, no. 3 (April 1968): 2.

Appy, Christian. *Working-Class War: American Combat Soldiers and Vietnam.* Chapel Hill, N.C.: The University of North Carolina Press, 1993.

Arato, Andrew, and Jean Cohen. "Social Movements, Civil Society, and the Problem of Sovereignty." *Praxis International* 4 (1984): 266–83.

Arendt, Hannah. *Eichmann in Jerusalem: A Report on the Banality of Evil.* Harmondsworth, U.K.: Penguin Books, 1979.

"Armed Forces Day." *The Bond* 4, no. 6 (17 June 1970): 3.

The Armed Forces and Resistance or Let's Cut the Crap. Madison, Wisc.: The Wisconsin Draft Resistance Union, 1967.

Armstrong, David. *Trumpet to Arms: Alternative Media in America.* Los Angeles: J. B. Tarcher, 1981.

"Army Attacks Union in Hearing." *The Bond* 4, no. 8 (26 August 1970): 2.

"Army Clear Present Danger." *The Ally* 23 (January/February 1970): 3.

"Army Backs Off: Drops Charges against Union Organizer Mitch Smith." *The Bond* 4, no. 4 (1970): 7.

"The Army Is Out to Get You." *The Last Harass* 1 (October 1968): 3–4.

"Army Screws GI Editor." *The Ally* 16 (May 1969): 3.

"As the Bond Expands." *The Bond* 1, no. 5 (ca. September 1967): 2.

"As You Were—A Mirror Of Non-Violent Revolution in America." *As You Were* 13 (April 1970): 1.

Aster, Henry. "And Other Works of Dogma." *Miami Free Press* 1 (18 April–1 May 1969): 2.

"ASU Aids Wounded GIs." *The Bond* 4, no. 6 (17 June 1970): 4.

"ASU History-Part One." *The Bond* 4, no. 8 (26 August 1970): 3.

"ASU Organizers Transferred." *The Bond* 4, no. 7 (22 July 1970): 1.

"ASU Power." *Rap!* 10 (November 1970): 3.

"ASU Power/We Demand." *The Bond* 4, no. 11 (18 November 1970): 4.

"ASU Spreads and Grows Stronger in Japan." *The Bond* 4, no. 11 (1970): 1.

"Attention Civilians." *The Bond* 1, no. 2 (7 July 1967): 3.

"AWOL Needs You." *The AWOL Press* 1, no. 11 (ca. 1969): 1.

"*AWOL* Needs Your Support." *The AWOL Press* 1, no. 6 (ca. 1969): 1.

Bailyn, Bernard. *Ideological Origins of the American Revolution.* Cambridge, Mass.: The Belknap Press, 1967.

Baker, Mark, ed. *NAM: The Vietnam War in the Words of the Men and Women Who Fought There.* New York: Berkley Books, 1983.

Baker, Ross K. "The Underground Press Has Fallen on Evil Days." In *The Media Reader.* Edited by Joan Valdes and Jeanne Crow. Dayton: Pflaum, 1975, 278–81.

Barthes, Roland. *Mythologies.* Translated by Annette Lavers. New York: Noonday Press, 1988.

———. "Myth Today." In *Mythologies.* Translated by Annette Lavers. New York: Noonday Press, 1988, 109–59.

Barton, Alan. Unpublished report on the attitudes of Columbia students and faculty. New York: Columbia University, 1968.

Baskir, Lawrence, and William Strauss. *Chance and Circumstance: The Draft, the War and the Vietnam Generation.* New York: Knopf, 1978.

"The Battle Hymn of the Republic." Final verse. [http://www.choraegus
.com/csm/csm0001.html].

Baudrillard, Jean. *Simulations.* Translated by Paul Foss, Paul Patton, and Philip
Beitchman. New York: Semiotext(e), 1983.

———. *Ecstasy of Communication.* Edited by Sylvere Lotringer. Translated by Caro-
line Schutze and Bernard Schutze. New York: Semiotext(e), 1988.

Baxandall, Lee. "Games in the Arena: New Players, New Integration." *Liberation*
(May 1971): 21–27.

"Behold the Passion of the Pen." *The Liar* 1 (6 November 1968): 2.

"Ben Het: An Experiment with American Lives." *The Ally* 18 (July/August 1969): 1.

Bergerud, Eric. *Red Thunder, Tropic Lightning: The World of a Combat Division in Vietnam.* Harmondsworth, U.K.: Penguin Books, 1994.

Berke, Joseph, ed. *Counter Culture: The Creation of an Alternative Society.* London:
Peter Owen Ltd., 1969.

Berks, John. "The Underground Press." *Rolling Stone* (10 April 1969): 11–32.

Berlet, Chip. "How the Muckrakers Saved America." In *Alternative Papers.* Edited
by Elliot Shore. Philadelphia: Temple University Press, 1982, 16–20.

———. "Muckraking Gadflies Buzz Reality." In *Voices from the Underground: Volume 1. Insider Histories of the Vietnam Era Underground Press.* Edited by Ken
Wachsberger. Tempe, Ariz.: Mica Press, 1993, 63–80.

Berry, Thomas Elliott. *Journalism in America.* New York: Hastings House, 1976.

"Bill Brakefield Gets 3 Years." *The Bond* 4, no. 1 (15 January 1970): 4.

Bimson, Howard. "Undergrounds—Here They Come or There They Go." *Media
Scope* (October 1969): 68–91.

"The Birth of the Black Brigade." *Bragg Briefs* 2, no. 5 (December 1969): 3, 7.

"Black and Puerto Rican GIs Resist Brass." *The Bond* 4, no. 8 (26 August 1970): 1.

"Black and Red Is an Experiment." *Black and Red* 1 (September 1968): inside front
cover.

"Black GI Power Grows in Germany." *The Bond* 4, no. 10 (21 October 1970): 1.

"Black GIs in Germany." *Fatigue Press* 25 (October 1970): 7.

"Black GIs in Germany in Mass Meeting." *The Bond* 4, no. 7 (22 July 1970): 1.

"Black GIs Organize." *The Ally* 28 (July 1970): 3.

"Black Unity." *Black Unity* 1 (August 1970): 7.

"Black Unity Band." *Black Unity* 1 (August 1970): 3.

Bloom, Marshall. "HUAC Confronts Underground Press." *Notes from The Underground* 1, no. 20 (1–15 December 1967): 4, 7, 11.

Blumer, Herbert. "Social Unrest and Collective Protest." *Studies in Symbolic Interaction* 1, no. 1 (1978): 1–54.

Borenstein, Rosa, and Alan Howard. *Liberation News Service: Bourgeois or Revolutionary Journalism.* New York: self-published, 1973.

Bowart, Walter. "EMERGING: A Fifth Estate." *The Paper* 2, no. 1 (29 September
1966): 10.

Brackman, Jacob. "The Underground Press." *Playboy* (August 1967): 83–96, 151–57.

"*Bragg Briefs* Distribution under Consideration." *Bragg Briefs* 2, no. 1 (August
1969): 1.

Brann, James W. "The Changing Student Press: Underground Papers Vie with
Regular." *The Chronicle of Higher Education* (12 August 1968): 4–5.

"Brass Back off Harvey and Daniels." *The Bond* 4, no. 7 (22 July 1970): 3.

"Brass Fink Out. Ft. Bragg Brass Break Word." *Counterpoint* 2, no. 12 (2 June 1969): 3.

"Brass Harass, Harass the Brass." *Attitude Check*, special issue (May 1970): n.p.

"Brass Jail Organizer—Fear Truth." *The Bond* 4, no. 3 (18 March 1970): 2.

"Brass Loses Round 1." *Aerospaced* 3 (ca. 1969): 1, 8.

"Brothers and Sisters." *Stars-n-Bars* 1 (27 October 1970): 2.

Bryan, Gene. "Underground Press Panel Holds Stormy Session." *Quill* (December 1969): 30.

Buford, Bill. *Amongst the Thugs*. New York: Vintage Books, 1991.

"Bulkhead Editorial." *Up against the Bulkhead* 1, no. 3 (15 June 1970): 2.

Burns, Stoney. "Notes Is a Year Old." *Notes from the Underground* 2, no. 1 (March 1968): 1, 6, 12.

Burns, Stuart. *Social Movements of the 1960s: Searching for Democracy*. Boston: Twayne, 1990.

Burroughs, William. "Storm the Reality Studios." In *The Underground Reader*. Edited by Mel Howard and the Reverend Thomas King Forçade. New York: Plume Books, 1972, 32–35.

"Call for GI Awareness." *Broken Arrow* 2, no. 2 (15 October 1970): 6–7.

Callison, Bill. "Why the Bond." *The Bond* 1, no. 1 (23 June 1967): 1, 3.

Caputo, Philip. *A Rumor of War*. New York: Ballantine Books, 1978.

Chambers, Iain. *Border Dialogues: Journeys in Postmodernism*. London: Comedia Books, 1990.

"Check Us Out." *Attitude Check* 1, no. 1 (1 November 1969): 3.

"Check Us Out." *Attitude Check* 1, no. 2 (1 December 1969): 5.

"Check Us Out." *Attitude Check* 1, no. 3 (1 February 1970): 5.

Chomsky, Noam. "Propaganda Systems: Orwell's and Ours." [http://www.contrib.andrew.cmu.edu/usr/tp0x/chomsky.html]. 1998.

Clarke, John. "Skinheads and the Magical Recovery of Community." In *Resistance through Rituals*. Edited by Tony Jefferson and Stuart Hall. London: Hutchinson, 1976, 99–102.

———. "Style." In *Resistance through Rituals*. Edited by Tony Jefferson and Stuart Hall. London: Hutchinson, 1976, 175–91.

Clarke, John, Stuart Hall, Tony Jefferson, and Brian Roberts. "Subcultures, Cultures and Class." In *Resistance through Rituals: Youth Subcultures in Post-War Britain*. Edited by Tony Jefferson and Stuart Hall. London: Hutchinson, 1976, 9–74.

Cohen, Jean. "Strategy or Identity: New Theoretical Paradigms and Contemporary Social Movements." *Social Research* 52, no. 4 (1985): 663–716.

Cohen, Jean, and Andrew Arato. *Civil Society and Political Theory*. Cambridge, Mass.: MIT Press, 1993.

Cohen, Phil. "Subcultural Conflict and the Working Class Community." *Working Papers in Cultural Studies* 2 (spring 1972): 5–52.

Cohen, Stan. *Folk Devils and Moral Panics: The Creation of the Mods and Rockers*. New York: St. Martins Press, 1980.

Cohen, Stan, ed. *Images of Deviance*. Harmondsworth, U.K.: Penguin Books, 1971.

Cohn-Bendit, Daniel, and Gabriel Cohn-Bendit. *Obsolete Communism: The Left-Wing Alternative*. New York: McGraw Hill, 1968.

Conlin, Joseph R. *The American Radical Press 1880–1960*. Westport, Conn.: Greenwood Press, 1974.

Corrigan, Paul. "Doing Nothing." In *Resistance through Rituals.* Edited by Tony Jefferson and Stuart Hall. London: Hutchinson, 1976, 103–5.

Cortright, David. "Black GI Resistance during the Vietnam War." *Vietnam Generation* 2, no. 1 (1990): 51–64.

———. "GI Resistance." In *Give Peace a Chance: Exploring the Vietnam Antiwar Movement.* Edited by Melvyn Small and William D. Hoover. Syracuse, N.Y.: Syracuse University Press, 1992, 116–28.

———. *Soldiers in Revolt: The American Military Today.* New York: Anchor Press, 1975.

———. Untitled report prepared for the National Convention of the U.S. Antiwar Movement, held in Chicago in December 1970. Found among the David Cortright Papers housed at the Swarthmore College Peace Collection.

"A Counterpoint Challenge." *Counterpoint* 2, no. 14 (7 August 1969): 8.

"Courageous GIs Defy Brass on April 15 Strike Day." *The Bond* 4, no. 4 (1970): 1.

Crandall, William F. "They Moved the Town: Organizing Vietnam Veterans against the War." In *Give Peace a Chance: Exploring the Vietnam Antiwar Movement.* Edited by Melvyn Small and William D. Hoover. Syracuse, N.Y.: Syracuse University Press, 1992, 141–54.

"Credo." *Ann Arbor Argus* 1 (January 1969): 1.

Crocker, Steve. "What Is The Underground." *The Paper* 3, no. 1 (16–30 September 1967): 2.

Crowell, Joan. *Fort Dix Stockade: Our Prison Camp Next Door.* New York: Links Books, 1974.

Dana, Joe. "Statement of Purpose." *The Oracle of Southern California* 1, no. 1 (March 1967): 2.

Dane, Barbara. *Guardian.* Barbara Dane: San Francisco, 1968.

"Dare to Struggle." *Dare to Struggle* 1, no. 1 (ca. August 1970): 1.

"Dear Congressman." *All Ready on the Left* 2 (September 1970): 8.

"Death to Lifers." *Anchorage Troop* 1, no. 1 (January 1970): 3.

Debord, Guy. *The Society of the Spectacle.* Detroit: Black and Red Books, 1983.

———. *Comments on the Society of the Spectacle.* London: Verso, 1990.

———. *Society of the Spectacle and Other Films.* London: Rebel Press, 1992.

"A Declaration." *Head-On!* 1 (25 December 1968): 6.

Dellinger, David. *Revolutionary Nonviolence: Essays by David Dellinger.* Garden City, N.Y.: Doubleday Anchor Books, 1971.

DeMaio, Joe. "Our Thing." *Distant Drummer* 4 (1968): 1.

Dennis, Everette E., ed. *Magic Writing Machine.* Eugene, Oreg.: School Of Journalism, 1971.

———. "The Underground Press." In *Magic Writing Machine.* Edited by Everette E. Dennis. Eugene, Oreg.: School Of Journalism, 1971, 7–8.

Dennis, Everette E., and William L. Rivers. *Other Voices: The New Journalism, in America.* San Francisco: Canfield Press, 1974.

Department of Defense. "Article 88." *Uniform Code of Military Justice.* 1950. [http://www4.law.cornell.edu/ uscode/10/888.html].

Department of Defense. "Article 91." *Uniform Code of Military Justice.* 1950. [http://www4.law.cornell.edu/ uscode/10/891.html].

Department of Defense. "Article 134." *Uniform Code of Military Justice.* 1950. [http://www4.law.cornell.edu/ uscode/10/934.html].

Department of Defense. *Uniform Code of Military Justice.* 1988. [gopher://
    wiretap.Spies.COM:70/11/Gov/UCMJ].

"Desertion and Other Trips." *The Ally* 5 (June 1968): 4.

Diamond, Stephen. *What the Trees Said; Life on a New Age Farm.* New York: Dela-
    corte Press, 1971.

Didion, Joan. "Alicia and the Underground Press." *The Saturday Evening Post* (13
    January 1968): 14.

Diller, Elizabeth, and Ricardo Scofidio, eds. *Visite aux armées: Tourismes de guerre/*
    Back to the Front: Tourisms of War. New York: F.R.A.C. Basse-Normandie and
    Princeton Architectural Press, 1994.

———. "Introduction." In *Visite aux armées: Tourismes de guerre/Back to the Front:*
    Tourisms of War.. Edited by Elizabeth Diller and Ricardo Scofidio. New York:
    F.R.A.C. Basse-Normandie and Princeton Architectural Press, 1994, 18–34.

"Disclaimer." *A'bout Face* 1, no. 1 (4 July 1970): 1.

"Disclaimer." *Aerospaced* 2, no. 1 (ca. 1970): 1.

"Disclaimer." *All Hands Abandon Ship* 2 (October 1970): 3.

"Disclaimer." *Attitude Check* 1, no. 1 (November 1969): 1.

"Disclaimer." *Broken Arrow* 1, no. 10 (30 May 1970): 5.

"Disclaimer." *Counter-Attack* 1, no. 1 (ca. 1970): 8.

"Disclaimer." *Duck Power* 1, no. 3 (24 September 1969): 1.

"Disclaimer." *Dull Brass* 1, no. 2 (15 May 1969): 2–3.

"Disclaimer." *Fatigue Press* 1, no. 16 (1969): 1.

"Disclaimer." *Fun Travel Adventure* 1, no. 6 (December 1968): 1.

"Disclaimer." *Up Front* 1, no. 2 (June 1969): 1.

"'Dissident' Views." *The Graffitti* 4 (ca. 1970): 5–6.

"Distribution Denied." *Aerospaced* 2, no. 1 (ca. 1970): 1, 6.

"Distribution Denied (But Read All about It)." *GI Press Service* 2, no. 3 (26 February
    1970): 38.

"Distribution Suits Filed." *Bragg Briefs* 3, no. 1 (April 1970): 3.

"DOD Document Attempts To Handle 'Dissent.'" *GI Press Service* 1, no. 8 (2 Octo-
    ber 1969): 116.

Do GIs Have Rights? The Case of Lt. Howe. Denver, Colo.: Freedom for Lieutenant
    Howe Committee, 1966.

Dohrn, Bernadine, Billy Ayers, Jeff Jones, and Celia Soujourn. *Prairie Fire: The Politics*
    of Revolutionary Anti-Imperialism. San Francisco: Communications Co., 1974.

Domhoff, G. W. *Who Rules America Now.* Englewood Cliffs, N.J.: Prentice Hall,
    1983.

Dower, John. *War without Mercy: Race & Power in the Pacific War.* New York: Pan-
    theon Books, 1986.

Downing, John. *Radical Media: The Political Experience of Alternative Media.* Boston:
    South End Press, 1984.

Dreyer, Thorne. "The Rag." *Other Scenes* 4 (April 1967): 3.

Dreyer, Thorne, and Victoria Smith. "The Movement and the New Media." *Libera-*
    tion News Service News Packet 144 (1 March 1969): 13–30.

Dreyer, Thorne, Victoria Smith, Dennis Fitzgerald, and Judy Fitzgerald. "Edito-
    rial." *Space City!* 1, no. 4 (July 1969): n.p.

Eder, Klaus. "A New Social Movement." *Telos* 50 (1981): 5–20.

"Editorial." *A'bout Face* 1, no. 6 (12 September 1970): 1.

"Editorial." *The Ally* 1 (February 1968): 3.

"Editorial." From *The Ash,* reprinted in *WE GOT THE brASS* (German ed.) 2 (ca. 1969): 8.

"Editorial." *Attitude Check* 2, no. 3 (1 April 1970): 5.

"Editorial." *Black and Red* 1 (September 1968): inside front cover.

"Editorial." *Capitalism Stinks* 1, no. 1 (25 June 1968): 1.

"Editorial." *Connections* 2, no. 5 (December 1967): 2.

"Editorial." *Counter-Attack* 3 (ca. 1970): 11.

"Editorial." *Counterpoint* 2, no. 9 (ca. April 1969): 2.

"Editorial." *The Eggman* 1 (April 1968): 6.

"Editorial." *Fight Back* (undated and unnumbered issue): 1.

"Editorial." *Flag in Action* 1, no. 3 (ca. 1969): 2.

"Editorial." *The Free Venice Beachhead* 1 (12 December 1968): n.p.

"Editorial." *Fun Travel Adventure* 8 (May 1969): 9.

"Editorial." *Graffitti* 1 (June 1969): 2.

"Editorial." *Humanitas* 10, no. 2 (September 1968): 1.

"Editorial." *Kaleidoscope* 1, no. 1 (6 October 1967): 1.

"Editorial." *The Liar* 1 (6 November 1968): 2.

"Editorial." *The Logistic* 1 (ca. 1968): 1–2.

"Editorial." *Morning Report* 1 (May 1970): 1–3.

"Editorial." *The Retaliation* 1 (1969): 2.

"Editorial." *San Diego Free Press* 1, no. 1 (14 November 1968): 1.

"Editorial." *Scimitar* 1, no. 6 (ca. 1968): 1.

"Editorial." *Top Secret* 1, no. 2 (21 March 1969): 2.

"Editorial." *Up against the Bulkhead* 1, no. 3 (15 June 1970): 2.

"Editorial." *Up Front* 1 (May 1969): 1, 4.

"Editorial." *USAF* 1, no. 1 (1 April 1969): 3.

"Editorial." *WE GOT THE brASS* (German ed.) 2 (ca. 1969): 8.

"Editorial." *WE GOT THE brASS* (German ed.) 3 (ca. 1969): 2–3.

"Editorial." *The Whig* 1 (4 July 1970): 1.

"Editorial." *The Williamette Bridge* 1 (7–20 June 1968): 2.

"Editorial Policy." *The Illustrated Paper* 1 (June 1966): 2.

"Editors' Note." *Counterpoint* 2, no. 5 (24 March 1969): 2.

Edwards, Verne, ed. "Promising Signs of Success." *Journalism in a Free Society.* Dubuque, Iowa: Wm. C. Brown & Co, 1970.

Ehrhart, W.D. *Busted: A Vietnam Veteran in Nixon's America.* Amherst, Mass: University of Massachusetts Press, 1995.

———. *Passing Time: Memoir of a Vietnam Veteran against the War.* Amherst, Mass: University of Massachussetts Press, 1995.

———. *Vietnam-Perkasie: A Combat Marine Memoir.* Amherst, Mass: University of Massachussetts Press, 1995.

———. "Who's Responsible." Originally published in *Vietnam Generation Journal & Newsletter* 4 (1–2). Edited by Kali Tal. Sixties Project web site. [http://lists.village.virginia.edu/sixties/HTML_docs/Scholar.html]. 1992.

———. "Why My Daughter Won't Grow Up in Perkasie." Originally published in *Viet Nam Generation Journal & Newsletter* 4 (1–2). Edited by Kali Tal. Sixties Project web site. [http://lists.village.virginia.edu/sixties/HTML_docs/Scholar.html]. 1992.

Eichel, Lawrence, Kenneth W. Jost, Robert D. Luskin, and Richard Neustadt. *The Harvard Strike.* Boston: Houghton Mifflin, 1970.

Elliott, Thomas Berry. *Journalism in America.* New York: Hastings House, 1976.

Ellis, Donna Lloyd. "The Underground Press in America, 1955–1970." *Journal of Popular Culture* 5, no. 1 (1971): 102–24.

Emerson, Gloria. *Winners and Losers.* New York: Random House, 1976.

Emery, Edwin. *The Press and America.* 3rd ed. Englewood Cliffs. N.J.: Prentice Hall, 1972.

Emery, Michael, and Edwin Emery. *The Press and America.* 5th ed. Englewood Cliffs, N.J.: Prentice Hall, 1984.

———. *The Press and America.* 7th ed. Englewood Cliffs: Prentice Hall, 1993.

———. *The Press and America.* 8th ed. Boston: Allyn and Bacon, 1996.

Emery, Michael, and Ted Curtis Smythe. *Readings in Mass Communications.* Dubuque, Iowa: William C. Brown and Company, 1974.

Ericson, Richard, Patricia Baranek, and Janet Chan. *Visualizing Deviance.* Toronto: University of Toronto Press, 1987.

Estrin, Marc, ed. *Recreation.* New York: Dell, 1971.

"Exiles in Canada." *The Ally* 23 (January/February 1970): 11.

An Exciting Career Awaits You in the GI Movement. Oakland, Calif.: SOS, 1970.

"An Explanation." *The Underground Oak* 1 (22 December 1968): 1.

Fact Sheet on GI Dissent. Washington, D.C.: The Servicemen's Link to Peace, 1969.

Farber, David, ed. *The Sixties: From Memory to History.* Chapel Hill, N.C.: The University of North Carolina Press, 1994.

———. "Introduction." In *The Sixties: From Memory to History.* Chapel Hill, NC: The University of North Carolina Press, 1994, 1–10.

"Farmworkers' Children Go Hungry as Generals Gorge on Grapes!" *Rap!* 2 (ca. 1969): 4.

Farrell, Barry. "For the Only Freak in Ohio." *Life* (20 November 1969): 32.

"FBI/MI Pressure." *Aboveground* 1, no. 5 (December 1969): 1.

Feldman, Sam. "To Publish Underground Newspapers." *Journalism Education Today* (fall 1968): 7–18.

———. "Going Underground." *Journalism Education Today* (fall 1970): 10–12.

Fenger, Merilee. "Fuel for Revolt, The Underground Press." *Montana Journalism Review* 12 (1969): 13.

"Fight On." *The Bond* 4, no. 1 (15 January 1970): 7.

Filler, Louis. "Truth and Consequences: Some Notes on Changing Times and the Muckrakers." *Antioch Review* (spring 1968): 27.

Fiske, John. *Understanding Popular Culture.* Boston: Unwin Hyman, 1989.

Forçade, Rev. Thomas King, ed. *Underground Press Anthology.* New York: Ace Books, 1972.

———. "Introduction." In *The Underground Reader.* Edited by Mel Howard and Rev. Thomas King Forçade. New York: Plume Books, 1972, 1–4.

———. "Obscenity, Who Really Cares?" In *The Underground Reader.* Edited by Mel Howard and Rev. Thomas King Forçade. New York: Plume Books, 1972, 159–72.

"Fort Jackson: Soldiers Try to Hold Anti-War Meeting." *The Bond* 2, no. 2 (18 February 1968): 1.

"Fort Riley Fight Builds against Racism." *The Bond* 4, no. 10 (21 October 1970): 4.

Foster, Walter. "The Workshop." *Free Press of Springfield* (December 1968): 2.

"Free Our Jailed GI Brothers." *The Bond* 4, no. 3 (18 March 1970): 1.

"Freedom of Speech?" *Anchorage Troop* 1, no. 4 (March 1970): 2.

"Freedom of the GI Press." *The Ally* 19 (September 1969): 3.

"Freedom of the Press?" *Bragg Briefs* 2, no. 2 (September 1969): 2.

"Freedom vs. Bullshit." *Aerospaced* 1 (ca. 1969): 3.

Frith, Simon, and Andrew Goodwin, eds. *On Record.* New York: Pantheon Books, 1990.

"From a Black Brother." *Pay Back* 1, no. 1 (July 1970): 5.

"From Apathy to Action." *Rough Draft* 1 (February 1969): 3.

"From the GI Underground." *WE GOT THE brASS* (German ed.) 1, no. 2 (ca. August 1969): 7.

"From the Organizing Fronts." *The Bond* 4, no. 7 (22 July 1970): 6.

"From the Organizing Fronts." *The Bond* 4, no. 8 (26 August 1970): 6.

Frontispiece. *GI Press Service* 1, no. 1 (26 June 1969): 1.

Fruchter, Norman. "Games in the Arena: Movement Propaganda and the Culture of Spectacle." *Liberation* (May 1971): 4–17.

"An FTA Birthday." *Fun Travel Adventure* 9 (June 1969): 1–2.

"Ft. Eustis Approves GI Paper." *Bragg Briefs* 2, no. 2 (September 1969): 1.

"Ft. Hood GIs Said No! And ASU Gave Full Support." *The Bond* 4, no. 9 (ca. September 1970): 3.

"Ft. Jackson GIs Win Victory!!!" *Dull Brass* 1, no. 2 (15 May 1969): 3.

Fulbright, Newton H. "Underground Press Strives to Fuse Sex with Politics." *Editor and Publisher* 102 (1969): 34.

Gardner, Fred. "Case Study in Opportunism: The GI Movement." *Second Page Supplement* (October 1971): 4–6.

———. "Hollywood Confidential." Originally published in *Vietnam Generation Journal and Newsletter* 3 (3). Sixties Project web site. [http://lists.village.virginia.edu/sixties/HTML_docs/Scholar.html]. 1991.

Garrett, Banning, and Katherine Barkley, eds. *Two, Three . . . Many Vietnams.* San Francisco: Canfield Press, 1971.

"George Washington." *Fatigue Press* 21 (June 1970): 12.

"Getting It Together." *The Ally* 27 (June 1970): 3.

"GI Broadcaster Tells the Truth." *Aerospaced* 2, no. 1 (ca. 1970): 1, 6.

Gibson, James William. *Warrior Dreams.* New York: Hill and Wang, 1994.

"GI Goes It Alone." *The Ally* 6 (July 1968): 1.

GI Legal Self Defense. Clarksville, Tenn.: The People's House, 1972.

"The GI Movement up to Today." *Peace* 1, no. 3 (1 October 1970): 4.

The GI Press. New York: Liberation News Service, 1969.

"GI Rights." *The Ally* 18 (July/August 1969): 3.

"GI Rights." *Green Machine* 1 (ca. 1969): 1.

"GIs and Supporters Turn Armed Forces Day Around." *The Bond* 4, no. 6 (17 June 1970): 1.

"G.I.'s [sic] and the Right of Free Speech." *Top Secret* 1 (14 February 1969): 3–5.

GIs Appeal to All Union Workers. New York: American Servicemen's Union, 1970.

"GIs Can Stop the War." *Fatigue Press* 26 (November 1970): 6.

"GIs Continue to Oppose Vietnam War." *The Ally* 1, no. 6 (July 1968): 1.

"GIs Defy Brass on April 15." *The Bond* 4, no. 4 (1970): 1.

"GIs Fight Back." *A Four Year Bummer* 2, no. 7 (September 1970): 2.

"GI's Jailed for Distribution." *Bragg Briefs* 2, no. 2 (September 1969): 1.

"GIs Organize in Japan." *The Bond* 4, no. 4 (22 April 1970): 6.

"GI's Organizer Ripped Off." *Fatigue Press* 23 (August 1970): 6.

"GIs to Voice Opinion." *About Face* 1, no. 1 (March 1969): 1.

"GIs Who Expose War Crimes Jailed." *The Bond* 4, no. 3 (18 March 1970): 7.

Gitlin, Todd. "Games in the Arena: Behind the Lights." *Liberation* (May 1971): 18–21.

———. "Sixteen Notes on Television and the Movement." *TriQuarterly* 23/24 (winter/spring 1972): 335–66.

———. "The Underground Press and Its Cave-in." In *Unamerican Activities*. Edited by Anne Janowitz and Nancy J. Peters. San Francisco: City Lights, 1981, 19–30.

———. *The Whole World Is Watching*. Berkeley: University of California Press, 1980.

"GI Underground." *The AWOL Press* 3 (ca. 1969): 2.

"G.I.V.A.W.V." *Broken Arrow* 1, no. 7 (23 September 1969): 5, 8.

Glessing, Robert. *The Underground Press in America*. Bloomington: Indiana University Press, 1970.

"God Zen and Socrates." *Grafitti* 1 (December 1966): 1.

Goodman, Mitchell, ed. *The Movement toward a New America, the Beginnings of a Long Revolution, (a Collage,) a What?* Philadelphia: Knopf and Pilgrim Press, 1970.

"Gordon Brass Attack *Last Harass*." *GI Press Service* 1, no. 4 (7 August 1969): 61.

Gramsci, Antonio. *Prison Notebooks*. New York: International Publishers, 1971.

"Growth of GI Power." *The Ally* 17 (June 1969): 3.

"Guidance on Dissent." *Dull Brass* 1, no. 4 (ca. 1969): 4–5.

Habermas, Jürgen. "New Social Movements." *Telos* 49 (1981): 33–37.

———. *Theory of Communicative Action*. Vol. 1. Boston: Beacon Press, 1984.

Haines, Harry W. "Hegemony and the GI Resistance: Introductory Notes." *Vietnam Generation* 2, no. 1 (1990): 3–7.

———. "Soldiers against the War in Vietnam: The Story of *Aboveground*." In *Voices from the Underground: Volume 1. Insider Histories of the Vietnam Era Underground Press*. Edited by Ken Wachsberger. Tempe, Ariz.: Mica Press, 1993, 181–98.

Hall, Stuart. "Cultural Studies and the Centre: Some Problematics and Problems." In *Culture, Media, Language: Working Papers in Cultural Studies, 1972–1979*. Edited by Stuart Hall, Dorothy Hobson, Andrew Lowe, and Paul Willis. London: Hutchinson , 1980, 15–47.

———. "On Postmodernism and Articulation: An Interview with Stuart Hall." *Journal of Communication Inquiry* 10, no. 2 (1986): 45–60.

Hall, Stuart, Chas Critcher, Tony Jefferson, John Clarke, and Brian Roberts. *Policing the Crisis: Mugging, the State, and Law and Order*. London: Macmillan, 1978.

Hall, Stuart, Dorothy Hobson, Andrew Lowe, and Paul Willis, eds. *Culture, Media, Language*. London: Hutchinson, 1980.

Hallin, Daniel. *The "Uncensored War": The Media and Vietnam*. Berkeley: University of California Press, 1989.

Halstead, Fred. *GIs Speak Out against the War: The Case of the Fort Jackson 8.* New York: Pathfinder Press, 1970.

"Hamburger Hill, Was It Worth It?" *The Ally* 17 (June 1969): 1.

"The Hard Contract." *Next Step* 1, no. 3 (3 August 1970): 4.

Hardt, Hanno. *Critical Communication Studies: Communication, History & Theory in America.* London: Routledge, 1992.

Hayes, James. "The Dialectics of Resistance: An Analysis of the GI Movement." *Journal of Social Issues* 31, no. 4 (1975): 125–39.

———. "The War within a War: Dissent in the Vietnam-Era Military." *Vietnam Generation* 2, no. 1 (1990): 8–19.

"Heads and Arms." *Rap!* 1, no. 8 (July 1970): 2.

Heath, G. Louis. *Mutiny Does Not Happen Lightly.* Metuchen, N.J. . . : Scarecrow Press, 1976.

Hebdige, Dick. "Aspects of Style in the Deviant Sub-Cultures of the 1960s." Master's thesis, Birmingham University, 1974.

———. "The Meaning of Mod." In *Resistance through Rituals.* Edited by Tony Jefferson and Stuart Hall. London: Hutchinson, 1976, 87–98.

———. *Subculture: The Meaning of Style.* London: Methuen Inc., 1979.

———. *Hiding in the Light: On Images and Things.* London: Routledge, 1988.

———. "The Bottom Line on Planet One: Squaring Up to *The Face.*" In *Hiding in the Light.* Edited by Dick Hebdige. London: Comedia, 1988, 155–76.

———. "Postmodernism and the Other Side." In *Stuart Hall: Critical Dialogues in Cultural Studies.* Edited by David Morley and Kuan-Hsing Chen. London: Routledge, 1996, 174–200.

Heinl, Robert. "The Collapse of the Armed Forces." *Armed Forces Journal* (7 June 1971)" 30–38.

"Help." *The Ally* 10 (October 1968): 3.

"Help." *Gigline* 1, no. 2 (August 1969): 10.

"Help!" *Rap!* 1, no. 9 (August 1970): 11.

"Help Aerospaced—The Best Peace at GAFB." *Aerospaced* 1 (ca. 1969): 3.

Help Us to Organize for Justice! New York: American Servicemen's Union, ca. 1969.

Herr, Michael. *Dispatches.* New York: Avon Books, 1978.

Herring, George. *America's Longest War.* New York: Alfred A. Knopf, 1986.

Herron, Jerry. *AfterCulture: Detroit and the Humiliation of History.* Detroit: Wayne State, 1993.

Hickey, Neil. "Publisher as Revolutionary. Neil Hickey and John Wilcock Rap about the Alternative Press." *Bitman* 3 (1971): n.p.

Hicks, Ronald G. *A Survey of Mass Communication.* Gretna, La.: Pelican Publishing Co, 1977.

———. "Underground Papers." In *A Survey of Mass Communication.* Edited by Ronald G. Hicks. Gretna, La.: Pelican Publishing Co, 1977, 70–71.

Hoffman, Abbie. *Revolution for the Hell of It.* New York: Dial, 1968.

Hon. Richard Ichord (D. Missouri). "Contributing Factors to the Morale Crisis in the Armed Services." House Committee on Internal Security, *Investigation of Attempts to Subvert the United States Armed Services.* 92nd Cong., 1st sess., 1971. Committee Print 6381–6385.

Hopkins, Jerry, ed. *Hippie Papers: Trip-Taking, Mind-Quaking, Scene-Making Word from Where Its At.* New York: Signet Books, 1968.

Horkheimer, Max, and Theodor Adorno. *Dialectic of Enlightenment.* Translated by John Cumming. New York: Continuum, 1989.

———. "The Culture Industry: Enlightenment as Mass Deception." In *Dialectic of Enlightenment.* Translated by John Cumming. New York: Continuum, 1989, 120–67.

House Committee on Internal Security. *Subversive Involvement in the Origin, Leadership, and Activities of the New Mobilizing Committee to End the War in Vietnam and Its Precessor Organizations.* 91st Cong., 2nd sess., 1970. Committee Print.

———. *Investigation of Attempts to Subvert the United States Armed Services.* 92nd Cong., 1st sess., 1971. Committee Print.

———. *Investigation of Attempts to Subvert the United States Armed Services.* 92nd Cong., 2nd Sess., 1972. Committee Print 7310.

Howard, Mel, and Thomas Forcade, eds. *The Underground Reader.* New York: New American Library, 1972.

Hulteng, John L., and Roy Paul Nelson. *The Fourth Estate.* New York: Harper and Row, 1971.

———. "The Underground Press." In *The Fourth Estate.* Edited by John L. Hulteng and Roy Paul Nelson. New York: Harper and Row, 1971, 201–6.

"Hundreds of GI's Sign Antiwar Ad." *GI Press Service* 1, no. 11 (13 November 1969): 164.

Hynds, Ernest C., ed. *American Newspapers in the 1970s.* Toronto: Saunders of Ontario, 1975.

———. "Alternative Newspapers." In *American Newspapers in the 1970s.* Toronto: Saunders of Ontario, 1975, 119–23.

"In Country: Vietnam." Vietnam Veteran's Terminology and Slang web page. [http://www.vietvet.org/glossary.htm].

"In General." *Out Now* 1 (May 1970): 2.

"An Injury to One is an Injury to All." *Fatigue Press* 16 (November 1969): 2.

"In Whose Interest." *Fatigue Press* 24 (September 1970): 3.

Ingelhart, Louis Edward. *Press Freedoms.* New York: Greenwood Press, 1987.

"It's Legal!" *Atitude Check* 2, no. 1 (1 March 1970): 1.

"Iwakuni-ASU Grows in Spite of Repression." *The Bond* 4, no. 7 (22 July 1970): 1.

"Iwakuni: Japan GIs in Rally." *The Bond* 4, no. 5 (13 May 1970): 5.

"Iwakuni Resistance." *The Ally* 28 (July 1970): 2.

"Jackson's Doin It." *Fun Travel Adventure* 8 (May 1969): 11–12.

Jacobs, Harold, ed. *Weatherman.* San Francisco: Ramparts Press, 1970.

Jacobs, Paul, and Saul Landau, eds. *The New Radicals: A Report with Documents.* New York: Vintage Books, 1966.

Janowitz, Anne, and Nancy Peters, eds. *Unamerican Activities.* San Francisco: City Lights Books, 1981.

Jefferson, Tony, and Stuart Hall, eds. *Resistance through Rituals.* London: Hutchinson, 1976.

Johnson, Dale. "On the Ideology of the Campus Revolution." In *The New Radicals: A Report with Documents.* Edited by Paul Jacobs and Saul Landau. New York: Vintage Books, 1966, 96–101.

Johnson, Susan. "Bundles, Packets and How the News Gets Around Underground." In *Magic Writing Machine.* Edited by Everette E. Dennis. Eugene, Oreg.: School of Journalism, 1971, 49–53.

"Join us Now!" *Broken Arrow* 1, no. 9 (10 February 1970): 1.

Jones, Steve. "One." *The Electric Newspaper* 1 (1967): 2.

Jurenas, Ed. "Statement of Policy, Purpose and Scope." *Anchorage Troop* 1, no. 1 (January 1970): 1.

"Just the Facts Man." *B Troop News* 3 (May 1970): 3.

Karnow, Stanley. *Vietnam, a History*. New York: Penguin Books USA, 1991.

Katz, Elihu, and Paul Lazarsfeld. *Personal Influence*. Glencoe, Ill.: Free Press, 1955.

Katzman, Allan. "Underground Press Syndicate." *East Village Other* (15 June 1966): 2.

"Keep The Pressure On!" *The Bond* 1, no. 10 (16 October 1967): 3.

Kenny, Timothy. "In the Land of the Blind the One-Eyed is King." In *Magic Writing Machine*. Edited by Everette E. Dennis. Eugene, Oreg.: School Of Journalism, 1971, 54–59.

Kern, Greg. "The Underground Press." *Haight Ashbury Maverick* 2, no. 7 (1968): 8–9.

———. "What Does it Mean?" in *Countdown* 1 (1 February 1970): 183.

Kerry, John. "How Do You Ask a Man to Be the Last Man to Die for a Mistake." *The New Soldier*. Edited by John Kerry with the Vietnam Veterans against the War. New York: The Macmillan Company, 1971.

Kessler, Lauren. *The Dissident Press: Alternative Journalism in American History*. Beverly Hills: Sage Publications, 1984.

Kimball, Jeffrey. "The Stab-in-the-Back Legend and the Vietnam War." *Armed Forces and Society* 14, no. 3 (1988): 433–58.

Kindman, Michael. "The Newspaper as Art Form." *The Paper* 2, no. 3 (13 October 1966): 2.

———. "The Underground Press Lives." *The Paper* 2, no. 10 (8 December 1966): 1.

Klare, Michael. "IDA, Cold War Think-Tank." *The Rat* (8 May 1968): 8.

Knabb, Ken, ed. "All the Kings Men." *The Situationist Anthology*. Berkeley: Bureau of Public Secrets, 1981.

Knabb, Ken, ed. *The Situationist Anthology*. Berkeley: Bureau of Public Secrets, 1981.

"Know Your Rights." *Aboveground* 1, no. 5 (December 1969): 4.

Kolko, Gabriel. *Anatomy of a War*. New York: The New Press, 1994.

Kopkind, Andrew. "America's Fifth Estate." *The New Statesman* (1 September 1967): 249.

Kornbluth, Jesse. "This Place of Entertainment Has No Fire Exits: The Underground Press and How It Went." *The Antioch Review* 29, no. 1 (1969): 95–96.

Korpsak, Joe, ed. *Underground Press Guide*. Los Angeles: Other Press Publishing Company, 1967.

———. "What the Underground Press Represents." In *Underground Press Guide*. Edited by Joe Korpsak. Los Angeles: Other Press Publishing Company, 1967, 2.

Lane, Mark. *Conversations with Americans*. New York: Simon and Schuster, 1970.

Langguth, Jack. "Force 'Strictly Defensive' Arrival Is Protested by Hanoi and Peking; U.S. Marine Units Arrive in DaNang." *The New York Times* (3 March 1965): 1, 3.

Law, Larry. *Fin de Spectacle*. London: Aldgate Press, 1980.

"Law N Order." *Fatigue Press* 24 (September 1970): 3.

Lawson, Paul "The Non-Electric Circus." In *Counter Culture*. Edited by Joseph Berke. London: Paul Owen Limited, 1969, 342–51.

Lazarsfeld, Paul, Bernard Berelson, and Hazel Gaudet. *The People's Choice*. New York: Duell, Sloan and Price, 1944.

Leamer, Lawrence. *The Paper Revolutionaries*. New York: Simon and Schuster, 1972.

Lefebvre, Henri. *The Critique of Everyday Life*. Vol. 1. London: Verso, 1991.

———. *Everyday Life in the Modern World*. New York: Harper Touchstone, 1971.

"The *Left Speak Out* Speaks Out Leftly." *Left Speak Out* 1 (ca. 1968): 3.

"Let's Talk about It." *Counterpoint* 1, no. 4 (14 December 1968): 2.

"Letter to Lt. General Lewis W. Walt." *Up Front* 2 (June 1969): 1, 3.

Levin, Jack, and James L. Spates. "Hippie Values: An Analysis of the Underground Press." *Youth and Society* 2, no. 1 (1970): 59–73.

Lewes, James. *GI Resistance: An Interactive Database*. Iowa City: Porky Prime Design, 1996.

———. *The Visualization of the Columbia Crisis*. Unpublished master's thesis, Annenberg School of Communication, University of Pennsylvania, 1990.

Lewis, Lloyd. *The Tainted War: Culture and Identity in Vietnam War Narratives*. Westport, Conn.: Greenwood Press, 1985.

Lewis, Raymond. "Editorial." *The Black Panther* 2, no. 6 (27 October 1968): n.p.

Lewis, Roger. *Outlaws of America; The Underground Press and Its Context*. Harmondsworth, U.K.: Penguin Books, 1972.

Liberation News Service Collective. "Dear Friends" (15 November 1967): 1.

———. "Dear Friends" (19 December 1967): 1.

———. "Liberation News Service (Speaks) Freaks Out . . . Again" (13 November 1967): 1

———. "Letter to Subscribers" (25 September 1967): 1.

"Lies and Half-Truths?" *Broken Arrow* 2, no. 3 (17 November 1970): 8.

"Life in Ben Het." *GI Press Service* 2 (10 July 1969): 21.

"Life in the Military." *Anchorage Troop* 1 (January 1970): 3.

"Lifers React." *Aerospaced* 1, no. 2 (ca. 1969): 5.

London, Jack. "To Be a Soldier." *OM* 4 (October 1969): 12.

"Los Patricios." *Gigline* 1, no. 2 (August 1969): 5.

Lowitz, Rick, and Mike Hood. "The Image." *The Los Angeles Image* 1, no. 1 (2–15 May 1969): 1.

Luke, Timothy W. *Screens of Power*. Urbana and Chicago: University of Illinois Press, 1989.

Lynd, Alice, ed. *We Won't Go: Personal Accounts of War Objectors*. Boston: Beacon Press, 1968.

Lynd, Straughton, and Michael Ferber. *The Resistance*. Boston: Beacon Press, 1971.

Marcus, Greil. *Lipstick Traces*. Cambridge, Mass.: Harvard University Press, 1989.

"Marines Rebel in Iwakuni." *The Bond* 4, no. 7 (22 July 1970): 1.

Marx, Karl. *Capital*. Vol. 1. New York: Vintage Books, 1977.

———. *Wage Labour and Capital*. Peking: Foreign Language Press, 1978.

———. *The Eighteenth Brumaire of Louis Bonaparte*. New York: International Publishers, 1984.

Marx, Karl, and Friedrich Engels. *The German Ideology*. New York: International Publishers, 1985.

———. *Karl Marx and Frederick Engels, Selected Works in Three Volumes*. Edited by the Institute of Marxism-Leninism under the Central Committee of the Communist Party of the Soviet Union. Moscow: Progress Publishers, 1983.

McKenzie, Angus. *Secrets: The CIA's War at Home.* Berkeley : University of California Press, 1997.

————. "Sabotaging the Dissident Press." In *Unamerican Activities.* Edited by Anne Janowitz and Nancy J. Peters. San Francisco: City Lights, 1981, 159–70.

McLaughlin, Lisa. *Breaking the Chains to a Sickness: Feminism, the Public Sphere, Media and Democracy.* Ph.D. thesis, University of Iowa, 1993.

McRobbie, Angela. "Working Class Girls and the Culture of Femininity." In *Women Take Issue.* Edited by the Women's Study Group. London: Hutchinson, 1978, 96–108.

————. "Postmodernism and Popular Culture." *Terminal Zone* 1 (1986): 25–34.

————. "Settling Accounts With Subcultures: A Feminist Critique." In *On Record.* Edited by Simon Frith and Andrew Goodwin. New York: Pantheon Books, 1990, 66–80.

————. *PostModernism and Popular Culture.* London: Routledge, 1994.

Mead, George Herbert. *Mind Self and Society.* Chicago: University of Chicago Press, 1967.

————. "The Genesis of the Self and Social Control." In *Selected Writings: George Herbert Mead.* Edited by Andrew J. Reck. Chicago: University of Chicago Press, 1981, 267–93.

"Media Lies." *Fatigue Press* 23 (August 1970): 2.

Menzel, Herbert. "Quasi-Mass Communication: A Neglected Realm." *Public Opinion Quarterly* 35, no. 4 (1971): 406–9.

Merton, Robert. *Social Theory and Social Structure.* Glencoe, Ill.: Free Press, 1957.

"Message to Black GIs." *Fatigue Press* 23 (1970): 3.

Miles, Joe. *For Immediate Release.* New York: GI Civil Liberties Defense Committee, 1969.

"Military Claw Reaches Out." *The Bond* 4, no. 2 (18 February 1970): 2.

"Military Rights, MDM Demands." *Out Now* 1, no. 7 (ca. 1970): 7.

Miller, Corey. "The Lost Mutiny." *As You Were* 3 (June 1969): 1.

Mills, C. Wright. "On the New Left!" In *The New Radicals: A Report with Documents.* Edited by Paul Jacobs and Saul Landau. New York: Vintage Books, 1966, 110–14.

"Mitch vs The Army." *The Bond* 4, no. 7 (22 July 1970): 3.

Modleski, Tania. *Feminism without Women.* New York: Routledge, 1991.

Molwana, Hamid, and Paul Geffert. "Vietnam Veterans against the War: A Profile Study of the Dissenters." In *The New Soldier.* Edited by David Thorne and George Butler. New York: The MacMillan Company, 1971, 172–75.

Morgan, Robin. "Goodbye to All That." In *Underground Press Anthology.* Edited by Rev. Thomas King Forcade. New York: Ace Books, 1972, 118–27.

Morley, David, and Kuan-Hsing Chen, eds. *Stuart Hall: Critical Dialogues in Cultural Studies.* London: Routledge, 1996.

Moser, Richard. *The New Winter Soldiers: GI and Veteran Dissent During the Vietnam Era.* New Brunswick: Rutgers University Press, 1996.

"Movement for a Democratic Military is You." *Duck Power* 2, no. 3 (April 1970): 7.

"Movement Spirit." *Catharsis* 2 (October 1970): 6.

Mungham, Geoff, and Geoff Pearson, eds. *Working Class Youth Culture.* London: Routledge Direct Editions, 1976.

Mungo, Raymond. *Famous Long Ago: My Life and Hard Times with Liberation News Service.* Boston: Beacon Press, 1970.

————. "The Movement and Its Media." *The New Left: A Documentary History.* Edited by Massimo Teodori. New York: The Bobbs-Merrill Company, 1969, 386.

Murdock, Graham, and Robin McCron. "Youth and Class: The Career of a Confusion." In *Working Class Youth Culture.* Edited by Geoff Mungham and Geoff Pearson. London: Routledge Direct Editions, 1976, 10–26.

"Myers Wins." *Flag in Action* 3 (December 1968): 4.

"Need GI Participation." *The Last Harass* 1 (October 1968): 2–3.

"The New Free Press." *Free Press Underground* 3, no. 1 (October 1967): 3.

"The New Media." *San Francisco Oracle* 1 (20 September 1966): 2.

Nelson, Cary, Paul Treichler, and Lawrence Grossberg, eds. *Cultural Studies.* London: Routledge, 1992.

————. "Cultural Studies: An Introduction." In *Cultural Studies.* Edited by Cary Nelson, Paul Treichler, and Lawrence Grossberg. London: Routledge, 1992, 1–18.

Nelson, Jack A. "The Underground Press." In *Readings in Mass Communications.* Edited by Michael Emery and Ted Curtis Smythe. Dubuque, Iowa: William C. Brown and Company, 1972, 212–25.

Neville, Richard. *Play Power: Exploring the International Underground.* New York: Random House, 1970.

"The New Counterpoint." *Counterpoint* 2, no. 1 (24 February 1969): 2.

"News and Letter Policy." *The AWOL Press* 1, no. 4 (ca. 1969): 1.

"News from the Staff." *Flag in Action* 1 (November 1968): n.p.

"News in Capsule for Our Armed Forces." *As You Were* 5 (July 1969): 2.

"Notes." *Last Harass* 1, no. 1 (October 1968): 2.

"A Note for Lifers." *Broken Arrow* 1, no. 6 (1969): 6.

"Notes from the Staff." *Flag in Action* 1, no. 1 (November 1968): n.p.

O'Brien, Ann. "The Bridge." In *Underground Press Guide.* Edited by Joe Korpsak. Los Angeles: Other Press Publishing Company, 1967, 11.

O'Brien, Tim. *If I Die in the Combat Zone.* New York: Laurel Books, 1987.

"Obscenities." *Fun Travel Adventure* 8 (May 1969): 7.

Offe, Claus. "New Social Movements, Challenging the Boundaries of Institutional Politics." *Social Research* 52, no. 4 (1985): 817–68.

Ogelsby, Carl. "Trapped in a System." In *The New Left: A Documentary History.* Edited by Massimo Teodori. New York: The Bobbs-Merrill Company, 1969, 182–88.

Olson, James S., ed. *Dictionary of the Vietnam War.* New York: Greenwood Press, 1988.

"On What We Need to Be Doing." *The Old Mole* 4 (November 1968): 12.

"One Reason for *ABOUT FACE!*" *About Face!* 2 (April 1969): 1.

Orwell, George. *Politics and the English Language.* Originally published in 1946. [http://www.bnl.com/shorts/patel.html]. 1998.

"Our Existence Depends Almost Entirely upon You People That Buy This Rag." *Finger* 1 (October 1968): 1.

"Our Goal—Protest or Power." *The Bond* 4, no. 7 (1970): 6.

"Our Position." *GI Voice* 1 (February 1969): 1–2.

"Our Thing." *Harbinger* 1 (May 1968): 2.

Pach, Chester, Jr. "And That's the Way It Was: Vietnam on the Nightly News." In *The Sixties: From Memory to History.* Edited by David Farber. Chapel Hill, N.C.: The University of North Carolina Press, 1994, 90–118.

"The Patriotism of Protest." *Bragg Briefs* 2, no. 3 (November 1969): 4.

"Pay Raise." *Fatigue Press* 23 (August 1970): 4.

"Peace is the GIs Cause." *The Ally* 9 (September 1968): 3.

Peck, Abe. "Faded Flowers." *The Quill* (June 1985): 34–37.

———. *Uncovering the Sixties.* New York: Pantheon Books, 1985.

Pelz, William. "The Decline and Fall of the Underground Press, 1969–74." *The Indian Journal of American Studies* 10 (1980): 58–66.

Pember, Don R., ed. "The Subterranean Mine Shaft beneath the Sod Press." In *Mass Media in America.* Chicago: Science Research Associates, 1974, 104–11.

"The Pen Is Mightier than the M-16." *Gigline* 2, no. 3 (March 1970): 2.

Perrin, Richard. "Blind Nationalism." *Act* 1, no. 2 (ca. 1968): 1.

"Petitioning Drive Succeeds on Bragg." *Bragg Briefs* 3, no. 1 (April 1970): 3.

Pfaff, Alma. "Testimony of Alma Pfaff." House Committee on Internal Security, *Investigation of Attempts to Subvert the United States Armed Services.* 92nd Cong., 1st sess., 1971. Committee Print 6386.

"Pfc Dennis L Davis (15 and a Wake Up) Gets An Early Out!!!." *Fun Travel Adventure* 8 (May 1969): 3.

Phillips, Dale. "Editorial." *Canada Goose* 2 (6 September 1968): 6.

"Policy." *Aurora* 1, no. 2 (2 August 1968): 2.

"Powell Challenge." *Fatigue Press* 25 (1970): 2.

"Pressure Wins Big Presidio 27 Victory." *Task Force* 1, no. 4 (25 March 1969): 8.

Preston, William, Jr. *Aliens and Dissenters: Federal Suppression of Radicals, 1903–1933.* New York: Harper Torchbooks, 1963.

"The Priest." *Left Face* 2, no. 1 (April 1970): 6.

Priest, Roger. "Bobby Seale's Parable." *OM* 3 (June 1969): 2.

———. "Bring the War Home." *OM* 3 (June 1969): 8.

———. "A Call to Resist Illegitimate Authority." *OM* 2 (May 1969): 1–2.

———. "Does This Pig Speak for You?" in *OM* 3 (June 1969): 5.

———. "1st Amendment: "It's Crap"." *OM* 4 (October 1969): 2, 3.

———. "The Great Disloyalty Trial." *OM: Special Court-Martial Edition* (ca. 1970): 2.

———. "Looking Toward the Future." *OM* 2 (May 1969): 9.

———. "On Organizing Pigs." *OM* 2 (May 1969): 10.

———. "Remember the Pig Is Armed and Dangerous." *OM* 3 (June 1969): 2.

———. "Slogan." *OM* 2 (May 1969): 8.

———. "Super Pig." *OM* 3 (June 1969): 5.

———. "Up against the Pentagon." *Up against the Bulkhead* 1 (ca. 1970): 3.

"Problems of GI Organizing." *Out Now* 1, no. 2 (June 1970): 7.

"Rank and File Storm after Arrest." *The Bond* 4, no. 9 (ca. September 1970): 1.

Ransom, David. "Starting a Community Newspaper." In *The Movement Toward a New America.* Edited by Mitchel Goodman. Philadelphia: Knopf Pilgrim Press, 1971, 426–28.

The Rat Women. "Women Take Over 'Rat'." In *BAMN: Outlaw Manifestos and Ephemera 1965–1970.* Edited by Peter Stansill and David Marovitz. Harmondsworth, U.K.: Penguin Books, 1971.

Rather, Dan, et al. *The War in Vietnam.* CD ROM. New York: Simon & Schuster, Macmillan, CBS Inc., and The New York Times Company, 1995.

"A Real Election/EM Vote CO Out." *The Bond* 4, no. 11 (18 November 1970): 1.

"Rebellion at Ft. Hood." *Fatigue Press* 25 (October 1970): 1.

Rechy, John. *Conduct Unbecoming . . . Lieutenant on the Peace Line.* Denver: Freedom for Lieutenant Howe Committee, 1966.

Reck, Andrew J., ed. *Selected Writings: George Herbert Mead.* Chicago: University of Chicago Press, 1981.

———. "Introduction." In *Selected Writings: George Herbert Mead.* Chicago: University of Chicago Press, 1981, xii–lxii.

"Remember the Ft Hood 43." *Fatigue Press* 24 (September 1970): 7.

"Repression at Iwakuni." *The Bond* 4, no. 6 (17 June 1970): 5.

Reservists Committee to Stop the War Newsletter 2 (April 1970): 1.

"Resistance in the Military." *The American Exile in Canada* 1, no. 15 (May 1969): 8.

Resistance inside the United States Armed Forces. Paris: RITA, 1968.

"The Right-Wing Responds." *Fun Travel Adventure* 10 (August 1969): 6.

Rips, Geoffrey. "The Campaign against the Underground Press." In *Unamerican Activities.* Edited by Anne Janowitz and Nancy J. Peters. San Francisco: City Lights, 1981, 37–158.

———. "Dirty Tricks on the Underground Press." *Index of Censorship* (April 1981): 47–50.

Roberts, Tom. "Army Acts to Silence Paper." *Aboveground* 1, no. 3 (October 1969): 3.

———. "Our Promise." *Aboveground* 1, no. 4 (1969): 2.

Roberts, Tom, and Curtis Stocker. "Disclaimer." *Aboveground* 1, no. 1 (October 1969): 2.

———. "Know Your Rights." *Aboveground* 1, no. 5 (December 1969): 4.

"Roger Priest: Guilty until Proven Guilty." *Gigline* 1, no. 4 (November 1969): 4.

"Roger Priest—OM." *Fun Travel Adventure* 10 (September 1969): 7.

Rogers, Carl. "An Interview with Mendel Rivers." *Link News* 1 (November 1969): 1.

Romm, Ethel. "Campus Protest Movement: You Go Underground for 'Inside' Report." *Editor and Publisher* 101 (1970): 12, 82.

———. *The Open Conspiracy.* Harrisburg, Penn.: Stackpole, 1970.

———. "Psychedelics by Offset: Protest Tabloids Turn on to Color Printing." *Editor and Publisher* 101 (1970): 68, 70.

Rorabaugh, W. J. *Berkeley at War: The 1960s.* New York: Oxford University Press, 1989.

Roush, Gary. "Statistics about the Vietnam War." [http://www.vhfcn.org/stats.htm]. 1996.

Rowe, John Carlos, and Rick Berg, eds. *The Vietnam War and American Culture.* New York: Columbia University Press, 1991.

Rudnick, Bob. "A Fifth Estate." *Canada Goose* 1, no. 3 (10 April 1968): 6.

Sale, Kirkpatrick. *SDS.* New York: Random House, 1973.

Sanford, David. "The Seedier Media." *The New Republic* 157, no. 23 (1967): 7–8.

Santouli, Al, ed. *Everything We Had.* New York: Random House, 1981.

Savage, Jon. *England's Dreaming: Anarchy, Sex Pistols, Punk Rock, and Beyond.* New York: St. Martin's Press, 1992.

"Save the Priest." *Last Harass* 6 (May 1970): 6.

Scherr, Max. "Editorial." *Berkeley Barb* 1, no. 1 (12 August 1965): 2.

Schmitz, Hon John. *The Viet Cong Front in the United States.* Boston: Western Islands, 1971.

"Secret Document Bares Army's Fear of ASU." *The Bond* 3, no. 4 (15 April 1969): 1, 4.

Shay, Jonathan. *Achilles in Vietnam: Combat Trauma and the Undoing of Character.* New York: Athenaeum, 1994.

"Shelterhalf." *Fatigue Press* 21 (June 1970): 3.

Shero, Jeff. "Editorial." *The Rat* 2, no. 2 (3 May 1969): 2.

Sherrill, Robert. *Military Justice is to Justice as Military Music is to Music.* New York: Harper and Row, 1969.

Shlee, Deanna Gail. Glossary of Military Terms: Slang from the Vietnam War A–Z. Sixties Project web site. [http://lists.village.virginia.edu/sixties/HTML _docs/Scholar.html]. 1998.

"Showdown—GI's Refuse to Fight." *The Ally* 19 (September 1969): 1, 3.

Sinclair, John. "White Panther Statement." In *Underground Press Anthology.* Edited by Rev. Thomas King Forçade. New York: Ace Books, 1972, 92–95.

Sinclair, T. C. "The Military and Freedom of Speech." Unpublished term paper. Austin: The University of Texas, 1968.

Small, Melvin. *Covering Dissent: The Media and The AntiVietnam War Movement.* New Brunswick: Rutgers University Press, 1994.

Small, Melvin, and William Hoover, eds. *Give Peace a Chance: Exploring the Vietnam Antiwar Movement.* Syracuse, N.Y.: Syracuse University Press, 1992.

"Solidarity in Thailand." *The Bond* 4, no. 12 (16 December 1970): 1.

"Special Processing Explodes." *The Ally* 29 (August 1970): 1.

Spector, Ronald H. *After Tet.* New York: Vintage Books, 1993.

Spencer, Michael J. "Why Is Youth So Revolting Nowadays." *Wilson Library Bulletin* (March 1969): 640–47.

Stacewicz, Richard. *Winter Soldiers: An Oral History of the Vietnam Veterans against the War.* New York: Twayne Publishers, 1996.

Stamberg, Marge. "About Liberation News Service." In *Recreation.* Edited by Marc Estrin. New York: Dell, 1969.

Stansill, Peter, and David Marovitz, eds. *BAMN: Outlaw Manifestos and Ephemera 1965–1970.* Harmondsworth, U.K.: Penguin Books, 1971.

Stanton, Shelby L. *The Rise and Fall of an American Army.* Novato, Calif.: Presidio Press, 1985.

Stapp, Andy. *Up against the Brass.* New York: Simon and Schuster, 1970.

Statement of Aims. New York: GI Civil Liberties Defense Committee, ca. 1969.

"Statement of Purpose." *The Blue Bus* 1, no. 3 (April 1968): 2.

"Statement of Purpose." *Open Ranks* 1, no. 5 (February 1970): 3.

"Statement of Purpose." *Stars-n-Bars* 1 (27 October 1970): cover.

Stocker, Curtis. "AG Unclassified." *Aboveground* 1, no. 5 (December 1969): 9.

"Stolte, Amick Get Four Years for Free Speech." *The Ally* 5 (June 1968): 1, 6.

"Subscribe." *Bragg Briefs* 2, no. 5 (December 1969): 8.

"Subversive Propositions about Ethical Action." *Reveille* 1, no. 1 (April 1968): 2.

Summers, Harry G, Jr. *Historical Atlas of the Vietnam War.* New York: Houghton Mifflin, 1995.

"Support the Priest." *Fun Travel Adventure* 17 (May 1970): 4–5.

Surowiec, Mike. "Alienated or Aligned." *The Midwestern Activist* 2 (20 October 1966): 1

Surrey, David. *Choice of Conscience: Vietnam Era Military and Draft Resisters in Canada.* New York: Praeger, 1982.

"Take the Offensive." *Fatigue Press* 24 (September 1970): 2.

"Tarnished Brass." *The Ally* 31 (October 1970): 1.

Task Force 2 (October 1968): 3.

Teodori, Massimo, ed. *The New Left: A Documentary History.* New York: The Bobbs-Merrill Company, 1969.

Terry, Wallace, III, "The Angry Blacks in the Army." *Two, Three . . . Many Vietnams: A Radical Reader on the Wars in Southeast Asia and the Conflicts at Home.* Edited by Banning Garrett and Katherine Barkeley. San Francisco: Canfield Press, 1971, 227.

"There Is No Turn-in." *Huachuca Hard Times* 1 (April 1969): 1–2.

"They Use Us against Each Other." *The Bond* 4, no. 1 (15 January 1970): 1.

Thompson, E. P. *The Poverty of Theory and Other Essays.* New York: Monthly Review Press, 1978.

Thorne, David, and George Butler, eds. *The New Soldier.* New York: The MacMillan Company, 1971.

"The Time is Now/We Need Unity." *Fatigue Press* 27 (December 1970): 2.

Tischler, Barbara. "Breaking Ranks: GI Antiwar Newspapers and the Culture of Protest." *Vietnam Generation* 2, no. 1 (1990): 20–50.

"To Our Readers." *The Ally* 12 (December 1968): 3.

Tollefson, James W. *The Strength Not to Fight: An Oral History of Conscientious Objectors of the Vietnam War.* Boston: Little Brown and Company, 1993, 185.

Touraine, Alain. "An Introduction to the Study of New Social Movements." *Social Research* 52, no. 4 (1985): 749–89.

———. *The May Movement, Revolt or Reform.* New York: Irvington Publishers, 1971.

"Toward GI Power." *The Ally* 10 (October 1968): 3.

"Toward GI Power." *Harrass the Brass* 1 (May 1969): 3.

Tracy, James. *Direct Action: Radical Pacifism from the Union Eight to the Chicago Seven.* Chicago: University of Chicago Press, 1996.

"Tricky Dick Wants Peace; or Does He?" in *The Ally* 17 (June 1969): 2.

"Two GIs [sic] Busted For Distributing Paper at Fort Sam." *GI Press Service* 1, no. 9 (16 October 1969): 137.

Turner, Fred. *Echoes of Combat.* New York: Anchor Books, 1996, 21.

"UFO Bust." *Fatigue Press* 23 (August 1970): 4.

"Underground Alliance." *Time Magazine* 88, no. 5 (29 July 1966): 57.

"Unfair." *Out Now* 4 (August 1970): 4.

"Union Demands." *Broken Arrow* 1, no. 9 (10 February 1970): 1.

"Unity." *Black Unity* 1 (August 1970): 3.

"Untitled." *About Face!* 4 (June 1969): 6.

"Untitled." *The First Amendment* 2 (ca. 1970): 2.

"Untitled." *Flag in Action* 1, no. 3 (November 1968): 3.

"Untitled." *GI Alliance* 1 (3 June 1970): 1.

"Untitled." *The Green Machine* 1 (ca. 1969): 4.

"Untitled." *Huachuca Hard Times* 1 (April 1969): 6.

"Untitled." *Rap!* 9 (August 1970): 8.

"Untitled." *Task Force* 1, no. 3 (25 October 1968): 3.

"Untitled." *USAF* 1, no. 1 (1 April 1969): 3.

"Untitled." *WE GOT THE brASS* (German ed.) 1 (ca. 1969): 11.

"Untitled Appeal." *All Hands Abandon Ship* 7 (ca. 1971): 2.

"Untitled Note." *A'bout Face* 1, no. 1 (4 July 1970): 1.

"Untitled Note." *Duck Power* 1, no. 3 (24 September 1969): 1.

"UPS." *The Paper* 2, no. 1 (29 September 1966): 10.

"USS Hancock Resistance." *The Ally* 28 (July 1970): 2.

Valdes, Joan, and Jeanne Crow, eds. *The Media Reader.* Dayton: Pflaum, 1975.

Vaneigem, Raoul. *The Revolution of Everyday Life.* London: Rebel Press and Left Bank Books, 1983.

Vermorel, Fred, and Judy Vermorel. *Sex Pistols: The Inside Story.* London: Omnibus, 1987.

"Vietnam and the Next Victim." *Rap!* 1, no. 11 (February 1971): 2.

"Voice of the Underground Press." *Williamette Bridge* (1–20 June 1968): n.p.

Volosinov, V. N. *Marxism and the Philosophy of Language.* Cambridge, Mass.: Harvard University Press, 1973.

Wachsberger, Ken, ed. *Voices from the Underground.* Tempe, Ariz.: Mica Press, 1993.

Wallerstein, Emanuel, and Paul Starr, eds. *The University Crisis Reader.* Vols. 1 and 2. New York: Random House, 1970.

"Wanted: For Freedom of Speech." *PEACE* 3 (1 October 1970): 1.

"War Crimes/Know Your Rights." *The Ally* 30 (September 1970): 2.

"War Ft. McClellan." *Left Face* 1, no. 5 (January 1970): 2, 6.

Wasserman, Harvey. "1968: Year of the Heroic Guerrilla Media." *Dallas Notes* (16 July 1968): 16.

Waterhouse, Larry G., and Mariann Wizard. *Turning the Guns Around: Notes on the GI Movement.* New York: Praeger, 1971.

Watson, Francis M. *The Alternative Media, Dismantling Two Centuries of Progress.* Rockford, Ill.: The Rockford College Institute, 1979.

"We Could Be So Good Together." *The Last Harass* 6 (May 1970): 2.

"We Disagree." *The Ally* 16 (May 1969): 3.

Wells, Tom. *The War Within: America's Battle over Vietnam.* Berkeley: University of California Press, 1994.

Welsh, Douglas. *The History of the Vietnam War.* New York: Galahad Books, 1981.

"We've Got the Power." *Broken Arrow* 1, no. 2 (20 August 1969): 1.

"What is Alice?" *Alice* 1, no. 1 (18 May 1968): 1.

"What is SDA (Soldiers for Democratic Action." *Call Up* 1 (26 September 1970): 1.

"What Next?" *The Ally* 26 (May 1970): 3.

"What We Want." *Fed Up!* (December 1970): 2.

"What We're About." *Broken Arrow* 1, no. 1 (ca. 1969): 1.

"What We're for and Why we're for It." *Duck Power* 1, no. 3 (1969): 2.

"Who is Counterpoint." *Counterpoint* 2, no. 1 (24 February 1969): 2.

"Who Knows What They Are Doing." *Fatigue Press* 26 (November 1970): 8.

"Why This Newspaper." *Demand for Freedom* 1 (7 October 1970): 1.

"Why We Marched, What We Demand." *Fatigue Press* 23 (August 1970): 4.

Wilcock, John. "How the UPS Papers Fill the Gap." *Other Scenes* 4 (April 1967): 2.

———. "Meet the Press." *Harbinger* 2, no. 7 (24 July 1969): 10.

———. "Other Scenes." *Open City* 2, no. 2 (12–18 May 1967): 2.

————. "These Are the UPS Papers." *Other Scenes* 4 (April 1967): 2.

————. "Underground Press Syndicate Members Hold First Meeting." *Other Scenes* 4 (April 1967): 1, 4.

————. "Will Success Spoil Our Underground Newspapers?" *Other Scenes* 4 (April 1967): 4.

Willener, Alfred. *The Action Image of Society: On Cultural Politicization.* New York: Pantheon Books, 1968.

"Willing to Fight but Not to Be Inoculated." *The Ally* 6 (July 1968): 8.

Willis, Paul. *Learning to Labour: How Working Class Kids Get Working Class Jobs.* Farnborough, U.K.: Saxon House, 1977.

————. *Profane Culture.* London: Routledge, 1978.

Wright, Charles. *Mass Communication: A Sociological Perspective.* New York: Random House, 1975.

"Write-on Roger." *The Right-on Post* 1 (May 1970): 3.

"Your Constitutional Rights as a GI." *Anchorage Troop* 1, no. 2 (February 1970): 8.

"Your Rights about Your Paper." *All Hands Abandon Ship* 1 (August 1970): 5.

Zaroulis, Nancy, and Gerald Sullivan. *Who Spoke Up?* New York: Holt, Rinehart and Winston, 1984.

Zinn, Howard. *Dow Shalt Not Kill.* Washington, D.C.: Liberation News Service, 13 November 1967, 4.

Index

About the Author

JAMES LEWES received his doctorate in Journalism and Mass Communications from the University of Iowa.